PHIL LOVESEY

DEATH DUTIES

HarperCollins*Publishers*

HarperCollins*Publishers*
77–85 Fulham Palace Road, London W6 8JB

This paperback edition 1999
1 3 5 7 9 10 8 6 4 2

First published in Great Britain by
HarperCollins*Publishers* 1998

A catalogue record for this book
is available from the British Library

ISBN 0 00 651060 4

Printed and bound in Great Britain by
Caledonian International Book Manufacturing Ltd, Glasgow

1

August, 1969

She knew the boy, a classmate but no particular friend. Just one of two dozen others, an acquaintance sharing her school days. In truth, she didn't have particular friends, and didn't seem especially bothered if she never did.

She watched his tears, absorbed in his distress. 'Wait till I tell Miss Harris I saw you crying.'

'Won't tell nobody,' he replied sorrowfully, wiping his nose with the back of his hand.

'Will.'

'Won't!'

'Will!'

Deadlock. The two children watched each other warily in the yellow front room of her home. His shoulders trembled, causing a slight ripple to course through his grey school jumper.

She sat quite still, fascinated. She'd never seen a boy cry before, not this close, anyway. There'd been grazed knees in the playground, sobbing children led by sympathetic friends to a disinterested teacher, but this was different, stiflingly real and snotty. She studied the boy with scientific fascination. No blood, no bruises, yet still he continued to blub and sniffle. She decided to prod him further.

'I'll tell Janet,' she threatened, then added: 'And she loves you.'

'Doesn't!'

'Does. Told me yesterday. Me and Maureen Hawkins.'

'So?' He turned away, looking towards the murky window to escape the taunts. From another room a dog began to whine. Instinctively the boy turned towards the haunting cry.

'Sergeant . . . ?'

'Is he yours?' she asked brightly.

He nodded, swinging his legs against the creaking wooden chair.

'Bet he's your mum and dad's, really.'

'He's mine!' he suddenly shouted. 'And your dad's bloody killing him!'

She froze, scarcely believing her scrubbed young ears. Were all seven-year-old boys this grown-up? She'd heard her mother say the 'b'-word many times, but to hear it from a boy in her own class? She found herself looking at him afresh; suddenly his trembling lip and snot-streamed nose seemed unexpectedly heroic. She wondered if she should love him, tell Janet in the morning that he was her boyfriend now. After all, he could swear, was three months older than her and had his own dog. He'd do, she decided.

'Wanna game of kiss-chase?' she offered, determined this would clinch it.

'You smell funny,' he countered, eyes screwed up in disgust. 'And you're weird, everybody knows it!'

A familiar accusation which she rode with a slight shrug of contempt. 'Ain't got a filthy mouth, though. Ain't a big crybaby.'

The sudden approach of grown-up feet signalled a temporary cease-fire. A woman's head peered angrily round the door.

'Will you be quiet!' came the terse command.

'But, Mum,' he blubbed. 'I want to go home. And I want Sergeant back!'

The little girl noticed that her new boyfriend's mother was also holding back tears. Perhaps his whole family were secret weepers. She wondered if she should cry too. She loved joining in.

'You'll get a thick ear if I hear any more from you!' the grown-up threatened. 'Now play with your friend. We'll be going in a minute.'

'She's not my friend!' he insisted, tiny voice squeaking with indignant rage. 'Nobody likes her! I want to go! I want Sergeant! Where is he?'

The grown-up scowled and left the room, leaving the unanswered question hanging in the air like a dying plea. The boy

2

fought to recover some credibility. 'I'll get a new dog, you wait and see. A really big one with sharp teeth to eat Mrs Harris. You see, I will. And your dad won't be able to kill him. He'll be eaten all up if he tries!'

Now it was an affront to her father. The honeymoon was over. 'My dad isn't killing your dog.'

'Is!'

'Isn't!'

'Is!'

'Isn't!'

Proof was required to break the stalemate. He looked her in the eyes and brought out the biggest argument in his armoury. 'My mum says that if Sergeant can't get better, your dad will put him to sleep. So there!'

'He always does that.'

He pointed a stubby finger and delivered his trump card. 'Sleeping is killing, stupid!'

'Not!'

'Is!'

'Not!'

The dispute was silenced by the return of grown-up feet, moving more slowly this time. The door opened and this time both her father and his mother stood in the yellow waiting room talking of 'arrangements' and agreeing it was 'the best thing possible under the circumstances'.

The girl watched the boy's mother dab at her face with a paper tissue, before sticking her tongue out at her classmate, re-establishing their original boundaries before school the next day. She was right, the dog was asleep, he was wrong, and, what made it worse – a crybaby. She slipped out of the room and headed across the darkened hallway into her father's surgery.

It wasn't the shock of the dead labrador on the chipped Formica table which upset her, more the possibility that her father had somehow misled her. She wasn't allowed to lie, grown-ups told her that. So why had he? She heard the others leaving, the front door closing, then her father marching back to join her in the bleached, bare room.

'Come on now. You shouldn't be in here, precious.'

'Billy Whittle was right!' she said, pointing to the floppy

tongue hanging absurdly from the dead animal's damp jaws. 'You killed him!'

The tired vet stooped to her side. 'He's sleeping, precious,' he soothed. 'Best thing for him. He was in a lot of pain.'

She surveyed the corpse, checking for life.

He fetched a green surgical sheet to cover the dog. It had been a long day; kittens, ducks, guinea pigs, sheep, two lizards, a rogue owl and now finally, Sergeant's last stand. Then this. The time had arrived, to tell his beloved daughter what he'd always dreaded – Daddy sometimes killed animals too.

He sat and beckoned her on to his lap. 'So what did Billy say, then, precious?'

'That you were going to kill his dog.'

He nodded, considering his approach. He smoothed her brown hair, gazing into the young face struggling with the deceit. He loved her utterly, yet wrestled with warning his only child against the ways of the world, with shielding her from them. It seemed to him the saddest thing that time replaced innocence with cynicism, strangling all shoots of childish joy like a constricting weed.

'You know,' he began, 'sometimes it's better to put an animal to sleep than to let it suffer.'

'But did you kill Billy's dog?' she pressed.

'I suppose that depends on how you look at it.'

She said nothing, awaiting the full explanation.

'Just imagine if you were a dog.' She giggled at the thought. 'And you had an accident, or were very poorly.'

'Squished by a big lorry?'

He smiled, charmed by the innocent violence of her imagination. 'Then you'd come to me.'

'I know that,' she sighed. 'You're a vet.'

'Listen now,' he said, anxious she'd understand. 'You might be so badly hurt, or so ill, there's really nothing I can do to make you better.'

'Take me to a cleverer vet, then,' she helpfully suggested, enjoying the charade.

He shook his head sadly. 'Sometimes, there's simply nothing any of us can do.'

She glanced over at the covered dog. 'And cats?'

'All animals, I'm afraid.'

'That's sad.'

He cleared his throat. 'But there is one thing I can do to make them feel better. And I did that for Sergeant.'

'Killed him?'

'Put him to sleep.' He held her tiny hand in his. 'A nice long sleep using special medicine, so that when he wakes up, he's in heaven, and all the pain has gone.'

'Real heaven?' she asked suspiciously. 'With God and Jesus and all the angels?'

He nodded. 'I expect God has a special little place just for dogs.'

'Doggy heaven!' she cried, picturing the scene. 'With bones in all the clouds!'

He slid her off his lap and stood. 'So you see,' he said, attempting to sum up in as palatable a way as possible, 'I don't really "kill" the animals at all. Helping them go somewhere special isn't really the same as killing, is it?'

She mulled it over, a serious expression clouding the innocent face. 'If you say so . . .'

'I do, precious,' he concluded. 'Now why don't you run along and see if you can help your mum with the supper?'

But the kitchen didn't appeal. She was prepared to accept the theory; now came the interesting bit. 'Do you read them stories to make them go to sleep?'

'Who?'

'The animals.'

'No. It's not like that.'

'What do you do, then?'

'Like I said. I give them some special medicine.'

'With a spoon, like Mummy does?'

He sighed, admiring her persistence, but wishing it could be deflected elsewhere. Instinctively, he knew her hunger for knowledge would only be satisfied by straight answers. Fatally, he wondered if seven was too young. But then again, what right had he to deny her the mechanical truth? 'I give them a little injection.'

She flinched.

'They don't feel anything, precious, I promise.'

5

'A needle? Bet they do!'

'They're already ill. A tiny prick makes no difference to them.'

'Then they go to heaven?'

He nodded, pleased at his honesty.

But she was hooked. 'Will you show me, Daddy? Next time?'

'No,' he insisted.

She thought for a moment, wondering what she might say to turn events. Even at her tender age, she had a powerful grasp of the use of childish charm to overturn the 'no' word. Especially with Daddy. When he said 'no', that was always the opening gambit rather than the final say. Besides, the whole business was still cloaked in mystery. And if it really was so nice for the animals, why couldn't she watch? She found a new way in. 'Can I see the needle, Daddy?'

'I don't think so, precious.'

'Is it like one of Mummy's sewing ones?'

'A little. Now don't you think you'd better . . .'

'Where does the special medicine go?'

His tired eyes searched the eager, unrelenting face. What harm could it do, he thought, walking to a wall-mounted cabinet and producing a small, black, leather-bound box.

He dropped on one knee, opening the box to reveal the steely tubular insides to her fascinated gaze. 'This is the needle,' he said, pointing to a large syringe. 'And this is where I push the medicine in.' He mimed the plunging action before her fascinated gaze.

She seemed fairly satisfied. 'But isn't there another way to heaven?' was her last effort. 'Without that big needle?'

'They don't feel a thing,' he repeated, gathering the giggling child into his arms. 'Now go and help Mummy.' He kissed her on the forehead.

'But I want to talk to you.'

'Scram!' he growled, playfully chasing her from the surgery, listening to her contented giggles drift towards the kitchen. 'Well,' he quietly congratulated himself. 'That didn't go too badly. Not too badly at all.'

She was glad they'd taken her mother into another room. She

didn't like being told off, and all Mummy seemed to want to do was scream at her. It wasn't fair. She liked these policemen, though, especially the lady. She wasn't calling her 'stupid' or 'bitch', whatever that meant. It was like Miss Harris said at school, the police were children's friends. She wondered if they'd give her a lollipop.

The lady wanted to talk to her again. 'Can you tell us what happened when you went into Daddy's surgery?'

She smiled, anxious to please. 'I got his sleeping machine. The one with the needle.'

'Did Mummy know what you were doing?'

'She was in the kitchen, with Aunty Jude.'

'And they had no idea where you were?'

She shook her head earnestly. 'Mummy tells me off if I go in there. But I wasn't naughty. Honestly. Daddy was ill.'

The nice police lady offered her a blue cotton hanky. She wiped her eyes. 'Can I keep it?' she asked. 'Show school a real police hanky?'

The WPC mustered a weak smile, as others in the interview room shuffled feet and cleared throats unnecessarily.

'Mummy's really angry with me, isn't she?' The bottom lip trembled, the young face prepared to crack again.

One of the young male officers knelt by her side. 'Once you'd got the "sleeping machine", did you give it to your mummy?'

She frowned. Didn't they understand? This was all her idea, nothing to do with Mummy. 'Daddy was sick,' she explained forcefully. 'I wanted him all better. He's in heaven now, with Jesus and all the angels. He told me, he told me so.'

The WPC nodded, averting her gaze. 'So Mummy never went near Daddy?' she asked. 'You gave him an injection, did you? On your own?'

'While he was asleep. To make him live in heaven. With Billy Whittle's dog, and lots of others.'

'And what happened next?'

The girl appeared to struggle with the memory of recent events. 'Well,' she slowly replied. 'It wasn't exactly like Daddy told me. He said that you don't feel nothing. Just a little prick, and then you wake up in heaven. But it wasn't like that.'

'What happened?'

7

A single tear rolled down her flushed cheek. 'It wasn't fair! He shouted at me and made me cry . . . kept shouting, it was horrible, like I done wrong or something. I was really scared in case Mummy heard all the row. She did. She came upstairs and started shouting at me. I just run out, downstairs to Aunty Jude. I think Mummy must've phoned for an ambulance.' The desperate young face appealed to the room. 'He was ill, like Sergeant.'

'Sergeant?'

'Billy Whittle's dog.'

She watched nervously as others took notes, overhearing the phrase 'air bubble straight into the brain, poor bastard'. They were like the rest, just didn't understand. Nobody did. Except Daddy. Hadn't he told her, just yesterday, how he felt like 'death warmed up'; that he was 'dying from this bloody flu'? If anyone needed to wake up in heaven, it was Daddy. Couldn't they understand? What had she done wrong? Why was Mummy so angry with her? She began to cry in great racking sobs, exhausted by the trauma.

The nice police lady cuddled her and stroked her long fine hair. 'There, there,' she soothed. 'Everything's fine.'

She looked up. 'I haven't been naughty, have I? I won't go to prison, will I?'

Two more grown-ups entered the room. She watched as one of her uniformed friends shared a whispered conversation with the strangers. She didn't like these new men, didn't reckon much to her chances for a lollipop from them. She saw one flash a badge, and watched one of the policemen nod and leave the room with them.

'What's CID?' she asked.

'Nothing you need worry about,' the police lady replied.

Now a fat jolly policeman entered the room, stooping down to whisper something in the lady's ear. He smiled at her, then winked, so she reckoned he must be a nice one too. Maybe he'd understand. 'Daddy told me what to do,' she sniffed. 'He'll be the best vet in heaven, now. They have a place there, for all the doggies. He told me. He's there with them now, isn't he?'

The WPC smiled, cuddling the vulnerable child. 'I hope so,' was all she could say.

She held the handkerchief tight and wondered if she'd get some sweets now. After all, they weren't going to send her to prison, so she can't have done anything wrong. Nothing at all. Mummy just didn't understand, that's all. She yawned. All this being good was a tiring business. But at least Daddy would be happy now. She yawned again and drifted slowly into sleep, safe in the arms of her protector.

2

Ruth Jenkins stared at the tiny struggling bird, wondering what on earth to do.

If only she wasn't so cold; if only she'd remembered to wear her gloves. But her hands, thrust deeply into her warm coat pockets, were reluctant to brave the ravages of the frosty morning. And in truth, she knew she could never have actually handled the bird without them, needing the leather barrier to distance herself from its pain. She looked away, searching the white winter sky for an appropriate excuse to move on, guilt-free. Common sense told her the pathetic creature had only minutes to live, yet . . .

She walked on, cursing her inadequacy, wishing for all the world she could have picked up a nearby brick and ended the obscene flapping. Perhaps a cat would have it away, she tried to persuade herself. A quick pounce with sharpened claws and . . . Yes, better to let nature see to its own casualties.

Within seconds she was inside the stifling nursing home, all memory of the dying bird vanishing as the smell of bleach, stale urine and yesterday's roast potatoes invaded her freezing nostrils.

'Christmas,' she muttered, catching herself in a large oval mirror mounted in the soulless hallway. 'Bah bloody humbug!' Five foot four in one-inch heels, a little overweight, hazel eyes complete with the beginnings of serious bags underneath. She looked tired, dead beat, a potential customer for a last lingering holiday in the place she now stood.

Dyeing her hair hadn't really improved matters; a decision made on a whim, a faintly ridiculous attempt to inject some youth and energy from a packet. Doug had been true to form, of course, assuring her it looked 'terrific, doll' – the standard uninterested compliment she had grown to despise for its lazy dishonesty.

A white-uniformed nurse approached, managing to stretch her whole face into one smile completely lacking in warmth and humanity. 'Mrs Jenkins,' she beamed. 'Do come through. Rene's ready for you in the lounge.'

Ruth followed the officious body as it led her down a dark corridor towards her mother. The malodorous cocktail became stronger with each step.

'Mr Jenkins not with you?'

She fought the urge to laugh out loud at the idiocy of the question. What the hell did the stupid woman think? That Doug had disguised himself as wallpaper in order to slip past unnoticed? 'He's working.'

'Every penny counts, coming up to Christmas.'

'Right.' Ruth wondered if it would be that way for her, when her systems began to misfire. Whether she'd spend the last of her days patronized by plastic people uttering cosmetic gibberish as they wiped her bum and checked her plumbing.

'By the window,' the nurse said, pointing the way. 'No real change, I'm afraid. By the way, would you mind calling at the office before you leave? Mrs Watkins would like to see you.'

Ruth nodded, anything to get rid of the woman, and stepped into a large room, shoes rustling on the polythene-covered carpet. A large chalkboard dominated one wall, informing slowly dying residents of the correct day, month and year. An entry under 'weather' simply read 'cold' in faded chalk. Ruth assumed it hadn't been changed since September. Vinyl-covered armchairs had been pushed back to the walls, and here and there, a human being sat wrapped in a crocheted blanket, shaking slightly, biologically functioning until Death arrived to claim them.

Rene Golden sat by a large bay window, enjoying her view of the bins, privet bush and low brick wall. Ruth walked over and pulled up a chair to sit by her mother. Energetic youngsters on an unwatched television tried to teach body-surfing to the vegetating residents.

11

'Hello, Mum.'

'Sent you home from school again, have they? Your father will take his belt to you.'

Ruth sighed, repressing the urge to light up. Why the hell would they care, anyway? Surely they'd be grateful for any assistance in hastening the inevitable, begging her to pass the pack round, eagerly inhaling the lethal nicotine vapours. 'Dad's dead, Mum.'

'They won't let me see him. He's here, I know he is.' Her mother pointed to a large plastic dustbin. 'Lives in there,' she whispered conspiratorially. 'Comes out when only I can see him.'

'Dad's dead, Mum,' she repeated slowly. The nurses had told her to be honest. During the primary stages, shortly after her father's death, Ruth used to go along with the ramblings, unwilling to confuse her mother any further, complying with long, elaborate fantasies, assuming it could do no harm to keep his memory alive a little longer. Her mother would look so content, wrapped in a comforting bubble of unreality, that she hadn't the heart to burst it.

On her next visit, Ruth was taken into a side-room and treated to a patronizing explanation of senile dementia. A care-worker routinely described the impending atrophication of her mother's mind, together with the brief moments of clarity to be thankful for; diminishing bright spots in the shadows of a long descent into insanity.

Reality orientation were the latest buzz words. Psychobabble, imported from the States, looking good and sounding great on mental health trust literature everywhere. The theory was that visitors and staff should always attempt to re-route the fast-crumbling minds towards some semblance of reality. If the 'client' thought it was Tuesday, when in fact it was Wednesday, then they needed to be told.

Ruth had nodded politely, silently wondering why her mother would even care what day it was, when it was mostly occupied hoping for a glimpse of her dead husband leaping from the bins. She'd cried all the way home, mainly for herself.

'Still loves me, you know,' Rene announced. 'Wants to know when I'm coming home.'

12

'That's up to the experts, Mum. Not Dad.' And she wanted to say it, dear God, how she wanted to add, 'You deluded old bat.' One day she would, just for her own peace of mind, the chance to say what she really felt, express her anger at the living joke before her. Because in so many ways, it was already too late, her mother was already dead, all channels of conventional communication extinguished. A bizarre creature now sat in her mother's shell, a mindless parasite playing cruel games with those who loved its original owner.

She looked at the half-eaten bowl of porridge and bananas and suddenly wanted desperately for her mother to be offered something with more substance: crunchy apples, tart oranges, thick-sliced granary bread. It didn't seem right that those whose brains were turning to mush should have to eat it as well.

Sesame Street had started on television. A resident began clapping when Big Bird appeared. Ruth sat staring at the set, suppressing the lump rising rapidly at the back of her throat. It was so completely pointless. All the things she'd ever imagined asking her mother, all the answers she wanted to hear, all the little conversations she'd planned and fantasized over the years – all too late for any of them.

'You still seeing that Doug Jenkins?' Rene hissed.

Ruth sighed. 'We've been married twenty-seven years.'

'Villain, he is. Robs old folk. You steer clear of him, do you hear?'

'He drives a cab, Mum. He's totally straight, has been for years.'

Rene reached out and grabbed her daughter's hand. 'He's only after one thing.'

Ruth permitted herself the tiniest smile. Doug and her; sex? Only if she showered in Stella Artois, wrapped herself in back issues of the *Sporting Life*, and provided an ashtray and a bag of chips while he went through his pathetic paces. At forty-seven, sex didn't matter any more, not with Doug, anyway. 'I'll be careful, Mum.'

Rene suddenly pointed to Ruth's head, confusion showing. 'What's all that blood on your head? You've got blood on your head!'

'Mum, I've only hennaed my hair.'

13

But Rene was horrified. A thin string of saliva hung from her flaccid mouth. 'Somebody's killed my Ruth!' she screamed. 'Took an axe to her head! Look! She's dead!'

'Mother, calm down,' Ruth replied through gritted teeth, turning and smiling at other residents in order to reassure them she wasn't dead.

'Did it hurt, dear? Can I kiss it better?'

What was the point of any of it? Ruth asked herself. Ten-minute walk to the station, fifteen minutes spent waiting for the train, seventeen-minute journey from Chelmsford to Shenfield, twelve-minute walk to the home itself – all for a forty-minute, fortnightly ramble through her mother's ruined mind. But not today; three minutes and she'd had enough. Ruth rose from the chair. 'I've got to go and speak to the commandant,' she said wearily. 'I'll see you over Christmas. Bring Doug next time. You'll love that, won't you?'

'All right, dear,' Rene replied brightly, turning her attention back to the window. 'Don't be late for school, now.'

Ruth sighed and kissed her oblivious mother lightly on her over-powdered cheek, praying to all the known gods in the spiritual universe that senility wasn't hereditary. Turning slowly, she left the bleak room and made her way back down the dreary corridor towards the warden's office. She knocked twice before a woman's voice invited her into the small, well-ordered room.

Mrs Watkins rose, offering a fragile hand and yet another processed smile. Perhaps it was company policy here, Ruth mused, all recruitment dependent on the successful candidate's ability to maintain maximum insincerity no matter what hand you shook, whose arse you wiped.

'Mrs Jenkins. So glad you could drop by.'

Drop by? Drop dead, Ruth thought. What was it this time, an increase in bed-wetting allowance, a global shift in tranquillizer prices? Had to be money, she surmised. Always more money to be milked from the estates of the dead and dying.

'And how's our Rene today?'

Now Ruth's mother was shared property? It was too much to take. She tried biting back the rising bubble of sarcasm, but failed. 'Apparently my dead father now lives in one of your rubbish bins, and I'm the living victim of an axe murderer.'

14

Again, the corporate smile. 'Please, Mrs Jenkins. Sit down.'
She sat.

'It's about Christmas, Mrs Jenkins.' She paused, savouring Ruth's momentary confusion. 'A family time, wouldn't you agree?'

'Well, I . . .'

'She'd be much happier with you, you know. Safe in the welcoming bosom of her family.' Mrs Watkins hushed her voice to a confidential whisper. 'Really gives them something to live for. And you'd be surprised how little trouble Rene would be. Star resident, really. Very little incontinence, easy-to-follow medication plan . . .'

The penny was dropping, word by unbelievable word. Ruth frowned, bombarded by the sales drive, unwilling to accept the proposal at its core. The ridiculous woman wanted her mother to stay with her and Doug for Christmas? For real?

'Last year,' Mrs Watkins continued, 'Mr Gimblar's family took him to the Canary Islands. He died a very happy man that Easter. Quite the envy of the other residents with his tan, he was.'

'Let me get this straight,' Ruth slowly replied to the earnestly nodding head before her. 'You want me to have my mother for Christmas? In my house?'

One final nod, and the tone changed to brusque professional. 'We'll provide transport to and from your home, a five-day course of medication, and fully comprehensive insurance.'

Ruth was too stunned to object. One half of her fevered mind grappled with the motive behind such a ludicrous scheme – though in truth her cynical side had already put that one down to cash; the less residents the home had at Christmas, the less staff they had to pay double-time to keep their drug-swallowing customers profitably living. The other half swam with the ghastly possibilities of the intended scenario.

Mrs Watkins spotted the hesitation, and was in. 'You'll have forty-eight hours to think about it, Mrs Jenkins. Rene will be so excited when I tell her.' She rose from her chair, signalling that her precious time with Ruth had already expired. 'Yes. A family time. You won't regret it.'

Dumbstruck, shocked, speechless at the sheer unexpected

insanity of the plan, Ruth found herself walking from the office and closing the door quietly behind her.

Forty-eight hours, that was the key. Ruth let out a sigh of relief. She'd ring the woman later that afternoon, explain what a hopeless idea it was, that she'd stop by and see her mother on Boxing Day as originally planned.

Then another, fainter voice begged to be heard inside her bamboozled brain. What if? What if this Christmas was Mum's last? How on earth could she . . . ?

She'd talk to Doug about it, then decide. Although, in truth, she already held a tender vision of chopping her mother's turkey into spoonfeedable-size chunks, as Doug sat in heavy silence in their tinselled dining room. Maybe it wouldn't be so bad.

Ruth began the ten-minute walk back to Shenfield station, footsteps crunching on the frosted gravel of the drive. At the gates, she looked briefly for the dying bird. Nowhere to be seen. She walked on, out into the silent avenue.

From under a nearby bush, a black cat watched her huddled departure, licking its lips and purring contentedly in the mid-December morning.

A lone black feather lay caught on its needle-sharp claws.

3

'Downsizing?' The term shot straight over Doug Jenkins's bemused, close-cropped head. 'What's that all about, then?'

Margaret Simmons lit another Marlboro and decided it was time to revert to basics. This was the one meeting she'd dreaded for almost a month, playing the oncoming scene over and over during quiet anxious moments. There'd been no problems with the other drivers, just an occasional shrug, disappointed gestures. But with Doug, she knew it'd be different. He simply wasn't accepting. Of anything. 'I'm winding the business up, Doug.'

'Winding me up, ain't ya?'

Margaret exhaled high into the nicotine-stained ceiling. How she hated every inch of the shoddy Portakabin she laughingly called her office. 'I've had enough, that's all.'

Still the penny hadn't dropped. 'Going to have to give me some clues, Margaret.'

'I'm selling up, Doug. Fed up with the lot of it. The cabs, the problems, the people, all of it.'

Doug's steely blue eyes registered a faint comprehension of his predicament. 'I'm out of a bleedin' job, you mean? At Christmas?'

'Sorry, Doug,' she replied softly. He wasn't the sort of bloke you wanted to antagonize. But with their history, Margaret figured she knew a little more about Doug than most bosses would've done. At the bottom, deep down where real character lies, she was tougher than he was. Why else would she be doing this, anyway? 'I'm just too bloody bored of it all. Mind's made up, I'm afraid. I'm selling up after Christmas, then getting out while I've still got the nerve to do it.'

Doug sat, gobsmacked by the unexpected announcement. 'Why?' was all he could muster.

Margaret leaned back in her creaking chair and smiled. 'Because', she said slowly, 'I've spent the last nine years stuck in this dump getting people from A to B, then going absolutely nowhere myself. When, more than anything, I just wanted to be out there with them. Living.'

'Behave,' Doug scoffed intolerantly. 'Can't go gadding around like a bloody teenager at your age!'

'I want out, is all.'

'So sod off to Florida for a fortnight. Treat yourself. But don't sell the fucking business, love. Christ's sake, there's people's homes at risk.'

'Doug,' Margaret sighed, 'businesses go down every day.'

An uneasy silence settled between them.

'You're serious, aren't you?' He rose and walked round to her side of the cluttered desk, reaching out a grimy paw to stroke her neck.

'Leave it, Doug. It's over. Everything's over.'

'No way, kitten. Let me . . .'

'Please.'

He slowly retreated and sat slumped once more in the dirty plastic bucket chair. 'Thought we had something, you and me.'

'So did I, at first.'

'And now?'

'Don't make me say it.'

A frown crossed his face, thick neck settling back on to powerful shoulders. 'Tell me, Margaret. Come on, I'm dying here. Turn up for work to discover you're shipping out on some personal-fulfilment bullshit, and it's all over between you and me. Just tell me why. You owe me that much, love.'

'OK,' she relented, realizing only the cold impact of the truth would convince him. She took a deep breath. 'What we had . . . was just a bit of fun, all right. And . . .'

'Well, maybe to you . . .'

'Please, Doug. Let me finish.'

He nodded, jaw jutting proudly to maintain some morsel of his fast-crumbling dignity.

'It made me realize that I wanted more. From life.'

'Shirley fucking Valentine, now, is it?'

She ignored the barb. 'Besides, the business is going nowhere. Chelmsford's full of damn cab companies. Too many cars chasing too little business.'

'Tool up, then. Adverts, new premises.'

'Got a spare fifty grand, Doug?'

'The banks. Get one of them business loans.'

Margaret shook her head at the indignant figure, wondering how she'd ever found a single cell of him the remotest bit attractive. Boredom, most probably. Then there was the guilt to consider, Ruth being a friend, unsuspecting, innocent to their sordid Portakabined procreation. 'You've got till the end of January. I'm writing all the drivers' references, ringing other firms, but I can't make any promises. If it comes to it, you'll have to take your chances on the ranks.'

'With what?' Doug spat contemptuously. 'A fucking push-bike? Rickshaw rides round the town?' He suddenly rose and splayed both hands on the desk, leaning over her like a snarling bull. 'You're selling the fucking motors, remember?'

'Try the banks, Doug. Take your chances like everyone else.'

'That's it, then, is it? Margaret fucks off and leaves us all in the shit?'

'I'm sorry. I really am.'

'Bollocks!' His eyes held hers, pupils locked in anger, defiance, fear and hurt. 'Seems I'd better get on then, doesn't it?' he said eventually, turning and ripping a piece of paper from the wall. 'These my pre-booked jobs?'

Margaret nodded, exhausted by the intensity of the conversation. But she knew it was done, sensed a bright light at the end of her dark tunnel. One month and she'd be out of there. Free. 'Thank you,' she said quietly.

'For what?' he snarled.

Her eyes met his one final time. 'Showing me how low I'd fallen.'

Doug said nothing, choosing to applaud the sentiment sarcastically for several moments before stepping from the cabin and slamming the flimsy door behind him. 'Bloody bitch,' he muttered, feeling the unforgiving chill of cold night air as it rushed to envelop him.

19

Still cursing, he climbed into his cab, started the ageing engine on the fourth attempt, then reached into the cluttered glove compartment for a quarter-bottle of Scotch. The amber spirit was warm on the back of his raging throat, greeting him like an old and trusted friend – more, much more than could be said for that selfish old hag back there.

The bitch had sacked him! For fuck's sake, what the hell was wrong with her? They had a good thing going, money was rolling in, no one was getting hurt – then she decides to act out some menopausal whim and bring the whole damn scene crashing down around his feet. Fuck! It was bloody madness! Where in God's name was he going to get work at his age?

He'd had over a third of the bottle by the time he reached Chelmsford's town centre. He gazed hatefully at the steady stream of laughing, joking office workers heading for beckoning pubs. Garish illuminations completed the greedy spectacle; hundreds of red and yellow bulbs strung out and twinkling above the pedestrianized high street, beguiling the consuming masses to scour hundreds of shop windows for pointless presents for eager friends and relatives.

How Doug suddenly loathed every square inch of it. Dumped, redundant, fifty-four with minimal prospects. Oh, happy Christmas, Margaret, you cold-hearted bitch!

What in God's name was he going to tell Ruth? Jesus, what a nightmare! How would he explain this one? That Margaret had decided to sell up, and the final straw was their affair? A hundred unanswerable questions raced around his exploding mind, as sweat began trickling from behind his ears.

And suddenly, a movement behind him. The back door opened as he sat waiting by the traffic lights at the top of Duke Street. A reeking, suited body slid uninvited into the back seat. Mid-twenties, loose-tied, lipstick kisses confirming he had enjoyed a significantly better evening than Doug, so far.

'Little Waltham,' the young voice confidently ordered.

Doug turned to the would-be punter, in no mood for any invasion of his schedule. 'Out the cab, pal, or your next trip'll be in a fucking ambulance!'

'Sorry, mate. I didn't mean to . . .'

'Out! Now!'

20

The youngster scrambled for the door. 'It's bloody Christmas, you know!'

Doug exhaled a blast of Scotland's finest after the retreating figure. 'Don't I fucking know it, son,' he said menacingly, before roaring off to his first pre-booked job.

It was ten to eight on Friday, December the nineteenth, and Mrs Ida Sharansky of Nightingale Road, Chelmsford was ten minutes from her premature appointment with her maker.

4

Mrs Wallace's funeral. Once again she sat in confused silence, wondering at the tears which fell noiselessly around her.

Funerals. Always the same. Always the black suits and dresses, maudlin faces staring respectfully towards the polished coffin draped in lily of the valley before the altar. Why couldn't anyone see with the clarity of religious vision that she did? Wasn't everyone always harping on about rewards waiting for us all in the kingdom of heaven? Harping on – she liked that, something unintendedly angelic about the expression.

It should have been a cause for celebration, the end of a pained struggle in this life, the beginning of an eternal carefree existence up above. Indeed, why fear death at all? According to the 'experts' – her religious education teacher at school, vicars, priests, bishops, and nearly every grown-up she knew – this life on earth was surely just a tiny blip on an everlasting journey to paradise. And if times got too bad, one had only to shed one's mortal coil to enjoy a far better life on 'the other side'.

She sat in the front pew listening intently, Aunty Jude on one side, Uncle William the other. It would be a while before they would all stand and sing again, so she'd opted to look her most attentive – after all, God was probably watching.

She was thirteen now, so they kept reminding her; pubescent, menstruating, biologically able to propagate her kind. But it seemed so blindingly obvious: creation at the end of life was as paramount as at its beginnings. The world had simply got the order wrong. And as far as she could gather from overheard playground conversations, there was a marked tendency to spend too much time speculating about the giddy processes involved in baby-making. The time would surely be better spent seeing it safely back into the forgiving arms of God at its end.

Back to heaven. With Daddy. Warm, safe, curled up amongst the clouds. When times got bad, she thought of this, the reward that awaited her for a lifetime's selfless devotion. Just like Jesus, she'd be sitting at the right hand of the Father, her father. And he'd be so proud. And the others would all come and thank her, she was sure of that.

There seemed to be other striking similarities between the acts of life and death. Both were supposed to involve suffering, maybe excruciating pain. Both involved a great deal of tears and relief from concerned relatives. And both involved the central characters being placed in wooden box-like structures, often appearing to sleep peacefully as a procession of faces stared gently down in silent adoration.

The minister began to read from a huge bible wrapped in the wings of a fearsome brass eagle. She'd often looked at the sharp beak and wicked talons and wondered why His holy book didn't sit in the middle of a fairy ring instead. And if God was such a nice man, why did His churches have horrible monsters nestling in the roof, staring down on all His devout followers? And if He'd created everything, why had He made thunder, snakes, wars, disease, bad people and mummies who were always angry? Surely if He was such a good and clever man, He'd never have let teachers and macaroni cheese into the grand scheme of things.

There were lies too, hidden in the bible's cramped, dusty pages. The one about walking free from your tomb three days after death was a complete untruth. She'd tested this several times, searching the streets for stray cats before ending their suffering as quickly as possible. And in the manner of any true pioneer, she'd suffered for her 'art', building a little collection of thin scars courtesy of many an outraged feline claw. She'd even built a miniature tomb, modelled on the line illustration from her bible, carefully wrapping each dead cat in one of Aunty Jude's pillowcases before sealing the entrance with a large stone. Then she'd waited. Three long days and nights, often sitting for hours by the tomb entrance in total silence, young ears carefully attuned to the faintest signs of life from within.

Nothing. Each time – nothing. The Bible had lied. She re-read the same miraculous event in all four Gospels and was about to crown the whole procedure with an actual crucifixion of the subject animal before entombment, when she realized where the flaw in her researches lay.

Jesus was the Son of God. He could do anything. She was merely the daughter of a deceased vet. And as Jesus had stuck to the task set by his Father, she should abide by the one Daddy had given her.

Still the congregation wept respectfully around her. Ignorant fools!

Now here was a story which really held her.

'Why do you look at the speck in your brother's eye,' the vicar intoned. 'But pay no attention to the log in your own? How can you say to your brother, "Let me take the speck from your eye," yet cannot even see the log in yours? You hypocrite.'

It was as if the weasel-faced cleric was addressing her personally.

'Take it out, then you will be able to see clearly to take the speck from your brother's eye.'

She marvelled at the self-sacrifice. Imagine, a log sticking from your eye, and still being so kind as to worry over a speck in someone else's? At thirteen, she had no real idea what a 'hypocrite' was, but if it was the name Jesus had given to those who put the comfort of others above their own, then she wanted to be one. Wasn't she one already? Hadn't she done the very same for her father? And the others . . . ?

Hypocrite – it sounded to her so very good and biblical that she half-expected the sun to stream through the blue and purple stained glass and illuminate her alone amongst the congregation, as His voice boomed, 'Behold, people of Danbury! You have a hypocrite in your midst! Look to the innocent, giving heart of the young girl, and be sure she gets riding lessons for Christmas!'

She had no time for the official explanation – some twaddle about looking towards one's own faults rather than those of others; after all, what could the vicar possibly have to teach a proven 'hypocrite' like herself?

They all rose to sing another song, 'Oh Jesus, I have promised; to serve you to the end'. She looked around, smiling at the others. She knew most of them personally, patients in Aunty Jude's rest home. Her home, too. She liked it there, didn't really miss her mother any more, and much preferred Uncle William's shepherd's pie.

The old people were nice for the most part, and frequently pressed a cold ten-pence piece into her hand if she read their letters aloud, or bought fresh flowers for their rooms.

There were bad points, but none too serious. Uncle William wasn't as much fun as Daddy had been, spending most of his time aproned in the kitchen, cooking, washing up and tending to the permanent laundry pile. Aunty Jude would never venture in, claiming the smell gave her 'one of my headaches', for which, it seemed, the only cure was a trip to Maldon for a coffee and a chat in the dress shop. She loved these trips, Aunty Jude driving the new white Ford Escort as she wound down the window and thrust her head into the summer breeze, alive with the salty smell of the Blackwater Estuary.

Her mother used to visit once a month, usually bringing a stranger who she insisted be addressed as Uncle Mick. He said little, but always seemed to have a sherbet fountain in his pocket, so that was OK. Aunty Jude had asked how she would feel if Mummy married again. She was completely stumped. Daddy was in heaven; how could she marry him again?

One day, her mother visited and this time Uncle Mick had two sherbet fountains for her. He'd married her mum, and they were sorry, they couldn't really think about taking her back as they were going to have a baby themselves. They hoped she didn't mind.

She heard later that her mother had 'lost' the baby, and was very upset. It seemed like a very careless thing to do, and she prayed hard that someone would hand it in at the police station – they were such nice people there.

Her mother didn't visit as often after that, blaming money troubles. She'd heard Uncle William and Aunty Jude talking about the same thing; raised voices in the middle of the night which kept her from sleep. The car had gone, and they had to use the bus into Maldon. The dress shop didn't give them coffee either, and Aunty Jude began wearing the same clothes two days running.

The collection plate began its journey round the aged congregation. She watched Aunty Jude, splendid in last year's hat, drop a new fifty-pence piece on to the silver platter. She remembered other times, when Uncle William would pass a pound note to his wife, and she would hold it theatrically to the light for all to see before sliding it gently under the pathetic pile of change which constituted the others' meagre offerings. And after, she'd hold her aunty's gloved hand as they'd chat to the smiling vicar in the breezy church porch, as Uncle William and the helpers saw to all the old people. Nowadays, they'd both hurry past, anxious to depart the draughty house of God.

The old ones, too, seemed to have changed. They took her to one side and often complained about the food. Boring, they would say, not like it used to be. Day trips became less and less frequent, and the heating was switched off earlier at night, and on later in the morning. The television still hadn't been fixed, light bulbs hardly ever replaced. Relatives would take Aunty Jude to one side, and she'd watch the earnest conversation; Aunty Jude promising things would improve, relatives insisting this was the last chance or their mother or father would be moved somewhere more suitable.

Then, one bleak February morning, Mrs Wallace arrived – the woman with X-ray eyes. At eighty-six, she could spot a single speck of dust from twenty feet, summoning Aunty Jude to her wheelchair in order that she might remove the offending particle. 'It's all human skin, you know,' she'd loudly announce. 'Bits of people, lying around in your house. Should be ashamed.'

And perhaps Aunty Jude was, spending more and more time alone in her room. When she did venture out, the dwindling resident population would complain of drink on her breath, led by Mrs Wallace, whose nose seemed to possess the same extraordinary powers as her eyes.

'I could always smell it on my Victor,' she'd say. 'I always knew. Not that he was a drinking man, oh no. But if he'd stopped in for a quick half at lunch time, I'd catch it on his breath the moment he set foot through the door after work. And he wouldn't dare argue with me, either.'

It seemed no one was prepared to argue with the fearsome Mrs Wallace. Relatives were summoned to her beck and call, whilst other residents soon learned to shuffle, hobble or wheel themselves swiftly in any direction but hers.

'Bloody battle-axe,' Uncle William would confide. 'Can smell a cigarette from ten bloody miles, but can't recognize when she's messed herself. The sooner she goes . . .'

Which was when the whole thing started over again, the young girl weighing up the pros and cons. The experiments with the local stray cat population nearing completion, she decided it was time to move on to more deserving subjects.

While it was in little dispute they'd all be better off without the old witch, she felt duty-bound to consider things from Mrs Wallace's side. Just because the majority wanted her gone, was that enough to justify . . . ? Besides, surely a wicked old woman like Mrs Wallace would be sent straight to hell; not quite the same heavenly release from pain she'd given her father. She needed some more guidance.

She went to Aunty Jude's room, gently opening the door to the darkened bedroom, joining her on the bed, wondering why she'd put cucumber on her eyes. A brimming ashtray threatened to fall from the crumpled blankets.

'Aunty Jude?'

'Hmmmm?' The response was distant, languid.

'What if Mrs Wallace was to die?'

'Hallelujah!'

'Would she go to heaven?'

Her aunt began to laugh, a slight ripple coursing through the bed, sending the ashtray spilling on to the floor. 'Undoubtedly, Petal. Heaven is full of Mrs Wallaces. A vast army of fat, interfering old women, who've kept their houses as spotless as their lives. The gates will fly open for her, and Saint Peter will probably drop to one knee as she passes. Whereupon, she'll doubtless inform him that his halo needs a spot of Brasso, and she's just in time to stop standards slipping any further.'

'I thought people like her went to hell,' she replied, stooping to tidy ash from the carpet.

'Mark my words,' her aunt replied, 'Mrs Wallace has probably had her damned place booked since birth.'

27

'So if she was to die, everyone would be happier?'

Jude Farrow removed the cucumber, squinting and searching for her young niece. But she was already gone, and Jude felt too tired to call her back. It wasn't as if . . . Would she?

The business with her father, six dreadful years previously; six years of abject misery and disappointment. Simply too preposterous that the child might try to . . . She was thirteen now, for heaven's sake. The games had stopped, teddies been put away, secrets buried.

She lay back on the bed. It was simply too ridiculous even to contemplate. It was past, it was over, a means to an end, with no repercussions. And that was that.

Mrs Wallace was dead by dawn. The coroner recorded death by suffocation, concluding that the deceased had accidentally ingested then choked on loose bedding some time during the night.

The girl smiled. If only they knew how long it had taken her to wash the saliva out of her beloved police handkerchief.

5

Thick fog hung over Nightingale Road.

Detective Chief Inspector Frank Davies stepped from the squad car and nodded grimly at the two uniformed officers guarding the opened door to a stone-clad terraced house. An ambulance and two further police cars were already parked in the narrow street, attracting inevitable interest from Nightingale Road's other residents.

'Ghouls,' he muttered, wishing he'd worn a thick jumper underneath his five-year-old Marks and Spencer's overcoat. It was a sad fact that the longer he'd been employed to protect Chelmsford's general public, the more he'd grown to loathe their macabre voyeurism. Not that they could be blamed for stopping to stare. With less than a week to Christmas, the unexpected parade of emergency vehicles and yellow-jacketed officials made as entertaining a festive spectacle as Santa arriving to open his cardboard grotto in Debenhams. 'Parasites.'

Detective Sergeant Alan 'Boot Sale' Mason ambled out to greet his tall, silver-haired superior, notebook in hand. Shabbily dressed, thin-faced, with a pockmarked complexion, Mason made Worzel Gummidge look like a male model. Few who knew him back at the station disputed the nickname. Mason always looked like he'd dressed from a boot sale, an end-of-season one when he'd bought his entire year's wardrobe with a crumpled five-pound note.

Davies noticed with distaste that the soiled lapels of his sergeant's beige coat appeared to have picked up a fresh collection of mustard and ketchup stains.

'Mornin', Guv,' Mason beamed, exposing yellowing teeth to the foggy morning. 'What a result, eh?'

'Result?'

'Last Saturday before Christmas,' Mason explained. 'Gets me out of the bleeding shopping, that's for sure.'

'Very fortunate, Boot Sale,' Davies replied, anxious to get on. 'What's the situation, then?'

Mason consulted his notes, suppressing a belch before attempting to decipher his own handwriting. 'Old girl – Mrs Ida Sharansky – Neighbour popped round to see her this morning – No answer from the door – front, that is – Walks round the back – peers through window – sees deceased slumped in chair – calls ambulance – They arrive ten twenty – Break in – quick butcher's at the stiff . . .'

'Boot Sale!' Davies reprimanded, realizing the gibberish would have to be rewritten if any case arose out of the death. 'You've been watching those old Sweeney re-runs on your satellite again, haven't you?'

Mason blushed slightly. 'Top show, that,' he mumbled. 'Ground-breaking series.'

'Get on.'

'Paramedics inspect the body . . .'

'Better.'

'. . . Discover various things which point to DBSC.'

'DBSC?'

'Death By Suspicious Circumstances.'

Davies sighed, wrapping his thin coat tightly round his freezing body. 'I'm going to come round and personally rip that damn dish off your bloody wall, Boot Sale. Just speak the Queen's English, man, for Christ's sake!'

'Very good, Guv. Wanna butcher's . . . Would you like to inspect the scene, Detective Chief Inspector?'

'Less of the lip, or I'll have you working eighteen-hour shifts from Christmas Eve till New Year's Day, which'll mean YBF – You'll Be Fucked.' Davies walked through the open front door. 'You said "things". What things?'

'It's in here, Guv,' Mason replied, leading Davies up a darkened corridor towards a living room at the back of the house. Inside a team of CID and Serious Crimes officers moved silently round the sad little room, taking notes and photographs. The only noise came from a portable television re-running *Dumbo* for the umpteenth time.

'Can't we turn that off?' Davies barked, causing heads to turn in his direction. All except one, the lifeless figure slumped in a battered armchair, blissfully unaware of the solemn activity around it.

'Hasn't been dusted, yet, Guv,' Mason replied. 'We think there's a possibility it was switched on after the old girl . . .'

'After?'

'Perhaps you'd better take a look. Bit of an odd one, this.'

The moment Davies always dreaded: facing a corpse. He'd lost count of the number of times he'd swallowed hard and 'done his duty', but the impact was always the same, a gnawing fear in his gut as he was invited to inspect the remains of a once-living body. Some, of course, had been far worse than others; full-blown puking affairs, when just the merest glimpse had him rushing for the exit, hand pressed firmly over his mouth in a desperate bid not to be reacquainted with his last meal. Others were almost passable, barely memorable, the briefest encounters with the dear departed. Suicides were the worst; stinking dead testimonies to loneliness and despair.

Steeling himself, he moved round and stood between the television and its former owner. A group of black crows rowdily jeered the young Dumbo's attempts to fly, somehow mocking any false air of modesty and respect left in the stifling room.

Mason hadn't been wrong. It was indeed a 'bit of an odd one'. Ida Sharansky's death-blue head lay sadly on one shoulder, eyes closed to Davies's scrutiny. A garish lipstick grin had been daubed over her flaccid mouth. Rouge, blusher and foundation attempted to colour the greying face. 'Like she's been made up for the funeral parlour,' he muttered slowly, absorbed by the macabre spectacle.

Mason stood by his side. 'Like something out of an 'orror film, ain't she? "Demon Clowns" sort of thing. Puts the bloody willies up me.'

Davies stooped to inspect the body more closely, pulling on a pair of latex gloves and gently moving the neck from side to side. Large purple and maroon bruises were clearly visible beneath layers of crudely applied face powder. He stepped back, surveying the slumped corpse with some distaste. A red rose had been pinned to Mrs Sharansky's dress, just above her dead bosom. One or two petals had followed suit and dropped lifelessly into her twisted lap.

'Good grief,' Davies whispered. 'What the bloody hell's this all about, then?' He turned to Mason, shock receding, professionalism taking over. 'House to house?'

'Uniform are on it now, doing everyone in the street, with a view to extend if you want.'

'Relatives?'

Mason flipped open the notepad. 'None in Chelmsford. According to the old girl who found her, a Mrs Jackson, Ida here is . . . was seventy-eight, widowed four years ago, and had family in Ipswich and Cambridge. They're being informed. Our man's already pronounced death at the scene, and the ID's been done by Mrs Jackson.'

Davies stared at the body. 'What else do we know about her?'

'Running her through the computer at the moment, Guv. Mrs Jackson's still too traumatized to tell us much more, though she says she spoke to Mrs Sharansky over the garden fence at about five last night.'

'Any indications of anything?'

Mason shook his head. 'Nah, says the old girl was just collecting her bloomers off the line. Odd though, isn't it? Looking at her, you'd think she was dressed up for tea with the bleeding Queen.'

'Doctor Death here, is he?'

Mason nodded. 'Given her the once-over, wants her moved to the path lab for the full forensic treatment. Want me to get him?'

'Please,' Davies replied. 'And Boot Sale, this lot been photographed, yet?'

Mason glanced round at the thinning crowd in the room. 'They're more or less done. Uniform are putting tapes out the front and leaving a couple of their lads on the door.'

'There a back door in here?' Davies asked thoughtfully.

'Locked, Guv. In the kitchen. Yard leads out to the gate at

32

the end which joins an alley running the length of this street, backing on to houses in the next, Crumley Road, I believe.'

'Bolted?'

'The back door?'

Davies nodded.

'It's got bolts on it,' Mason replied. 'Top and bottom, but it's only locked with a Yale.'

'Go see if the latch has been dropped, will you? And send Cloth in.'

'Right y'are, Guv.' He disappeared, ushering the others out of the room. Davies, finding himself alone with the corpse, strolled round, idly scanning family photographs on the tiled mantelpiece, trying to reconcile the smiling woman he recognized as Mrs Ida Sharansky with the pathetic, cosmetically abused sight behind him.

'Detective Chief Inspector Davies, how are you?'

Davies turned to the elderly pathologist. 'Doctor Cloth,' he acknowledged. 'Grim task at this time of year, goodwill to all men, and all.'

'But not elderly Jewish women, it seems,' Cloth replied soberly. 'A penalty, one might almost assume, for not believing in our wondrous Christmas festival.'

'Time of death?'

Cloth walked over to the body. 'Can't be certain, of course. But I'd place it between seven and midnight last night. RM's worn off, the body's quite flexible. Strange little scene, though, wouldn't you say?'

Davies nodded. 'Strangled, though, I take it?'

Cloth stood behind the chair, leaning over the body. 'Most probably something like this,' he confirmed, placing both hands within millimetres of Ida Sharansky's neck, aligning his fingers with the subdued bruises. 'The tongue is quite distended and swollen. Your officers found a slipper behind the television, possibly alluding to some sort of struggle.'

'She kicked out, you mean, as the killer throttled her?'

'Maybe,' Cloth replied. 'I'll need to do more tests. An old woman like her, the chances are she may well have strained a muscle during the struggle.'

'But was it done here, in the chair?'

33

Cloth nodded. 'Highly likely. The bruising's consistent with an attack from above and behind.' He moved round and lifted an eyelid. 'Burst blood vessel to the left eye. Classic indication of enormous pressure applied to the throat.'

Davies turned from the lifeless eye. 'Read a book once,' he mused. 'Science fiction thing, cops of the future. All they had to do was pop out the victim's eyes and wire them up to some sort of computer. It developed them, spilling out a perfect image of the last thing they ever saw.'

'The murderer, presumably?' Cloth closed the eye.

'Not in this case,' Davies replied. 'The killer strapped a one-way mirror over his face. When the cops got the print, all they saw was the terrified expression of the victim, seconds before death.'

'I prefer romantic fiction, myself,' Cloth announced, checking nostrils for dried blood. 'Hero, heroine stuff. Unrequited love finally wins through after battling impossible odds.'

'Mrs Cloth know about this, does she?'

The pathologist smiled. 'Things like this, Detective, might never happen if we had a little more love and understanding in this world.' He turned his attention back to the body. 'She needs to be moved to the cold house before she loses any more fluids.'

'Do it,' Davies confirmed. 'Will you be able to tell me whether she was dressed after she was killed?'

Cloth mulled it over. 'It seems consistent with the overall scene. I can tell you now that the make-up was applied after death. These bruises are quite clearly underneath it, and there are no discernible prints on the face powder, gloved or otherwise.'

'So the killer made her up afterwards?'

Cloth turned to the DCI, irritation on his face.

'Just thinking aloud,' Davies apologized.

'Your case, Chief Inspector,' Cloth replied. 'She died, then was made up. By who, I know not. There could have been a dozen of them doing it, for all I . . .'

Davies held up his hands in mock surrender. 'You've made your point. Get her out of here and take a closer look. I'll be in touch.'

The pathologist nodded and left the room. Mason stuck his head round the doorway, beckoning Davies with an urgent hand. 'Got something for you, Guv.'

'Checked the back door?'

'Not yet. Just been talking to Uniform . . .'

'Bloody do it, Sergeant!' Davies replied irritably. 'Chances are, Mrs Sharansky's insane Avon lady legged it out that way after she gave the old dear her last makeover.'

'Could be a bit premature, Guv,' Mason replied. 'Uniform have interviewed a bloke over the road who says he saw a taxi-driver draw up outside at about half-eight last night.'

'Go on.'

'Says he heard the cab tooting its horn a couple of times, then he saw the driver get out, take a quick butcher's through the front window, then let himself in.'

'In here?'

'S'what he says. Won't breathe a dicky-bird about the rest of it until he's spoken to the top man.'

Davies strode from the room. 'Where is he?' He followed Mason back through the darkened corridor out into the foggy street. A figure strode up to meet them, notebook in hand. Davies recognized him instantly. The local press had arrived, called no doubt by the good folk of Nightingale Road.

'Chief Inspector Davies,' said the earnest young reporter, 'can you tell me what's happening?'

'I'm crossing the road,' Davies growled. 'And you're obstructing an investigation.'

'Rumour is that Mrs Sharansky's been murdered. When can we expect a statement?'

'Rumours are dangerous things,' Davies replied. 'You'll get the facts, when it's time, and if it's appropriate.'

'So you're not denying it, then?' the young man persisted.

Mason whispered something in the reporter's ear, and Davies watched in astonishment as he walked quickly back towards his car.

'Explanation?' Davies asked quizzically.

Mason grinned. 'Just told him there was nothing for us here, but reports were coming in of an armed robbery in the High Street. He's off for the exclusive.'

'Dishonest and disrespectful,' Davies replied, walking through a white garden gate towards an olive green front door proudly displaying a Neighbourhood Watch sticker in one of its glass panels. A uniformed WPC clutching a cup of tea ushered both men inside to a tidy front room. A middle-aged man with National Health spectacles and a knitted cardigan rose from an armchair placed right alongside the main window looking back out on to the street.

'Inspector Davies?' he asked hopefully, extending a white, puffy hand. 'Brian Phelps. Pleased to be of service.'

Davies tried never to prejudge, but he was human, and at first glance Mr Phelps seemed exactly the sort of individual who made it his life's mission to pursue triviality to its banal and inconsequential ends. Davies could imagine him writing a lot of letters to the local newspaper complaining of parking bylaws and planning permission infringements. 'It's Detective Chief Inspector Davies,' he corrected, shaking Phelps's hand as minimally as possible. 'I gather you saw something last night?'

Phelps sat back down and began stirring his tea, savouring the moment. This was his finest hour, something to really impress the Rotary Club at their forthcoming Christmas dinner. 'Indeed, Detective Chief Inspector. Indeed I did.'

Davies shot Mason a despairing look. 'Some time last night,' he prompted, attempting to speed matters along. 'A cab?'

Phelps took a sip of lukewarm tea, slurping noisily. 'Curious thing, the Neighbourhood Watch,' he said cryptically. 'One wonders, Detective Chief Inspector, as to its purpose –'

'Indeed,' Davies cut in, fast feeling he was losing the initiative. 'But you saw something last night?'

'Too late, though, isn't it?' Phelps replied, grinning with self-satisfaction. 'I've written letters to the paper about exactly this sort of thing. My argument is this,' he stared at Davies through thick-rimmed spectacles. 'It's all a bit like closing the stable door after the villain has bolted.'

'Getting back to last night . . .'

'You see my point, don't you?' Phelps looked back out across the road. 'Too late now, isn't it? All your cars, detectives and ambulances won't bring her back, will they?'

Davies rubbed his face in his hands. 'Mr Phelps, I have reason to believe you may have seen something which is extremely pertinent to this investigation . . .'

'She's been murdered, hasn't she?' Phelps replied. 'Must be murder to justify all this activity.'

'I'm not at liberty to say, sir.'

Phelps took another sip at his tea. 'And now you want me to tell you who's done it?'

'I want you to tell me what you saw.'

'We're treated like little unpaid policemen. You treat us like that.'

'I'm sorry?'

Phelps stood, pulling back lace curtains for a better view. 'If you had more police on the streets, Detective Chief Inspector, things like this need never happen.'

Davies ground his teeth. 'It's not me who makes the policies, Mr Phelps.'

Phelps ignored the protests, high on his moral soapbox. 'You spend thousands giving us stickers and telling us to look out for burglars and their like, when, in effect, all you're doing is letting us do your job for you.'

Mason butted in, unable to keep silent any longer. 'Are you on any medication, sir?'

Phelps was outraged. 'That is an insult!'

'Please, Mr Phelps,' Davies attempted one final time. 'Just tell us what you saw.'

'Will I be assured of a Community Action Trust reward? I trust that I will. After all, without my evidence, your investigation would fall flat on its feet.'

'Not up to me, sir,' Davies replied bitterly, knowing Phelps would most likely pursue the matter through the courts if he had to. 'Though I'll see what I can do.'

Phelps sat back down. 'Very well. At about eight twenty-five last night, I was disturbed by the hooting of a car horn in the road outside. Abiding by the labour-saving principles of the police-sponsored Neighbourhood Watch scheme, I looked out of my window and saw a taxi belonging to Whizzcabs parked outside the entrance to Mrs Sharansky's house.'

Mason had already left the room, tracing Whizzcabs to verify the job.

'Go on,' Davies urged.

Phelps milked the moment. 'The driver, upon receiving no reply, left his cab and walked to the front door. I quite distinctly remember him looking through the front windows, as there were lights on inside. Next, he moved to the front door, then seconds later, I saw him slip inside.'

'You're absolutely certain of this? Did you see him leave the premises?'

'I returned to my television programme, a rather good nature documentary. I merely assumed Mrs Sharansky had left her door on the latch for him. I think I heard the taxi draw away some time later. Until all the fuss this morning, I quite naturally thought she had merely left in his taxi.'

'Quite. The driver,' Davies pressed. 'Would you be able to recognize him again?'

Phelps considered the question. 'A big chap,' he said. 'Stocky. But it was dark, so who can say?'

Davies nodded to the tea-drinking WPC. 'Get Mr Phelps down to the station and take a statement. Run some faces past him.'

'Now?' Phelps protested. 'But I still have some Christmas knick-knacks to buy.'

Davies shrugged. 'It'll all count for the reward,' he lied. 'Just the sort of thing to really impress the panel.'

'I'll get my coat,' Phelps replied, quickly draining the last dregs of tea from his cup.

Davies left the warm room for the freezing street. Mason was jogging back through the fog towards him.

'Whizzcabs confirms that one of their lads took the Sharansky booking last night at eight thirty.'

'And?'

'Someone called Jenkins,' Mason replied. 'Doug Jenkins.'

A frown crossed Davies' face. 'Doug Jenkins?'

'According to them.'

'Jesus Christ. Jesus bloody Christ.'

'We've got an address. Uniform are picking him up right now.'

'Tell them to take an extra man,' Davies warned. 'I know

38

him of old. He's a big lad with more form than Ladbroke's.' He searched the invisible sky, noting that, if anything, the fog appeared to be getting thicker. 'Doug Jenkins,' he muttered. 'Why you, for God's sake?'

6

Southend, 1986

Most of them simply wanted her for a few frantic minutes back at
the bedsit. Married men and sales reps, renting her wares on the
stained mattress behind dirty nets and faded curtains. And that's
how she preferred it: minimum chat, cash exchanged. The first
time had been the worst; she showing her inexperience, lying
back, eyes tightly shut, distancing herself from the wheezing
groans as he dribbled into her hair.

After, she'd spent an hour in the bathroom, scrubbing every
inch he'd touched before cutting her long brown locks with nail
scissors. Then, she'd gone shopping with the money and bought
food for the week. Three days later, she trawled the seafront
pubs again, and, that night, took another paying customer into
her bed.

When the month was out, she felt no shame, no remorse.
She had half a dozen regular clients, prospects for more, cash
in hand and time to spare. Life was good, very good. But she
never forgot how it was for the others, the unfortunate ones,
the lonely ones, the ones who'd simply had enough, the ones
who turned to her for the ultimate salvation.

During the long summer evenings, she'd visit local churches,
volunteering her good intentions to help run youth groups and
the like. She quickly became known as a tireless worker, well
founded in her pledge to help the needy.

One Thursday, she was asked to help deliver meals-on-wheels
to Southend's housebound community. She agreed, allowing
herself a two-week break from her normal afternoon 'work'
to tend to the appetites of the old and infirm. Besides, it was

what she'd always promised herself, the whoring just a means towards this end. She could amply afford the time, and it gave every sordid encounter a fresh new purpose. The money she'd been passed by dozens of trembling hands now put food into the mouths of the underprivileged.

Two of them worked the round: a young student home for the summer who drove the van and whistled, and the Angel of Mercy herself, smiling benignly while delivering foil-wrapped trays of tepid meat and vegetables.

After the first week, she'd got to know many of them personally, pushing through open front doors to bring lunch to the hungry. She'd often stay and chat a while, listening to tales of grown-up children who'd left these shores, and spouses who'd long since passed away, but still sparkled in the memory. Then there'd be an impatient blast on the horn from outside, and she'd have to press on, stroking cats and petting dogs on her way back out into the sunlight.

Mr Fabian was midway through the round. Fifty-seven and sprightly, his disability – an injury sustained during the same car accident which claimed his wife – qualified him for the free lunch. His mantelpiece held a tableau of remembrance to their marriage: faded photographs plotted the complete relationship, from the church gate to their last holiday together in Cleethorpes.

He'd always ask her to come back later, and she would, joining him for victoria sponge and listening as he unfolded the full sorrow of his dear wife's passing. Sometimes, she'd catch him looking at her knee, and she'd shift a little, allowing her skirt to rise fractionally, her mind already made up.

He'd turn away for a moment, before being drawn back to the exposed leg, and the promise of what lay above. Not that she ever set out to tease. She knew what he really wanted, really really wanted. And it would take an act of deep human compassion to give it him. But wasn't that what her life was devoted to, the chosen path – sending them away happy, to a better world than this?

Mr Fabian would talk of his son, the bitter disappointment of his own flesh and blood. He'd point to photographs of the once-happy family; picnics in the park with the wife who would

41

be crushed by his side; the uniformed boy with the cheeky smile, a living time bomb waiting to fall in with the wrong crowd. His son owed money, and now the lenders were coming for the father, demanding he pay the debt.

He'd cry, and no matter how much she tried to comfort him, he'd always blame himself for braking too late – for literally driving his whole family into a nightmare of death and despair.

One afternoon, Mr Fabian didn't want to talk about the past. He'd splashed on cheap aftershave and sat proudly in a new cravat. She'd always known it would happen, this sexual inevitability. Her previous experiences had prepared her well. The act, although uncomfortable, was far from impossible, and afterwards he clung to her and wept like a baby, unable to face the photo of his wife, smiling sweetly from the bedside table.

She gently freed herself, dressing quickly as he buried his head on the still-shaking bed. She wandered downstairs, totally focused, absolutely sure, looking for the correct tool. She found a cobwebbed half-brick in the back garden and took it back upstairs together with a kitchen knife. He had the pillow over his head, so, with heartfelt tenderness, she eased it from his sweaty grasp, watching his damp hair cling lazily to the underside.

Next, she bought the brick down with all her might, sending blood splashing on to the ceiling. A low moan escaped, then nothing. Quickly, she rolled him over, then slashed at his throat with the knife. In seconds, the lifeblood drained from the unconscious man. His limbs shook sporadically, but she knew enough about death throes not to worry about the pain of muscular spasms. She was pleased with this one, dispatched as quickly as possible with the efficiency of a skilled butcher working the busiest abattoir.

She shook with elation, rushing to the window and scanning the sky for any trace of his soul soaring to heaven to join the beloved Mrs Fabian, now beautifully restored and dressed in white. Nothing. She saw nothing. Yet in her heart she knew the two were united in paradise for ever, and they had her to thank for this singular act of unsurpassed charity.

But it was the consequence of the sad and lonely world she lived in that she could not rest in her triumph. Looking at the bloodstained bed and body objectively, she could only conclude the impression was of a particularly violent murder. Then it came to her in a blinding inspirational flash – divine intervention, perhaps? Fabian's son, the debt collectors – rough types by anyone's standards, certainly evil enough to . . . She turned from the body, realizing that the police would reach their own conclusions. And if a few thugs were wrongly imprisoned for murder, so what? She wondered if they could all be this way from now on, releasing the needy and blaming the greedy; killing both with one righteous stone.

A ray of sunlight broke from behind a threatening cloud, sending a shaft of gold into the stagnant room. Another sign? Her eyes alighted on the illuminated service revolver lying in the base of the open wardrobe, an illegal keepsake from Mr Fabian's army days. Now she wouldn't always have to look for half-bricks.

Humming cheerfully to herself, she stripped and washed thoroughly before letting herself out through the back door, wearing the dress, coat and shoes which had formerly belonged to Mrs Fabian, now surely the happiest woman in heaven.

7

Frank Davies looked at the lukewarm liquid with deep suspicion. 'Coffee?'

Mason shrugged. 'Detective, aren't I? Not a bleeding butler service.'

Davies took a wary sip, wincing at its bitterness. 'So what have you been detecting, Sergeant?'

Mason flopped in a chair, rubbing his eyes. One day, he mused, all this would be his: the office, rank, respect, the lot. DCI Mason; it just sounded so completely right, so very televisual. He imagined John Thaw could still be persuaded out of retirement to play Davies, while Dennis Waterman was obviously the only choice for the Mason role. A good old-fashioned beat-'em-up cop drama; less of the red Jags and real ale, more sheepskin jackets and black eyes. One day . . . 'Uniform have pulled Jenkins, booked him, shot him, printed him, and he's waiting downstairs.'

'Any trouble?'

'He kicked off a bit, but nothing they couldn't handle. Ranting and raving, you know.'

Davies could picture the scene with startling clarity. 'He's an old wide boy, Boot Sale. Knows all the tricks.'

'What's your connection then, Guv?'

Davies's eyes wandered to the wall, and a gallery of photographs depicting his career. PC Davies, fresh out of Hendon; DC Davies joining Chelmsford CID; various group shots as he rose steadily through the ranks; and the latest, DCI Frank Davies, posed against a marbled background, smiling reassuringly – the public's protector. 'I knew him as a beat bluebottle way back.

Thirty years or so.' He half laughed. 'The Maldon Hard Man, or so he reckoned. Petty stuff mostly – fights, B and E. He was up and down ladders faster than a whore's drawers.'

'Done time, then?'

'Few months, here and there. Married one of our mob.'

'A copper?' Mason was open-mouthed.

'A WPC,' Davies replied, his thoughts turning to Ruth. 'An idealistic upholder of the law. Good-looker, too. We popped out of Hendon together. And what she ever saw in him, I don't know.'

'Typical woman though, eh? Out looking for the squeaky-clean type who'll wash up, cook, and wipe the baby's arse, then settles for the first bit of rough she finds.'

Davies frowned. 'I daresay it was a little more complex than that, Sergeant. Got anything on the cab company?'

Mason coloured slightly. 'Yeah, er . . . sorry, Guv. Firm's Whizzcabs, owned by . . .' he opened his notebook. 'Margaret Simmons. Uniform's taken a preliminary statement. She's downstairs now with DC Hassloff giving him the widescreen version.'

'Widescreen?'

'Full monty, Guv. Complete picture.'

Davies sighed. 'The press?'

'One or two of the local lads sniffing round. Our liaison officer's keeping them at bay with promises of an announcement later. The game's up, though. They've more or less figured out that the old dear was done in.'

'And that's all I want them to know, Boot Sale. For now. What about other forces? You contacted them, got any crosschecks with the make-up business?'

'Nothing yet, they're still searching the records.' Mason finished his coffee, then paused and asked, 'Guvnor, you think maybe there's . . .'

'I can't think anything yet, Sergeant. And neither can you. Just following procedure. In cases like this, where a body is discovered which has been interfered with or mutilated after death . . .'

'The face-cake, you mean?'

Davies nodded. 'Chances are, this may not have been the first time, so we check with all our buddies in other forces, wait for

45

Dr Death to give us the postmortem; and that is the end of it. No further speculation is needed at this stage, Sergeant.'

'Like one of these . . . serial killers?' said Mason eagerly. 'You reckon that Jenkins bloke, your old buddy, is a fucking psycho? That's wicked.'

'I really don't know why I bother with any subtle hints in our relationship, Boot Sale, I really fucking don't.' Davies rose from behind his desk, leaving the coffee virtually untouched. 'Three years, we've worked together, and you still can't take a hint, can you?'

'Guv?'

Davies lowered his voice. 'It's your first murder, Alan. Just sit back and watch, eh? The last thing I want is anyone jumping to stupid fucking conclusions. As it is, I've got the Serious Crimes Squad breathing down my neck. It's about following procedure, Alan, that's all. It isn't exciting, or particularly glamorous.' He lightly banged the wall with his fist. 'See? Concrete, not cardboard.'

This had really thrown the junior man. 'No, no,' he replied, shaking his head. 'Not with this, at all.'

'Reality, Sergeant. Concrete reality. Not a shitty seventies cop show. Just procedure, and concrete boring reality. Get it?'

'I guess. We off downstairs to see Jenkins, then?' Mason asked, holding the door for his boss.

'Margaret Simmons,' Davies replied. 'Jenkins can sit and stew for a while.'

They had all they wanted from Mrs Simmons within twenty minutes, and, armed with a copy of her statement, they walked past the holding cells in the basement of the building to the interview rooms beyond. A flustered young man in a badly tailored bottle-green suit came racing up behind them.

'This came in last night,' said DC Hassloff breathlessly, all ginger hair and freckles. 'Uniform didn't follow up on it, but I thought it might be relevant.'

Davies read from the notepaper. 'More grist to our mill,' he said slowly, showing it to Mason. 'Keep on it, lad. Anything else, let us know.'

Hassloff grinned and proffered a second sheet. 'Results of the

46

search on Jenkins's motor, just in. Glove compartment makes for interesting reading.'

Davies read from the second piece of paper, nodding occasionally. 'All very illuminating,' he announced. 'Any news on the relatives?'

Hassloff shook his head. 'The odd visit every couple of months. Neighbours say Mrs Sharansky had no enemies to their knowledge. It's going to be like looking for a needle in a haystack.'

Mason grinned at the more inexperienced officer. 'Ain't a needle, son. It's a prick we're after. Most likely we've got him banged up in here. By the way, nice whistle. How much they choke you for that?'

Hassloff blushed slightly. 'It's linen,' he mumbled, trying to recover some dignity. 'My wife put it in the machine and . . .'

'Give you a fiver for it?' Mason offered.

'Leave him alone, Boot Sale,' Davies ordered, watching the custody sergeant approach down the long corridor. 'We're here to interview the suspect at –' he checked his watch – 'twelve forty-seven.'

The uniformed sergeant nodded, making a note on the pink custody record, and unlocked the door to Interview Room 3.

Davies followed Mason into the bare room and dismissed the uniformed officer in attendance. Doug sat glowering at the new arrivals, resplendent in a white paper suit. Davies nodded slightly at his old adversary, getting a scowl by way of return. How little things had changed, he thought, suddenly reminded of similar occasions many years ago, he and Doug on opposite sides of the table, opposite sides of the law. And even though time had taken its toll, piling on a few extra pounds, creasing both foreheads with extra worry lines, it was the same predictable situation – the past revisited in the murderous present.

'Long time, no see,' said Doug. He looked at Davies. 'You're supposed to say something like "What's a nice old boy like you doing in a dump like this?"'

'Hello, Doug,' Davies greeted him soberly. 'Let's get on, shall we?'

Mason slammed two new casettes into the twin-tape machine and made the necessary legal introductions. The interview had started.

'Know why you're here, Doug?' Davies began, staring the big man straight in the eye.

'You tell me,' Doug calmly replied. 'Your boys woke me up this morning and hauled me down here. Went through my clothes, nicked me car keys, then dressed me up like a fucking snowman. Happy Christmas, is it? A little present from you and the lads?'

'Ida Sharansky.'

'What?'

'Anything to say about her?'

Doug studied the battered table top. 'Dead, isn't she? According to your blokes, that is. Tough break at this time of year, for her family, I mean. And her, of course – not that she's . . . Look, the first I heard of it was when they brought me in here.'

'You went to her house in Nightingale Road last night.'

'I had a job booked at hers. Down to the bingo.'

'Tell us what happened, Doug.'

'Got there 'bout eightish. Couple of blasts on the horn, then nothing. Couple more blasts, the old dear's nowhere in sight.'

'You got out of the cab?'

Doug shook his head. 'Are you kidding? It's bloody freezing of a night. I left it a few minutes, in case she was on the bog or something, then radioed base to tell them it was a no-show.'

Davies leaned back in the wooden chair. 'This was a regular fare, though, wasn't it? Mrs Sharansky took a cab every Friday night for the bingo hall.'

'Not with me,' Doug replied. 'One of the other lads normally took the job. We've had . . . one or two problems with the company, so I took the job to fill in.'

Mason began sucking on a match. 'We've already spoken to Mrs Simmons at Whizzcabs, Doug. She told us about all the "problems".'

Doug was unimpressed. 'Bully for you. Then she'll probably have told you I phoned her from the cab and asked her to give the old woman a ring, just to check she wasn't asleep or something. She did, then called me back. Still no reply. I moved on, clocked off. It was my last job on the shift. Margaret – Mrs Simmons, that is – had just given me a bit of bad news, and I just wasn't in the mood for it.'

Davies watched his man closely. 'What sort of mood were you in, Doug?'

'Like I say, I'd just had a bit of bad news.' He began to scratch at the sides of his greying stubble a little nervously. He hated this, hated every minute of it. The two of them there, cleverer than him, trying to catch him out. It was like everyone always said, you needn't have done anything to feel guilty in a police station.

'How about extremely pissed off and abusive, Doug?'

'It's Christmas,' he replied, trying a winning smile that lost. 'We all get a bit stressed, don't we? Bet you lads do too, eh, Frank?'

'Ah, but we try to avoid making threats of physical violence to our customers.' Davies passed the statement taken from the unlucky punter who'd tried to hail Doug's taxi to take him to The Bell in Little Waltham. 'Seems you upset the wrong person, Doug. He filed a complaint, even suspected you of drinking at the wheel.'

'This is rubbish. I mean . . .' Doug read the statement with a trembling hand. 'He was just some tosser that jumped in when I was at the lights. Yeah, I told him to piss off. I was on a pre-booked job, for Christ's sake.'

Davies slid the second piece of paper across the table. 'Had you been drinking?'

'No.'

'Interesting, then,' said Davies, 'that we should find two quarter-bottles of Scotch in your glove compartment.'

'Medical reasons,' Doug boldly replied.

Mason leaned forward. 'What about the rubbers, then, Doug? Medical reasons, too?'

'Rubbers?'

'Condoms. You and Mrs Simmons's baby preventers.'

Doug shifted slightly. 'One of the other lads must've put them there for a joke.'

'What, a pack of twelve with five missing? Funny fucking joke, Doug.'

'They've got a strange sense of humour.'

'Ruth know, does she?' Davies asked. 'About your extramarital overtime?'

49

Doug's eyes pleaded with his old adversary. 'You wouldn't, would you? Please, Frank, I done nothing last night. I told you all I know. I'm sorry about the old lady, I really am. Please, don't start shouting off to the missus. Margaret and I was just a . . . thing, that's all. You know, wasn't ever serious. Don't tell Ruth. Play the fucking game, Frank, eh?'

'Bet Ruth wasn't too happy about you being picked up this morning.'

'She doesn't know.'

'Doesn't know?'

'She works mornings. Office cleaning, three times a week. Doesn't get home till lunch. You let me on my way now, and she doesn't have to know a thing about it.'

'Office cleaning?' Davies replied, trying hard to imagine his former colleague and promising police officer reduced to polishing desks for a living. 'Christ. She really screwed up when she met you, didn't she?'

'We've done all right up till now . . .' Doug started to protest, before a knock on the door stalled him.

'DC Hassloff enters the room,' Mason dutifully recorded for the tape.

Hassloff lingered in the doorway. 'A word, Guv?'

Davies nodded, walking into the corridor outside.

Mason checked his watch. 'Interview suspended at twelve fifty-nine.' He turned off the twin-cassette machine. 'You got a brief, Mr Jenkins?' he casually enquired.

'Solicitor, you mean? Don't need one, do I? Ain't done nothing.'

'Your choice.'

'S'right. My choice.'

They sat in silence for a few minutes before Davies re-entered the room, nodding at Mason to turn the tapes back on. He sat back down and placed a small see-through plastic bag on the desk. A shiny black wallet could clearly be seen inside.

Doug shifted uneasily.

'Recognize this?'

'It's a plastic bag.'

'Don't get smart on me, Doug.'

'Looks like a wallet.'

'Mrs Sharansky's wallet.'

'Is that so?' A bead of sweat broke from Doug's brow.

'Just handed in, Doug,' Davies continued. 'Member of the public found it on the grass verge by Parkway this morning. Nice gesture, don't you think? Good to see there's still some basic honesty at work within our happy little town.'

'If you say so.'

'Course, it might have had something to do with the fact that the bloody thing was empty. I mean, maybe if you'd left twenty quid in it, they'd have nicked the money then hidden it somewhere a little less public.' He picked up the plastic bag. 'Chucked it, did you? From the cab as you drove away?'

'I didn't do nothing!'

Davies half smiled, enjoying the ironic relevance of the double negative. He half considered pointing it out to Doug, but the sad truth was that the old boy was most probably too thick to understand he'd just inadvertently confessed. He returned to the wallet. 'Three sets of prints on this. One belonging to the deceased. One belonging to our honest member of the public . . .'

'I turned up at the house, hooted the horn . . .'

'And yours, Doug. Your prints on Mrs Ida Sharansky's wallet. We've just checked them with the set we took from you this morning.'

'Well, someone's fucked up, then! I never touched the bloody thing! God's honest truth!' Doug found the room had gone suddenly silent, and he seemed distantly to hear himself struggling to fill the stifling void with his familiar voice. 'I mean, how can they be my dabs, Frank, when I ain't never even seen the thing before? Answer me that, if you can, eh? I mean, I'm mystified, it just don't make sense, does it? Eh?'

Davies stood and began to walk slowly round the room, while Mason watched Doug like a hawk. 'You see, Doug, I've got a real problem.'

Doug nodded earnestly. 'You and me both, Frank. I'm really confused, too.'

'I've got an old woman, murdered and several clues which seem to contradict your version of events.' Davies sat back down, arms placed behind his head, staring Doug straight in the eye. 'Few beers last night was it?'

'That's not a crime, is it?'

'It is if you use someone else's money.'

'Jesus, Frank, why don't you listen to me? I never nicked her purse! I'm past all that shit. Christ, you know that as well as I do.'

Davies shook his head slowly and played his trump card. 'I've got an eyewitness, Doug. Says he's prepared to stand up in court and testify that he saw you leave your cab, look through Mrs Sharansky's windows, then walk inside.'

Doug sat open-mouthed. 'Eyewitness?'

Mason continued: 'We know you left Whizzcabs in a foul temper. Mrs Simmons told us about her plans to fold the business. She also told us your affair was one of the deciding factors. That must have hurt real bad.'

'Eyewitness? Who? They're lying, or . . . or mistaken. I was in the cab. I never left the cab.'

Davies cut in. 'Here's a possible scenario, Doug. You were fuming, abusive to anyone trying to hail the car, and most probably drinking Scotch. You got to Ida's. The old girl wouldn't come to the door. You went up to the house. The door was open –'

'No, no, no.'

'– You went in, pissed, angry. It all started coming back, the old days. Remember the old days, Doug? Bit of breaking and entering, robbing those you thought could well afford it? I do, Doug.'

'I've been straight for twenty-six years, for Christ's sake!'

'Come on, Doug,' Mason fired back. 'Just haven't been caught, have you? Once a villain, always a villain. You done her in. Topped her for her bloody bingo money! You filthy ba–'

'That's enough, Sergeant!' Davies cried, anxious not to give Jenkins's brief anything which might indicate that the suspect had been abused in any way.

'He's overstepping the bloody mark, Frank,' Doug protested. 'I want some legal representation here, now.'

Davies played at considering the request. 'Heard a story the other day, Doug. Real strange, it was. Want to hear it?'

'I want a solicitor.'

Davies nodded, then continued. 'On the radio, this was, so it must be true. Apparently this French hang-gliding bloke was flying around when he entered this enormous thundercloud and shot upwards like a bloody rocket. He entered the jet stream that circles the earth, suffocated, died, and his body froze. Even weirder, the bloody Russians have been tracking him on their radar as he circles the planet. Seems he could be up there forever, perfectly preserved, this frozen Frenchman dangling from a bit of canvas.'

Doug looked at him as if he was mad. 'I don't see . . .'

Davies thumped the table with his fist. Even Mason jumped with shock. 'The point is, Doug, I find that story a damn sight more convincing than yours!' He stood to leave. 'Let's hope your brief's a bloody good one, because the way it's stacking up, Doug, we'll be charging you with murder.'

8

Ruth Jenkins sat on her toilet, as comfortable as a forty-seven-year-old woman with occasional haemorrhoid problems could be. It wasn't nice or dignified, this growing-old business. Week by week, month by month, another line, another crease, another symptom of her inevitable march towards her mother's total immobilization appeared as if to taunt her with its ragged inevitability. What was the point, she idly wondered, in being so completely damn fit and healthy as a child, when life dictated that you really needed all that youthful energy to battle on your behalf years later?

Sod it, she decided philosophically, making a mental list of the forthcoming shopping trip. The last Saturday before Christmas, her last chance to brave the pedestrianized town centre and its gaudy year-on-year decorations, mingling with upwards of fifteen thousand disgruntled residents as they clamoured for food, presents, and all the largely unnecessary traditional trimmings.

The doorbell rang. Bloody hell! Wasn't it always the way whenever she settled down for a five-minute respite after a morning's office cleaning? It rang again, more urgently now, pushed four times in quick succession. Cursing, she re-dressed, flushed, and hurriedly washed her hands before making her way quickly downstairs towards the front door.

'Frank?'

Davies tried a smile, difficult in the circumstances. 'Hope I didn't disturb you, Ruth?'

For an instant, Ruth was all confusion. She couldn't remember the last time she'd seen her former colleague. He'd certainly never visited the house before. 'I was simply going through the motions. Christmas, you know? Long time, no see, Frank. I'm ... er ... shocked.'

He nodded, face fixed, serious, expressionless. 'Can I come in?'

She ran her hands through her short, hennaed hair and sighed. 'Classic timing, Frank. You turn up like a prodigal friend on the busiest Saturday of the year. I've got things to do. It's great to see you, but can't it wait? Another time, perhaps. Drop by over Christmas.'

'It's business, Ruth.'

'Oh.'

'I'm sorry.'

'What for?'

'Can I ... ?' He took half a step forward.

'I suppose so.' Ruth showed Davies inside, trying to ignore the bad feeling in the pit of her stomach. 'Tea?'

'If it's no problem.'

She busied herself in the kitchen as Davies stood awkwardly in the through-lounge.

'Got a cleaning job, then?'

'Needs must, Frank. How did you know?'

'Been talking to Doug this morning.'

'Doug? This morning?'

Davies walked into the tiny kitchen and watched Ruth make the tea. 'I've had to pull him in, Ruth.'

The words bit deeply into Ruth's fast-beating heart. All thought of Christmas was instantly forgotten. 'Oh God. The station?' she asked quietly.

Davies nodded. 'Had a big one come through, Ruth. Little old lady found dead in Nightingale Road.' He paused before adding, 'Doug's ... well, he's helping us with our enquiries.'

Ruth's hands shook as she poured boiling water over two tea bags. 'Sorry, Frank. I'm not quite with this. Someone's been killed, and you've taken Doug in for questioning?'

'I'm sorry, Ruth.'

'My Doug?'

Davies took the proffered cup, shifting nervously from foot to foot. 'Ruth, what time did he get in last night?'

Anger and panic began to override Ruth's shock. 'Hang on a minute, Frank. You don't come in here and tell me my husband's been arrested, then calmly start asking me bloody questions! Not before I see him, you don't! Besides, don't you think I've got one or two questions for you? Like what the hell is this all about, for starters?'

'He's in custody, Ruth. It doesn't look good.'

She held up a hand. 'What doesn't look good?'

Davies tried his most reassuring smile. 'Can we just sit down for a moment?'

'I want to know what's going on. Why have you arrested him?'

'Please,' Davies implored. 'Let's sit down, eh?'

They sat on a battered sofa, each cradling their steaming hot cups. Davies explained all he knew, a potted diplomatic version, as Ruth listened.

'That's as far as it goes,' he summarized. 'I can place Doug on the premises; I've got his dabs on Mrs Sharansky's wallet; past record to consider – the lot.' He turned to her. 'I've got to tell you, Ruth, I'm bloody close to charging him. I came to see you because . . .'

'Because?' Ruth repeated softly, her mind swimming with fact and detail.

'It's been a long time, you know, since the good old days. Guess we've all lost touch a little bit. The odd barbecue, friend's wedding, you know.'

'No,' Ruth calmly replied. 'I don't, Frank. I really don't.'

Davies placed his cup carefully back on the crowded table. 'What I'm trying to say, Ruth, is that you're the best judge of him now. He could be in really deep waters. I . . . er . . . need to know what he's really like. These days. If he could really . . . you know . . . ?'

'Kill someone?' Ruth was appalled.

'Maybe that. Yeah.'

'No. Never.'

'How do you know?'

Now she was incensed. 'How do I know? Twenty-six fucking years of marriage, Frank! Guess that gives me the inside edge, eh?'

56

He shifted slightly, hating every moment spent in the gloomy room. Ruth was one of his oldest friends, but this was one instance when professional duty overtook private emotions. 'Has he ever hit you at all, Ruth?'

She sat stunned by the question, mouth agape at the sheer audacity of it.

'Look Ruth,' he apologized, 'I don't want to ask you this —'

'Get out, Frank.'

'But an old lady's been murdered, and I'm looking at Doug as . . .'

'I said, get out!' Ruth demanded. 'And take your feeble insinuations with you! Of course he's never hit me! For Christ's sake, Frank, you've always had a down on Doug, ever since the old days. He's straight now; heaven knows how many times I've told you that!'

Davies bristled, embarrassed and flustered. He fought to recover some credibility. Then, before he could stop himself, it was out. 'I know about Doug and Margaret Simmons, Ruth. Their little games in the Portakabin when they thought no one was looking.'

Ruth was up on her feet, marching towards the hallway. 'It's time you left. Right now! Go on, out!'

But Davies stayed put. 'We interviewed her; she told us all about it. Confronted Doug with the truth, he didn't deny it.'

Ruth's head was beginning to spin. 'Truth?'

'The affair. Their affair.'

She was silent for a moment, deciding whether it would be more satisfying to slap his face or knee him where it hurts. She opted for neither, wishing to retain whatever dignity remained. Doug, an affair? It simply wasn't credible. And with Margaret Simmons? Overweight, dyed blonde hair, rotten teeth and piggy eyes? Ruth caught herself just in time. What the hell was she doing, carrying out a mental assassination on a good friend? Surely she wasn't jealous? Besides, the very idea of Doug and Margaret was completely preposterous, and frankly rather unsavoury. 'Doug's not the brightest of men,' she said defiantly. 'He's easy meat to dupe.'

'I think it was more a case of him duping her,' Davies replied.

'She told us she was so disgusted with herself that it was one of the reasons she was winding up the business.'

'Well, now I know this is complete fantasy. Margaret winding up Whizzcabs? At Christmas?' Ruth shook her head. 'For God's sake, Frank, they get sixty per cent of the year's takings over Christmas. Someone's been stringing you a long, long line.'

Davies nodded in feigned agreement. 'She told Doug last night that he and the other drivers should start looking for another job in the New Year. Apparently, Doug took it very bad.'

Ruth was flabbergasted. 'But she can't just do that,' she said, sinking down on to one of the dining chairs that might soon be going back to the shop if the HP payments weren't kept up. 'You sure of this? It doesn't make any sense. How's Doug going to get another job? It's not even his cab.'

Davies lowered his voice respectfully. 'The job might not be a problem, Ruth.'

She stared blankly back, wondering how much more she could stand.

'It seems he left Whizzcabs in a foul temper. He was drinking and he was seen entering the premises. Next morning a neighbour finds the old woman dead.'

'No,' Ruth replied. 'Not Doug.'

'How do you know, Ruth? How can you possibly say? You didn't even know about him and Mrs Simmons until I told you.'

She reached for a cigarette and lit up, tight-lipped and frosty. 'I'll say it again, Detective Chief Inspector. He's not blessed with the quickest mind. He'd admit to anything if he thought it'd get him out of trouble.'

Davies tried a new tack, something which had been bothering him since he'd first stared into the dead, painted face earlier that morning. 'Doug ever been into anything . . . unusual?'

The question ambushed her. 'Unusual?'

He blushed slightly. 'A bit . . . well, kinky, perhaps?'

'Kinky? You mean, sexually?'

'Please, Ruth,' he begged. 'It's important. And I'd far rather ask you off the record, so to speak, than down at the station.'

'She was raped, then, this old woman?'

'I can't tell you that, Ruth. You know the drill.'

Ruth screwed up her face. 'And you think Doug . . . ?' Words failed her. She felt quite sick with it all. 'I want to see him,' she said.

'He's with a brief. Like I said, it's not looking good. The circumstantial evidence is piled pretty high against him. Hopefully the duty solicitor is speaking some sense to him.'

She rose and walked out into the hallway, returning with her coat. 'Take me there,' she said sharply. 'I want to see him now.'

'S'difficult, Ruth.'

She half laughed. 'Christ almighty! Are you telling me that with all your rank, you can't let me in to see my own damn husband?'

'Is he into make-up, Ruth?'

'Make-up?'

'Lipstick, face powder?'

'I'm not even going to answer that!'

'Ruth, please,' Davies soothed. 'I have to ask.'

'And what do you expect me to say?' she snapped, buttoning her coat. 'That when Doug knocks off he races home and makes himself up like Danny La Rue every night?' She turned on him acidly. 'I'm going to see him. I'd appreciate a lift.'

'You can't, not yet. Not until we've finished with him.'

'Fine,' she replied defiantly. 'I'll go on my own.'

Davies stood and followed her out of the front door. If there was one thing he had always admired in Ruth Golden, it was her tenaciousness. Once the bright-eyed young policewoman had made her mind up . . . 'I'll take you,' he conceded. 'But I can't promise anything.'

'Big of you, Frank. Very big of you.'

9

It was normally a five-minute drive from Ruth's humble two-bedroom terrace to the imposing police station at the junction of New Street and Victoria Road. However, that Saturday, Christmas had clogged every road with thousands of overheating cars, their drivers anxiously searching for non-existent parking spaces.

'Whatever happened to chestnuts roasting on an open fire?' Frank gamely tried as they crawled forward another twenty yards. 'Shopping's all it seems to be about these days.'

Ruth said nothing, glad that Frank's was an unmarked car. Not that she needed to have worried about being spotted. Eighteen years in Chelmsford had left her with approximately one friend for every three years spent in the place, and even those couldn't be called trusted. Acquaintances, people to share an occasional evening at the pub, or a summer barbecue. Christ, she reflected, it was a miserable haul after nearly two decades.

The whole thing, she was sure, had to be a mistake. It couldn't be true. Not a word of it. Whatever Doug had got himself into, it had to be from colossal foolishness rather than downright wickedness. He'd been straight for too long. Beaten back by the system a few times, but honest, nonetheless. A few minutes with the great ape would sort the whole business out.

And this affair? Well, that had to be codswallop, didn't it? Doug and Margaret Simmons – preposterous. Margaret had been a friend, first in line to offer Doug a cab and prospects after he'd been laid off from Hoffman's four years earlier.

She shuddered. God, what a blow that had been. Three thousand manual labourers joining the dole queue, victims of a silent army of Japanese workers turning out cheaper engine bearings thousands of miles away. Ripped out the heart of the town, together with the self-esteem of many of its former employees. Totally destroyed Ruth and Doug's dream of a retirement cottage in Norfolk.

But they'd managed, struggled on. Their only child, Maria, had married and moved on, leaving the redundant empty-nesters to find other means to eke out their years. Ruth got the office-cleaning job, Doug took Margaret's offer, although sometimes, when the red bills piled up threateningly on the kitchen corkboard, Ruth would speculate on what would have happened if she'd stayed on in the force.

'You happy with it, Frank?' she heard herself suddenly asking.

'What's that?'

'The job. DCI. You've come a long way, Frank.'

He sighed, half-heartedly watching a raging argument develop between two drivers after the same illegal parking space. 'Never ends, though, does it?' He turned to her. 'I worry about the same stuff as you do. Bills, mortgage, kids, marriage, the lot. It's a different force to when you left it, Ruth. I've spent nearly thirty years climbing halfway up the ladder, yet come tomorrow, I could just as easily find myself at the bottom again.' He tried a clumsy conversational tack. 'How'd he seem last night?'

'Doug?' The distance settled easily between them again.

'Upset, or . . . ?'

'He slept on the couch. I was already in bed asleep when he got in off the shift.'

'That normal, him on the sofa?'

'When he doesn't want to disturb me.'

'Right.' And the conversation closed once more.

They drove in silence the remaining four hundred yards to the police station, parking in the underground car park and making their way up through a maze of corridors to the main CID squadroom. Ruth felt alert, composed, ready. It was all simply some huge misunderstanding.

Mason sauntered up, sniffed and wiped his nose on the back of his wrist, grinning broadly at them both. 'Our man Jenkins has had a change of heart,' he announced. 'Seems he's virtually coughed to the whole deal. Apparently the heartless bastard . . .'

'Sergeant Mason,' Davies cut in swiftly to silence his undiplomatic partner. 'This is Mrs Jenkins. She's here to help us with enquiries regarding her husband.'

'Sorry, Guv, Mrs J. Just getting a little carried away.'

Ruth stared at the dishevelled Sergeant. 'I think', she said deliberately, 'if anyone is entitled to call my husband a "heartless bastard", then that privilege should be mine, and mine alone.' She turned to Davies. 'So, can I see him now? Or do I have to march down and find him myself?'

All eyes rested on the senior man, awaiting the decision. And in classic British management tradition, he deferred it with another question. 'Any news from the lab?'

Mason nodded, then looked quizzically at his boss. Surely it wasn't done to discuss details of an investigation in front of members of the public?

'It's all right, Sergeant,' Davies reassured him. 'Mrs Jenkins is an old friend and completely trustworthy. Go on.'

Mason paused for an instant, taking a good hard look at Ruth. 'Guvnor told me,' he said. 'Used to be one of us. Sorry about all this.' He turned to Davies. 'Dr Death has given the body a quick once-over. Says none of the cosmetic samples match anything found in the old girl's house.'

'Not hers?' said Davies, considering the point. 'Then whose?'

'God knows, I've got a team taking samples from every cosmetics counter in town until we find a match. But it wasn't the old girl's.'

'Oh, I forgot to mention, Detective Chief Inspector,' said Ruth brightly; 'I've always wondered why Doug takes a little vanity case with him whenever he goes to work.'

'Not funny, Ruth,' Davies admonished, turning to Mason once more. 'The back door?'

Mason repressed a snigger. He rather liked seeing this feisty redhead humiliating his boss. 'Locked by the Yale on the inside, but no catch dropped. Bolts top and bottom open.'

'So they could have legged it out through the back garden?'

'Jenkins?' Mason replied, confused by the scenario. 'He just drove off, Guv.'

'I mean, Sergeant,' Davies explained wearily, 'if Jenkins isn't our man.'

'I think you'd better read the statement he's just made,' said Mason. 'According to PACE, we've got just about the full monty to charge the bast– . . . suspect.' He glanced shiftily at Ruth.

They walked into Davies's office and read the statement left lying on his desk.

'PACE?' Ruth asked Mason after she had finished.

'Police and Criminal Evidence Act, love. The damn bible of the job. New directives for all us hard-working coppers. Makes all the bleeding decisions for us, really.' He looked slightly embarrassed. 'I'm really sorry about your old man.'

She turned to Davies. 'Can I see him now?'

Davies sighed. 'It's up to him, I'm afraid, Ruth. Got to clear it through the custody sergeant.'

Ruth cast her eyes to the ceiling. 'Well, do it, Frank, for God's sake!'

'I've got to charge him first. Sorry, but that's how it is.'

'PACE?'

He nodded weakly.

'Bloody PACE-cadets, the whole damn bunch of you!'

She was left alone in the office as Davies went to talk to the people downstairs. She still felt oddly calm. She re-read Doug's statement three times, hearing his voice in her mind as she scanned the bland typewritten page.

Ten minutes later, Davies came for her, silently leading her down to the custody cells. She walked with her head held high, rehearsing every word, determined not to make a scene. She was angry now, bloody angry, but would give no one the pleasure of recognizing it.

'He says he'll see you for ten minutes,' Davies apologized as the custody sergeant opened the heavy iron door. She glanced at a small chalkboard to her left. JENKINS, D. 150152. 20–12 MURDER. She took a deep breath and entered the bare cell.

'Fancy meeting you in a place like this.'

She swallowed hard, containing her anger, taking her first look at her husband.

Doug sat on a wooden bench doubling as a bed on the far

wall. He tried again with a weak smile. 'Of all the cells in all the world, you walk into . . .'

'Shut up, Doug.'

He made a move towards her, wrapping his huge arms round her rigid body.

'It stinks in here,' she said, avoiding the kiss with her cheek.

He sat back down. 'Ruth,' he pleaded, struggling to meet her eyes. 'I didn't do anything.'

'Don't lie to me. I've just read your statement.'

He said nothing for a moment, considering his options. 'I never killed her.'

'You robbed her, Doug. Robbed a dead woman.'

'But I never killed her. I swear.'

'And I can believe that? From a man who openly admits he broke into an old woman's house –'

'The fucking door was already open!'

'– discovered her dead inside, then decided to steal her purse instead of calling an ambulance?' She regarded him with total disdain. 'Do correct me if I'm wrong, but that's your "story" isn't it, Doug?'

'I never killed her!'

'Why?' she said simply. 'After all these years. Why?'

He leaned back against the cold brick wall. 'You've read the statement. You work it out.'

She made a pretence of recalling the words. '"I've been straight for nearly thirty years. I'd just heard I was about to lose my job. I was a bit pissed, and then I saw the old lady was dead. I wasn't thinking straight. I saw the wallet on the table, and before I knew what was happening, I was out of there."'

'That's how it happened.'

Ruth nodded. 'Bound to convince a jury with that one, Doug.'

'Look,' he said, shaking his head, 'I know I've done wrong. When I saw her there, all made up like Widow Twanky, I thought she was sleeping. I gave her a little shove, to wake her, and she just slumps forward. Well, I wasn't even supposed to be in there, was I? I panicked, got the hell out.'

'After you'd stolen her purse, Doug. For Christ's sake, you stole from a dead body!'

A desperate frown crossed his haggard face. 'Like I say, I wasn't thinking straight. I knew someone would most likely discover her some time. They did, this morning. I've been proved right, haven't I?'

'And you and Margaret?' Ruth said icily. 'Thinking straight with her, were you?'

He hung his head. 'Guess not,' he mumbled.

She found it impossible to conceal the contempt. 'You and Margaret!' she exploded.

'It's history now. I never meant to hurt you.'

She laughed bitterly. 'It's just so completely sordid. And I wonder at the woman's sanity, I really do.'

'Look,' he pleaded, 'I've done bad things. A really bad thing. A really stupid bad thing. But I never killed her. You must believe me.'

She turned away. 'You still haven't told me why. I've been over and over it. Is it something I've done?'

Childish petulance overcame him. 'Why?' he whined. 'For fuck's sake, look at me, Ruth. In six years' time, I'll be sixty. What have I got to show for that, eh? Poxy little terraced house in Chelmsford, boring bloody life, crap marriage. And all because I went straight to please you. I've got fucking nowhere, while others have shot up the bloody ladder.' He rose from the bench. 'We've been married twenty-six years and we're still bloody struggling to pay the fucking phone bill!'

'It's been an honest struggle!'

'Wrong!' he roared. 'It's been a bloody nightmare. There's no reward for good behaviour in this damned life. Go straight and some other bastard'll rip you off!' He thumped his chest. 'Yes, I nicked the old girl's purse. What bleeding use did she have for it? And yes, I pissed the money away in as many boozers as I could. So fucking what? I've got no job and no prospects. I'm on the bloody scrapheap again, and I ain't done nothing to deserve it. I got pissed last night, well and truly hammered. 'Cause I deserve a break, too!'

Ruth turned away. 'You're pathetic,' she said. 'And why should I believe any of it? Maybe you killed her, Doug. You're stupid enough!' She banged on the cell door.

'Fuck off, then!' he snapped. 'Go on, sod off to that cosy little shithole we've slaved a lifetime over. Live the bleedin' good life. And don't come running to me when you discover someone's broke in and nicked the telly while you've been moralizing!'

The door opened and Ruth stepped back out into the corridor. Her eyes felt suddenly heavy with tears, salted rage and frustration threatening to stream down both cheeks.

Davies met her at the end of the corridor. 'Can I give you a lift back?'

'I'll walk,' she replied, avoiding his eyes.

'It's no problem, really.'

'I'll walk,' she repeated, realizing she had three important calls to make the moment she got home. Firstly to her daughter, Marie – though what in God's name would she tell her? Dad's in a spot of bother, so I'm afraid Christmas is cancelled? Next call: her mother's rest home. Best disguise the truth there, Ruth reasoned. A certain economy of truth was called for, the point being that Mrs Watkin's proposed bout of seasonal jollity was now definitely off the cards. Ruth resolved not to be dissuaded on this. She wouldn't be steamrollered. Not again. Things had changed. There was simply no way that that woman would convince her to change her mind. Probably. She'd leave a message, get one of the staff to pass it on. Cowardly, but necessary.

And finally, to Felix.

10

It had been a delightfully easy day. She always felt terrific after sending another poor soul on their way. A bit like a winning boxer might, she mused, after the title bout. Sheer relief it was over, that no harm had been done, the training, preparation and sacrifice all worthwhile. And why shouldn't she feel good about it? Her rewards were small enough for the life she had chosen to lead. No friends to trust, no permanent address she could call home, just an endless supply of clients to despatch.

And the killing itself – for that's what other people, all uninformed and ignorant, would call it: murder, slaughter, whatever. How much pleasure did she derive from sending others on their way a little ahead of schedule? A great deal, heaps of pleasure. Bucketfuls. It was her one driving reason for being. But not in a nasty way, she'd told herself. Not in a powerful way. Not like the psychos and sickos she occasionally followed in lurid videos rented in other people's names to pass a particularly dull day. Not like them at all. They didn't care, and there was the difference. She killed out of love, regarded her terminations with moral impunity; a travel agent of the tortured soul, offering cheap flights to an otherwise elusive netherworld.

She'd shopped for most of the day, wandering the crowded town, looking for the little something to give herself on Christmas morning. She found a plastic dolly set in the market for two pounds and settled on that. It had combs and brushes, together with a miniature taffeta dress to clothe the naked plastic mannequin. She loved dollies. Always had. So quiet, so kind, so loving to her, reassuring in their high-pitched squeals of encouragement. And they all had voices. But didn't everyone's? She'd call the new doll Ida, and paint some lines on her face to make her look much older.

She bought a can of pop and some crisps, and sat on a crowded bench in the covered shopping centre, watching the world and its worries pass mechanically by. Christmas carols wafted lazily through the body-warmed air. Tempers were fraying all around her, children crying, clinging to their mothers as fathers aimed unnecessary insults and slaps, weighted down with ridiculous purchases they couldn't afford. They were so stupid, these people, so short-sighted with all their bickering and frustration. If they really hated Christmas and the world so much, all they had to do was die. Heaven was always waiting for the best-behaved souls.

Indeed, it seemed to her that the longer one lived on earth, the more disconsolate one got, and therefore prone to the behaviour most likely to condemn one to hell in the next life. Better to leave while you were still bright, optimistic and happy. At least you were guaranteed a place among the clouds that way.

Perhaps, she mused, it would be best to only kill the nicest, kindest people for just these reasons. She'd have to think it over, consult her bible. It would tell her, it had all the answers.

She finished the crisps, and thought about another packet. It wouldn't do. One would lead to another, then she'd be fat and the men wouldn't want to lie with her any more, put their things in. No men, no money. No money, no salvation for those most in need. Sometimes she would almost laugh at the irony with which she herself had combined the processes of life and death via prostitution. Copulation to expedite termination. A closed circle with herself at its centre. Death's sexual catalyst.

As night fell, she returned to the bedsit to play properly with the new doll. She ate a tin of alien-shaped pasta, then turned on the television to catch the news. She liked the news, constantly affirming her chosen path with item after item depicting mass suffering from all four quarters of the globe.

It was the local news. She watched transfixed as a young reporter stood, microphone in hand, outside Ida's house. It couldn't be! How on earth had they discovered her so quickly? His sombre tones filled her cramped bedsit.

'. . . although Essex Police are loath to reveal more details, what I can reveal is this. Some time during last night, Mrs Ida Sharansky was visited by her killer, who strangled her in her chair, before most likely making off with her pension.

'Friends and neighbours I've managed to speak to today in this quiet, ordinary Chelmsford street assure me that the soft-spoken Jewish woman had no natural enemies. All are shocked and deeply saddened by this horrendous outrage so close to Christmas.'

The scene changed to a succession of Nightingale Road residents, each giving glowing testimonials and shaking their heads sadly at the futility of it all.

Rage gripped her like a vice. Confusion raced through every fibre. Murder? They were treating it as murder? How dare they? What right had they to judge her selfless act? It was happening again, just like Southend. The Fabian mistake. She still cringed at the long-buried memory. Her mistake, her bad judgement, letting the police believe the old man had been murdered. Her vow never to take that option again.

The papers had been full of it, sensational headlines, sadistic copy. The defenceless cripple, struck down by a brutal drugs gang demanding repayment of his wayward son's loan. They protested their innocence, sure enough, but the mere mention of the word 'drugs' was enough to have the jury send them down. Which was what she wanted. Or thought she did.

Every day, as more and more lurid details of Mr Fabian's blood-soaked bedroom were released, she became increasingly ashamed of her decision to leave the delightful widower so obviously 'murdered'. True, the police and press were a million miles from ever suspecting her of the 'crime', but it was too late, the damage had been done. Mr Fabian's beautiful passing at her own merciful hands had been turned into a gory media freak show – a total desecration of her mission of mercy.

She resolved that it would never happen again. Steps would be taken, measures considered, plans drawn up. In the intervening years, the fourteen despairing souls she had sent happily on their way to a brighter, more compassionate existence had all gone with dignity, without sensation, rating little more than a paragraph in the local papers.

And the truth was, she began to enjoy it so much more. Not in a self-indulgent or evil way, but as an artist – a creator of elegant catastrophes and domestic accidents. The old ones, the lonely ones, they were the most in need. Just like Ida, always willing to talk. Sometimes, during the winter, she'd stay all night, throwing open their windows, gently stripping them, lying on the same bed and chatting happily as hypothermia gradually took them away. They never felt the cold, their bodies ravaged by the toil of life, breaking down, systems fading . . . but not quick enough.

Occasionally, she would linger, mingle with the shocked crowd gathering on the frosty lawn next morning, watching the empty carcass being taken by a death-hardened ambulance crew to a final resting place, listening to the comments:

'How she would have wanted to go.'

'Reckon she never felt a thing.'

'Mind weren't right, was it? Going to bed naked on a night like that, eh?'

'Lived on her own. Where was the family? That's what I want to know.'

And she would smile and leave, ready for her next client, resolving to make their passing even more peaceful than the last. As little blood as possible, minimal bruising – which brought up the idea of make-up. Just like her dollies. She gave it a try. Nervously at first. Even though she felt she wasn't very good at it. She'd improve, given time, with practice. Besides, the men seemed to like it when her lipstick was a little too clumsy, the rouge a shade too red.

Yes, make-up. That would set the next client off a treat. Just like Daddy. The burial men had done that – powdered him and made him sort of smile. Looked quite good, as far as she remembered. No reason to cry like everyone else did.

So with Ida she'd spent some time experimenting with the new technique. It was difficult at first, the cold sagging flesh having little or no resemblance to either her own or the plastic dollies'. But she persisted. Had to. Owed it to this lovely woman.

And when she'd finished – well, it wasn't half bad. Perhaps a bit too garish, but it was her first attempt on someone else.

She even suspected that some of the men she knew would have paid good money to be with Ida – which must have been a compliment, mustn't it?

Yes, she decided, Ida looked OK, and this was how the near perfect release should be, would be from now on. A personal service conducted with artistic love and quiet dignity.

But now this!

Another wretched travesty sent to test her. An utter fabrication of the truth. Robbery – what robbery? It was lies, all lies. There hadn't been a robbery. She'd left Mrs Sharansky's things totally untouched. And now this further insult – the grand parade of concerned friends, crying their crocodile tears for the television cameras. She despised them all.

Where had they been when dear Ida had wept real tears of grief just four hours after they'd first met, unfolding her later life in vivid descriptions of lonely days and wakeful nights, still mourning the empty half of the double bed she'd shared for thirty-six years with her dear departed husband? Locked safely inside their own cosy brick boxes, she surmised, disinterested, oblivious to the old woman's pain a few feet from their cosy living rooms.

Ida, dear Ida, what have they done to you?

She remembered their first encounter, a chance meeting on a bus bound for Basildon. She'd beamed brightly at the sad old lady, recognizing the signs. Another one for release, another trapped in a cage of fear and loneliness. And she really hadn't wanted the task, not so soon after the man with cancer, but she'd put her own needs aside, staying, talking, and finally being invited back to Ida's miserable little house.

The first of four such meetings, leaf-tea and custard creams, listening to the life history, assessing the need, weighing up the options, deciding whether her intervention was really required.

And how poetically blissful it had been. One of the best, as near to perfection as she could ever aspire to. She recalled every detail: turning up at Ida's, walking through the open front door as they'd arranged, confident that the dark night had afforded total anonymity from spying eyes.

Ida, watching television in the gloomy room. 'That you, dear?

How nice. There's some tea in the pot. I'm just watching this nature programme.'

'That's fine. You stay right where you are.'

Creeping up behind her, gloved hands holding a small length of parcel tape, hovering above the old woman's unsuspecting head. Bending over the armchair slightly, waiting to offer the ultimate salvation. Swiftly taping the aged mouth. And pressing, thumbs over her thorax, fingers squeezing the sides, feeling vertebrae dislodging. Struggles decreasing, finishing within two minutes at the most. Textbook stuff. Ida would've been proud.

The next fifteen minutes were spent kneeling at Ida's feet, lovingly re-making her latest client's face, powdering over years of loneliness, smoothing away the ravages of hundreds of sleepless nights with caring hands. The final touch, glossing the blueing lips bright red and restoring their former, smiling glory, before slipping out of the back door and into the chill black night.

And this was murder?

She fought the urge to scream at the screen. There were others nearby. Bedsits were hypocritical pieces of twentieth-century architecture. Tiny rooms designed to seal one human from another, but whose wafer-thin walls afforded no privacy by their very flimsiness.

The reporter was back, concerned, milking the biggest story of his career to date. '. . . all police will confirm is that they're currently interviewing a local man in connection with their ongoing enquiry, following the handing in of Mrs Sharansky's empty purse earlier in the day. This is Ben Browne, Eastern News, in Nightingale Road, Chelmsford, where, for one day at least, the spirit of Christmas seems to have deserted a street in mourning for one of its oldest residents.'

The programme moved on to cover forthcoming sports fixtures. A man? Police were interviewing a man? She struggled to make sense of it. How? Who? And how had Ida's purse managed to be handed in, when the last time she'd seen it, it had been on the table in Ida's place?

She turned off the set and began pacing the room, replaying every detail over and over in her mind.

Someone was trying to steal her thunder. Someone very bad indeed. Someone wicked.

Steal? Of course! Ida had been robbed, after all. The front door, left so helpfully on the latch – she'd departed via the back door, leaving the front still open. That was how he'd got in.

But what sort of monster was he, not to notice the old woman dead? At the very least he should have called an ambulance . . . unless . . . her mind raced with the overwhelming implication – he wanted the glory for himself!

It had been the same at school. And always boys. Always keen to take credit for her work. Like the time she'd ended it for the yelping dog she'd seen run over outside the school gates. Others had stood there horrified, uselessly inactive. But not her, she knew what to do in a trice. Running from the playground, she found the nearest heavy stone and crashed it on to the bleeding animal's broken, dust-covered skull. Instantly a crowd gathered round the still twitching corpse, struck dumb by such a blood-vivid display of their own mortality. Silently, she'd slipped back inside the gates as a teacher ran from the playground to beckon the others inside.

Rumours soon swept the school, garish descriptions of the canine skull exploding under the weight of a rock hand-delivered by . . . a boy! Simon Jessop soon talked himself into school folklore, claiming false ownership of her mercy. Casually, he entertained small pockets of young girls with his heroic version of events – while she said nothing. While she seethed at the injustice of it all. Hers was the glory, not his!

Those who had witnessed the event stayed silent, knowing better than to dispute anything Simon Jessop laid claim to. Besides, it would mean having to stick up for 'Weirdo', as she was less than affectionately called, a sure way to teasing and humiliation in itself. They hated her at school – the loner who had joined late, two years after the pecking order of the class had been cruelly established. Weirdo – the girl who lived with her aunt up at the old folks' home, who read the bible instead of comics, who preferred to kiss the wet, pink end of a rabbit's nose than spend time fooling with the boys after school. Even children in the infants shunned her.

So Jessop took credit for the dog, together with admiring looks and whispered glances. He was hard, he was tough, so tough he could kill a dog with one blow to put it out of its misery. But above all, they thought how kind he was, to have ended it for the animal so quickly. Jessop – tough and kind, a legend born from her labour.

On the day she killed the poor dog, she discovered what true hate was – someone who stole your reputation. She despised Jessop with every breath in her body, vowing it would never happen that way again. Her work was her own. No one must know, it would be a secret between herself and the police, like with Daddy.

She tried to picture the scene, a crowded interview room down at Chelmsford police station. The monster, whoever he was, calmly telling CID that he'd done the deed. Taking her credit. Most probably telling them that he had helped himself to Ida's money as part-payment for his services.

The bastard! The contemptible bastard!

She knew what the police would be saying, remembered full well her own experience after she'd sent Daddy to heaven. They'd told her that she'd done no wrong. Again and again, cuddling her, soothing her. The ultimate endorsement for her work by the legal guardians of the state.

She'd done no wrong, they'd said.

Now he would be getting the same, this imposter, this parasite. She sat on the edge of her tiny bed, pulse racing. She wouldn't stand for it. She'd made vows. His time was over. He was a very sick and evil man. She only hoped Mrs Sharansky wasn't too distressed by all the fuss caused by her passing.

The next step was obvious. She would release another, and soon, while the monster was still in custody. Then there could be no mistake, no room for petty thieves and pale imitations.

Then they'd realize that the Angel of Mercy still had her wings!

11

Alan 'Boot Sale' Mason leered at the drunken girl in the pink lurex top as he sipped the froth from his third pint. Pure bloody bliss! A top day's work. His first murder enquiry as number two to the Guv'nor, and they'd brought the thing home in barely ten hours. Fucking mega result!

He rarely drank in the Wheatsheaf, even though it was directly opposite the police station. He was a real-ale buff, and the multicoloured display of bottled fruit cocktails and Australian lagers held no appeal for a man more at home in a quiet country boozer.

But this was the last Saturday before Christmas, and he'd told the wife he was working late on the case. 'Sorry, love, no details. Confidential.' There was an incredible selection of young women to ogle, and, the real clincher, the guv'nor had offered to buy him a few pints once he was through with the CPS.

Not that Mason could see any problems on that score. What more could the Crown Prosecution Service want? They'd handed Jenkins to them on a silver bloody platter. A murder conviction and life sentence had to be their only option. Idly he wondered what suit to wear as he gave his central testimony in Chelmsford's forthcoming trial of the decade. He might even get his mug in the local paper.

He was still fantasizing about his imminent celebrity status, when, out of the corner of his eye, a familiar figure began trying to push his way through the festive crowd. Mason noted with some admiration how smoothly Davies managed to slip past the girl in the pink lurex top.

'Get a rub, then?' he asked above the merrymaking, as Davies eventually sat down at the damp, beery table. 'Young enough to be your bleedin' daughter.'

'Behave, Boot Sale,' Davies growled, taking a great gulp from the flat pint Mason had bought for him some twenty minutes earlier.

'Cosmic bazookas, though, eh? Been dying for a piss for twenty minutes, only I'm too embarrassed to stand up!'

Davies shot him a withering look. 'You're a smutty little man, Boot Sale. Your missus know you're out eyeballing young totty?'

Mason winked, miming a phone to his head. '"Working late,"' he grinned. 'S'good to bleedin' talk, innit?'

Davies sighed and unbuttoned his tie. An imitation gas-effect fire roared away just a few feet from his legs; the crowd jostled all around, laughing, drinking, smoking. How he hated this place.

Mason soon noticed the scowl. Something was wrong. 'We all square, then?' he asked. 'CPS boys happy with Jenkins?'

Davies reached into his pocket and brought out a tin of Café Crème cigars, a sure sign something was amiss. 'They're not happy bunnies.' He lit up, drawing deeply on the cigarette-sized cigar. 'Don't think we've got enough.'

Mason's jaw dropped. 'Not got enough?'

'Doesn't stack up for them,' Davies replied. 'They admit we were probably right to charge him, but they're not sure they can bring it home in front of a jury.'

'Bollocks!' Mason scoffed. 'He's bang to rights, surely?'

Davies took another deep drag. 'It's the make-up business. They can't see him stopping to apply the face-cake if all he's after is nicking the wallet.'

'You're kidding, aren't you?'

'Maybe they've got a point.'

'He's guilty, Guv.'

'Then why? Why the make-up?'

Mason leaned closer, lowering his voice amidst the hubbub all around. 'Because he wanted to disguise the bruises. That's obvious, isn't it?'

'It is?'

'Course. Look, Jenkins, he's not the brightest of geezers, right?'

Davies was in no position to dispute the fact.

'He turns up at the old lady's pissed, and pissed off. She's expecting the cab to take her to the bingo hall, so the door's on the latch.'

'Dangerous, though.'

Mason shrugged. 'Who knows why these old dears do what they do. Probably hard of hearing or something. Chances are, she always left the door open for the cabby. We'll have to talk to the other drivers to verify it. Jenkins said he'd never taken the job before.'

'Go on.'

'Anyway, once he's in, he spots the wallet, then sees the old girl asleep in front of the telly.'

'Maybe.'

'He's just about to have it away with the pension, when she wakes up. He's got no choice, does the business, then realizes she looks a bloody mess. So he decides to let Boots No 7 cover up his handiwork. Then he legs it, hoping she won't be discovered for a few days, by which time she'll be rotten all over.'

Davies grimaced at the image. 'Then makes the call to Whizzcabs, to cover his tracks?'

Mason leaned back triumphantly. 'Exactly, Guv. Like I say, bang to bloody rights, guilty as sin itself.'

Davies mulled the theory over for a few moments. 'Where does he get it from?'

'The make-up?'

'It wasn't the old lady's – the lab's confirmed it.'

Mason set his pitted face in its most cunning smile. 'I've given this a lot of thought.'

'Oh, Christ.'

'This is serious, Guv,' Mason replied. 'You fancy another beer?'

'Just get on, Boot Sale!'

Mason finished his own pint, licking froth from his top lip. 'Well,' he began, 'we already know Jenkins was giving that fat bird at Whizzcabs a portion of an evening.'

'Margaret Simmons,' Davies confirmed, wishing he'd taken his eager young sergeant's offer of another drink. It had been a long day, and the thought of listening sober to another of Mason's bizarre *Sweeney*-inspired theories filled him with apathy. 'What about her?'

Mason appeared to blush a little. 'I'm no expert, mind,' he struggled. 'But it has to do with . . . shagging.'

'Is this at all relevant?'

'Bear with me, Guv.'

'And?'

'It's just that after he'd given her one, chances are, due to the illicit nature of their affair, she'd want to repair the cracks, so to speak.'

'Are you being obscene, Sergeant?'

'She'd put the make-up on, so no one would guess what she'd been up to.'

'You've got personal experience of this, have you?'

Mason blushed for the second time. 'Just take it from me, they all set about repairing the mascara and lipstick the moment it's all over. They have to, otherwise their husbands find out.'

'Like lipstick on your collar, you mean?' Davies mumbled, as a distant memory came racing up out of his past. The young PC, proudly strutting in his new blue uniform, afternoon assignations with a married woman. The interview, CID from Colchester asking him if his lover's marriage was a good one, and him, lying through his teeth, confirming nothing was wrong, desperate not to be found out. A promising career so very nearly cut short by his own lust. And the child, crying, when all the time it was probably the mother . . .

'Exactly!' Mason replied. 'So I got to thinking, if Jenkins and Simmons were having a spot of hanky-panky in the office, chances are he was giving her one in the car an' all.'

Davies was suddenly jolted back into the noisy present. 'And you think . . . ?'

'Her make-up,' Mason proudly replied. 'Most probably left in his glove compartment, just like the rubbers, remember?'

Davies mulled it over. 'So he dashes out and gets Margaret Simmon's make-up, dashes back in, then puts it on the old lady's face?'

Mason nodded, grinning from ear to ear.

'Get some boys over to Whizzcabs, first thing tomorrow. Interview the other drivers who normally took the Sharansky job. Find out if the old girl usually left the front door on the latch for them. Scour the place for cosmetics. Do her home as well. Anything you find, send it straight off for analysis. And put the thing to Mrs Simmons. Ask her if she's ever . . .'

'Shagged Jenkins in the motor?'

'Perhaps something a little more diplomatic than that.'

'Had sexual relations with Mr Jenkins within the confines of one of her fleet of taxi-cabs?'

Davies permitted himself the first smile of the evening. 'Something like that, Boot Sale.' He was happier now, far happier. Against all the odds, Mason had actually delivered a plausible hypothesis for the problem which had vexed him most over the day. Maybe he was right. Doug was certainly stupid enough to try clumsily to hide the strangling. Doubly stupid if he was drunk at the time. All they needed now was confirmation from Margaret Simmons's make-up samples, and they could go for a confession. He checked his watch – ten fifteen. They could hold Doug for another twenty-four hours, according to PACE. Time enough to have him safely locked away on remand for Christmas.

He beamed at Mason. 'Do I remember you asking me if I wanted another, Boot Sale?'

'Same again, Guv?' he lamely enquired, wondering how to remind Davies that the offer of drinks, the choice of venue, was originally his.

'Scotch,' Davies replied, feeling suddenly festive. 'A double, Boot Sale. On the double.' Then he watched with quiet content as his disgruntled sergeant fought his way back to the crowded bar.

12

A cruel wind had ripped the heart from the night.

Jude Farrow made her way cautiously down a long dark passage, drawn by the distant echoes of an excited child.

Her. It could be no other, leading her to the stairs.

There was something hideously familiar about the scene; too many secrets lay just around the corner. She felt for the light switch, trembling hands touching cold damp walls.

'No, Teddy. You must be careful.' The young voice drew her in. 'Don't want teddy to fall. Teddy going to break something.'

Jude's heart began to thump loudly in her restricting chest. The door to her left suddenly flew open. A huge china doll grinned back at her, bandaged, bloody, bruised. 'Gotta torch the kid, Jude,' it whispered obscenely. 'Hasn't worked out like you hoped, has it? I'm next. Next to heaven. Too late for me.'

She began to retch, breaking into a run as she tried to escape the never-ending corridor. They were all behind her now, a little army of broken dolls and severed teddies, some with syringes sticking from their necks.

Jude tried to scream, but no sound came.

Then she heard it, just around the corner. Whump, whump, whump, as another teddy with all the life and weight of a living bear-cub tumbled down the stairs. Instinctively, she stooped to save the wildly bleating creature, standing, arms outstretched at the bottom step. Too late – the bear fell, a sickening collision of hairy flesh on cold stone floor. The twisted animal lay in agony at her bare feet, eyes rolling, whining, screeching in its death throes.

The others stood behind, plastic hands and velvet paws clapping in the dead of night.

'My turn now!' the large doll announced, pushing past and clomping up the stairs. 'I'm coming, wait for me!' As it disappeared into the gloom, it turned to Jude one last time. 'Know what you've got to do, Jude?'

'Got to torch the kid,' she mumbled, mesmerized by the vanishing doll. 'Before it happens again.'

'Bye for now!'

'Don't!' She reached for the dirty cotton dress.

But the doll was gone, upstairs into the black, where the child waited in dreadful silence. Unnoticed, the bear died at her feet, thick blood pooling around her toes, matting lifeless fur.

'Mummy . . . Mummy . . . Mummy . . .' A chant rose from a hundred hideous voices, sending her hair grey in an instant. She turned to face them: mutated black-eyed toys, arms outstretched, walking on, closing in. A ghastly parade, hungry for her.

'Leave me!' she screamed, pushing at a sea of plastic arms and porcelain legs. 'Leave me be!'

But there were too many surrounding her, overwhelming her, tearing at her sweat-soaked nightie, exposing her breasts, fighting to suckle.

And still they came.

'Mummy . . . Mummy . . . Mummy . . .'

William Farrow shook his wife awake.

'Leave me!' she screamed, slapping at him. 'Leave me be!'

He reached over and switched on the bedside light. 'Jude,' he soothed. 'It's okay. You were dreaming. Just a nightmare.'

Outside, the wind howled round their tiny bungalow. She pulled the duvet tight about her neck, gasping for breath.

'The fire, again?'

She nodded, dreadful images still too vivid in her head.

He moved to comfort her. 'Just a nightmare, Jude. Another nightmare. I'll get you some water.'

She found her voice. 'No,' she insisted. 'I'll be all right. I'm sorry for waking you. Really.'

He yawned and smiled. 'Never had you down as a husband-batterer. Must have been the chilli con carne. They say spicy food can lead to bad dreams. I'll tone it down next time.'

'The food was fine,' she replied. 'I just need to get myself a cup of tea.'

He started from the bed. 'Let me.'

'It's OK, William. You sleep. I'll do it.'

'Sure?'

'Sure.'

He settled back down, beginning to drift off. She climbed out of bed and stepped into her slippers, stopping by the doorway to pull on a cotton dressing gown.

William turned over to face her. 'Can't go on blaming yourself, love,' he mumbled.

'Blame?'

'The fire. Wasn't your fault. Could've happened to . . .' but he was already asleep, breathing rhythmically in the howling darkness. Ruth left the bedroom and made her way into the kitchen, switching on the flickering striplight and illuminating William's immaculate workplace, pots and pans hanging by size order in neat rows from a copper rail above the cooker.

The evening classes were his life now. Twice a week he'd depart for the local college armed with a carrier bag of ingredients to cook some exotic new dish for their supper. She managed a small smile. Dear William, who'd once called the kitchen his domain, had always taken enormous pride in the meals he'd prepared, even when the lucky recipients were twenty ungrateful octogenarians. He'd held the Maltings together before . . . He'd soldiered on, against increasingly overwhelming odds, while she'd sought sanctuary in a bottle, day after day after day.

She dropped a tea bag into a mug and doused it with boiling water. There were bad things happening, she sensed it. The local news earlier that night, the old woman strangled in Chelmsford – it couldn't possibly be her, could it? Yet the hallmarks were the same: a sad, lonely individual suddenly removed from an uncaring society.

Her mind struggled to retrieve details of the news item which had teased her all night. A man. Police said they were interviewing a man about the incident. Something about stealing her pension, Christmas money. Bungled robbery, they'd concluded. A man. So it really couldn't be . . .

But the card, hidden from William like all the others, a crudely drawn affair, childlike in its naïvety, a seven-year-old's impression of a Christmas tree adorned with badly-glued glitter which fell from the envelope as she'd opened it.

The card, her Christmas card – postmarked Chelmsford. So she was there.

But what did it prove? Nothing. Yet that did little to relieve the dread gnawing at Jude Farrow's sterile insides.

> Dear Aunt Jude, Uncle William
> Happy Christmas
> Much love from Chloe

Coincidence. Just coincidence.

She sipped her tea, resolving, as she always did, that William must never, ever know. No matter how much she wanted to discover the truth, it would never fall on William's innocent ears. Yet the pain of living with all she knew ate constantly at her soul – and this was the cause of her desperate search for fertile fulfilment. How many had died in that search? She screwed her eyes tightly shut, unable to face the tragic reality of a life gone so terribly wrong.

She pictured herself in another time, years ago, victim to a hundred bustling hormones racing within, deadly chemical messengers mocking her inability to function as nature intended. The pain of it, the physical torment of looking into others' prams, admiring their contented gurgling offspring, so effortlessly conceived. And the rage of knowing that her time was slipping by with each depressing flood of menstrual blood.

Could no one understand her agony?

Tired, unkempt mothers burdened with two or three screaming kids would smile wearily and pathetically assure her that children tied you down, depersonalized you, sucked you dry, drained you of any ambition.

How she wished to be drained.

How she prayed to die slowly from the exhaustion of her natural role as mother.

How she hated the rosy glow of every woman heavy with imminent child, waddling from one shop to the next, basking in knowing nods and smiles from grandmothers everywhere.

She had to have a child of her own. It was the only way to arrest the constant pain even sleep wouldn't end. Naturally, or unnaturally, she would defy the doctors, amaze the sceptics, delight the sympathizers. With her own child.

How had it gone so horribly wrong? So terribly wrong.

The television, earlier that evening. Another, perhaps – the Jewish woman? Good God, how many did that make?

No – police said they had a man. Think straight, Jude. Think sensibly. But the card, postmarked . . .

Memories of the Maltings came flooding back. Awkward old biddies who died suddenly at night. And in the morning, waking to see the child's eager young face beaming at the bottom of her bed, not a word passing between then, but both knowing.

The solution, hitting her one afternoon as she lay in an alcoholic stupor. That the killing had to stop – they were all at risk. The girl had to die. The nightmare had to end.

And so the fire, late one night as the cause of Jude's nightmares slept soundly in her little boxroom. Put down to a faulty electrical connection by firemen in the smouldering aftermath. Three had died. But not her. It was as if she couldn't die, like some unseen force had shielded her from the flames, smashed her window, thrown her to the orange-glowing lawn to catch her lovingly in its demonic arms.

Jude vividly remembered the chill horror of seeing the young teenager, emerging like Satan through a cloud of billowing smoke and brick dust, alive and running towards her.

'Don't cry, Aunty Jude,' she'd cried excitedly. 'They're all in heaven now!'

Jude Farrow finished her tea, trying to persuade herself the whole notion was simply the ludicrous ramblings of a guilty conscience.

Outside, the wind began to drop a little. She resolved to do what she'd always done: wait and see. Yet the restless feeling wouldn't go away. Instinct told her someone was coming. The thing was going to end. They'd need answers. And when they did, she vowed to be ready.

She turned off the kitchen light and walked quickly to the bedroom without daring to cast a glance over her shoulder, too terrified that a hundred pairs of tiny eyes might have been staring right back.

13

Ruth turned and froze in horror as the grey shark swam straight towards her. The jaws opened slightly, and she gasped at the rows of razor-sharp teeth less than three feet from her face.

Instinctively, she overted her gaze, unable to watch the two black eyes staring deep into her own. However, at the last, the beast scythed away, powered by one lazy whip of its tail, spiralling upwards to join others circling a few feet above her head.

Where the hell was Felix?

Getting to Southend on a Sunday morning had proved a testing task in itself, waiting over an hour at Chelmsford's freezing bus station, then a further hour spent drifting to the wintry, dead resort at a little over thirty miles an hour. And now he had the gall to keep her waiting in a plastic tunnel at the bottom of Essex's largest fish tank.

She checked her watch again. Twenty-five minutes late. Typical bloody Felix Pengelly. The whole crazy scheme was typically his. What had he said on the phone the previous evening? Something about it being 'good for you to get out of Chelmsford for a while, see events in a new light'?

Typical bloody Felix Pengelly.

A few other disinterested punters wandered through the gloomy tunnel, drawn by the aroma of the café just yards from the exit. She wondered if Frank and his pals were finished going through the house yet.

What a bloody liberty that had been! Woken up before nine thirty to a crowd of uniformed and CID officers flashing a warrant to search the premises for cosmetics. Frank had flushed three shades of purple at her language, but Ruth figured he deserved every effing word of it.

Finally, thirty-three minutes after they'd agreed, Felix Pengelly strode into the narrow perspex tube, a huge grin on the familiar oval face framed with a shock of thinning blond hair.

'Ruthie!' he boomed, neatly sidestepping a lunging eel which bumped its nose silently on the clear, curved plastic. 'So what do you think, eh?'

'I think you could at least have made the effort to come and see me at home. I've been up most of the night worrying about Doug. I'm too confused to think straight. I've got a team of police going over my home with a fine-tooth comb, my marriage is most probably in tatters, and I'm wasting my time waiting for you in a bloody goldfish bowl. I'm not pleased, Felix.'

'Evidently not.' He tried another smile before sidling over to plant a kiss on her worried cheek. 'Sorry, Ruth. Just couldn't resist the irony of it.'

'Irony?'

He nodded. 'There stands our Ruthie Jenkins, drowning under the weight of it all, ravenous sharks closing in from all sides, when up pops Felix Pengelly to whisk her away for a coffee and a sandwich.'

'Do shut up, Felix.'

'You didn't feel hunted, threatened?'

'You miss the point. I already am.' She looked him up and down, glad he was as huggable as ever. Overweight and softly creased, the unmistakeable beginnings of a double chin provided a living testimony to the vital contribution played by the deep-fat fryer in his bachelor life. 'You look . . .' She couldn't find the words.

He blushed slightly. 'Fat? I've put on a few pounds, is all.' He smacked his portly belly, straining under a thin jumper two sizes too small. 'Sign of wealth in some countries, Ruth. Let's grab a bite, and you can tell me all about it, eh?'

Smiling, Felix led Ruth from the claustrophobic confines of the Shark Encounter to the brightly painted Sea Life Centre café. They bought coffee and sandwiches and sat at a table by the large window, overlooking the famous grey river estuary. To their right, Southend's pier extended a mile into muddy

87

saltwater for no real reason, save to make its annual entry into the *Guinness Book of Records*, whilst immediately outside, two gulls fought for a soggy pile of yesterday's chips, flapping and screeching in their efforts to steal from each other.

'So, what's the latest?' said Felix, oblivious to rogue scraps of egg and cress tumbling from the corner of his mouth. 'Has Davies got Doug to confess to the Whitechapel Murders, yet?'

Ruth narrowed her eyes. 'If you're just going to sit there and take the piss, Felix, I'm leaving.' She felt suddenly vulnerable, hurt by his lack of empathy. Then reality hit home. Felix may not have been an ideal choice as friend and confidant, but right now he represented the only option. For starters, he was another like her: an ex-copper, and, more to the point, the only consistent 'friend' of hers and Doug's over the preceding two and a half decades. Yes, he was taking the whole episode rather more lightly than she'd hoped, but he'd always cared, shared laughs with them both, and even acted as godfather to their only child.

He sighed, acknowledging his lack of tact. 'Done something to your hair, haven't you?'

'Dyed it.'

'Looks good. Really.'

'I did it for me. Look, is this going anywhere? I've dyed my hair, so what? I'm in trouble, Felix. I need support, not inane compliments.'

He reached over and took her hand in his. 'Listen, Ruthie, we both know Doug's no murderer, right?'

Reluctantly, she found herself nodding, glad of the unexpected physical contact.

His tone softened. 'Remember, you only just told me about all this nonsense last night. I find the whole thing incredible . . . even, dare I say it, rather amusing. That's me. How I am. It doesn't mean I don't care, or I'm not willing to help in any way I can.'

She looked into his smiling eyes, feeling slightly ashamed.

'From what you've told me, Doug's supposed to have murdered and robbed an innocent old lady merely because someone insulted his sexual prowess and gave him the sack. Furthermore, he smears make-up all over her face. Think about it, Ruthie.'

He squeezed her hand. 'It's bloody preposterous. You know it, I know it, and sooner or later that idiot Davies'll realize it.'

'But he admits stealing the woman's purse. He admits being in the house. And – maybe worse, I suppose – he doesn't deny the affair.'

Felix looked deep into her eyes. 'I want you to tell me honestly,' he said softly. 'Were you really surprised?'

'Of course I was!'

'Honestly?'

Ruth flinched a little. 'Things were never perfect between the two of us. Whose relationship is? But if he's shitty enough to have an affair, who says he wouldn't have murdered when he had the chance?'

'I do.'

'That's right,' Ruth snorted. 'Stick up for him. All boys sticking together.'

He shook his head. 'Doug's Doug. Solid, unchangeable. What he sees, what he wants, he takes. It's what attracted you to him in the first place. It doesn't make him a killer, though.'

'So you're the expert now, are you?' Ruth sneered.

'I've known you both a long time, Ruthie,' Felix answered, a little stung. 'Besides, I watch a lot of *Oprah*. This thing comes up all the time. Happens all over the world.' He finished the last of his coffee. 'Just sorry it's happened to you, that's all.'

Ruth felt her mind beginning to shut down. 'I don't want to talk about it any more.'

He reached for her unfinished sandwich. 'Waste – the biggest sin of the twentieth century.' He took an uninvited bite out of her cheese and tomato. 'Now, what can I do for you?'

Ruth managed a half-smile. 'I'm pretty much on my own. God, I know it's a depressing thought, but will you come back to Chelmsford and simply be there with me?'

'Depressing for who?'

'I need to talk to Margaret. Maybe she knows something, anything. No matter how I detest the man, no matter how much I despise him, I suppose deep down I know Doug didn't kill that old woman. It's just not him.'

Felix raised an eyebrow. 'So you'd take him back? And you

want me to be a part of some desperate crusade to prove his innocence?'

'I just want . . .' Her eyes scanned the distant grey horizon '. . . to know I wasn't wrong. That's all.'

He stood and walked round to her side of the table, taking her gently by the arm. 'Ruthie,' he said simply, 'I'd love to.'

They made their way out to a lonely pastel-blue Austin Morris waiting obediently on double yellow lines by the deserted seafront. Felix removed the crudely handwritten 'Doctor on call' cardboard sign from the windscreen before winking at Ruth and opening the passenger door.

'That works, does it?' she laughed.

'Ninety per cent of the time.'

'And you, an ex-copper?'

He tapped the side of his nose. 'Exactly, my dear. Know all the tricks, Ruthie. All the flaming tricks.' He climbed in and managed to coax the aged engine into life. Ruth lit up, wondering how she was going to squeeze another cigarette end into the already overflowing ashtray.

One thing was certain. Felix Pengelly would never have made CID. Not in a million years. He was simply too scruffy; a wild card, a loose cannon on the deck. He, of course, had his own theories, maintaining middle-management police bureaucracy had blocked his application after watching too many episodes of *Columbo*, feeling threatened by his rambling style. Ruth, however, had been at pains many times to point out that whereas the fictional crime-fighting lieutenant represented an absorbing dichotomy of a fastidious mind trapped in a dishevelled body, Felix was simply dishevelled.

It had always been this way, right from the moment the three of them had met in Maldon's police station back in 1969. Ruth and Frank Davies, fresh out of Hendon, had arrived twenty minutes early, all sparkling buttons, pressed uniforms and highly polished shoes. The duty sergeant had already completed the tour of the station when Felix ambled in, mouthing an apology, flies at half-mast. On their first ever beat together, a blackbird appropriately added its own airborne decoration to his ill-fitting helmet.

Davies soon established himself as the leading light amongst the three raw recruits, and the local community quickly learned to fear the earnest young law enforcer zealously carving out a meteoric career in the sleepy backwater. Truanting children puffing on Park Drives lived in fear of the approach of his regulation footsteps, catching them unawares to march them back to school. Local landlords swiftly recognized the folly of slipping PC Davies a bottle of Scotch to ignore an after-hours poker game in the snug. If they wanted Plod to turn a discreet eye, they waited until PC Pengelly took the beat.

For her own part, Ruth admired both men. Davies bore out her own aspirations, and frequently took the time to explain hours of laborious police procedure in the minutest detail. However, patrolling with Felix was more fun. There wasn't much that could match huddling on the quayside on a dark winter's night, giggling over a free portion of pineapple fritter and chips.

As time wore on, she began to understand why Felix's beats were so delightfully trouble-free. When she and Davies were called to a pub brawl, both ran at the double, arresting the culprits, taking statements, detaining suspects back at the station. However, if a similar incident erupted during one of Felix's patrols, he would merely stroll to the scene, arriving some minutes later to find both parties back drinking at the bar, and a grateful landlord willing to offer 'a tot of the usual' by way of thanks for the tardy response. A further six months and she saw the difference all the more clearly. Davies's attitude antagonized crime; Felix's lethargy strangled it.

She'd been on patrol with Felix the first night she'd clapped eyes on Doug's athletic backside, emerging rear-first from an upstairs bathroom window. Even in the yellow battery-powered light, his face radiated quiet danger. A strong jaw supported rugged features which seemed to offer an enticing cocktail of youth, excitement and adventure. She felt drawn to him, keen to see if the allure would fade in the harsh light of day. Like a startled night creature, Doug Jenkins offered the promise of rebellious passion as dark and mystifying as the inky blackness which surrounded him.

For his part, Felix had done his best to encourage their union, maintaining that this was Ruth's chance to save a petty thief from becoming a knife-toting gangster. Davies fully disapproved of any relationship other than the traditional custodial one between villains and police; but it seemed that the more he tried to cool her ardour, the more Felix and Doug would fan it.

Ruth left the force in 1970, marrying Doug in September the same year. With most of Doug's less law-abiding friends disowning him for taking one of 'the filth' for a wife, Felix stepped in as a beaming best man.

Maria Jenkins arrived in 1972, and for a while both parents doted on their only child, pouring their love into the young girl rather than each other. However, Ruth's feelings towards Doug had changed; the danger had vanished from his eyes. Marriage had tempered his free spirit, responsibilities had beaten the rebel from him. And although he now conformed to the 'perfect' husband stereotype, the truth was that he was boring. Straight, clean, but very, very boring.

They removed themselves emotionally, day by day, moving to Chelmsford, buying their first, and only place. All smiles in front of young Maria, silence and stifled yawns after she'd gone to bed. Doug began to drink. At first it was purely social, payday sessions with workmates from the factory, then, more dangerously, pursuing the habit on a solitary basis, slumped before the television bought from the meagre redundancy when Hoffman's laid him off, ranting about wasted opportunities and the stupidity of going straight.

During the long summer of 1976, Felix himself was becoming increasingly disillusioned with his job. As a result, he resigned, telling friends he could no longer bear to be a 'walking relic from a bygone era, a damn village institution struggling to cope with twentieth-century lawlessness'. No one had questioned him, simply accepting that Felix had always done whatever he felt drawn to do at the time. A succession of broken marriages and dismal business enterprises followed. But, mainly to Doug's annoyance, he always seemed to smile through life's many adversities, treating each crisis as another adventure, every disaster a potential window of opportunity.

He turned to Ruth as they approached Chelmsford's outskirts. 'Got any idea where to start, then?'

She started, brought sharply back to reality by his booming tones in the tiny car. 'I have to see Margaret,' she said.

'Doug's boss? The woman he was . . . ?'

'Having the affair with. You can say it, Felix.'

'Is this wise? I mean, is it going to help our Doug off big bad Franky's murder rap? You might not like what she has to say.'

'Agreed. But at least it'll stop me murdering the stupid sod myself the next time I see him.'

14

'Now then, Doug. Shall we try again?'

'Suit yourself.'

Davies signalled Mason to start both recorders and make the preliminary announcements. 'Sleep well?'

'I guess.'

'Want your brief in on this? We can arrange it.'

'How long you gonna hold me for, anyway?'

Davies paused. 'Until you tell us what really happened, Doug.'

'You already know that!' Doug replied. 'That's what I told you all bloody yesterday.'

'Tell us again, please, Mr Jenkins,' Mason asked as politely as possible. 'One or two little areas we're still not sure of. Such as, why make the old girl up like something out of a kiddies' panto?'

Doug ran his stubby fingers through his close-cropped hair. 'I never did that. I found her all made up. Jesus Christ, it's in the fucking statement!'

Davies leaned back on two legs of his chair. 'We've just had Margaret Simmons in again, Doug.'

'So?'

'DS Mason and myself have been rather worried about the make-up, you see.'

'She won't have given you much. Waste of a Sunday morning for you guys, I reckon.'

Davies nodded slowly. 'Not entirely, Doug. For starters, she told us that you and her sometimes had sex in your cab.'

'Her cab,' Doug corrected, looking increasingly worried. 'So what?'

Davies smiled. 'She also said she used to take her handbag with her. And that after you and her had finished, so to speak, she'd tidy herself up, using make-up.'

'She may have done. So?'

'The interesting thing', Mason pressed, 'is that when we had a little butcher's at her kit, surprise, surprise, one or two items matched brands found on Ida Sharansky.'

Doug struggled to follow the thread. 'So you reckon . . . ?'

Davies obliged. 'You probably had some of her stuff still in the car. You panicked when you realized what you'd done, rushed outside, got the gear, then gave her the botched Chanel treatment to cover up.'

The big man shook his head sadly. 'She was like that when I found her. It's the truth.'

Davies nodded unconvincingly. 'Why nick the wallet, Doug? Why not simply ring for an ambulance? If, as you say, Mrs Sharansky was already dead, why not do the right thing? It is Christmas, after all.'

Doug ground his teeth. 'I saw the cash. That was all I saw. Sure, I knew she was ill or something . . .'

'Ill?'

'I didn't think!'

'You killed her, then had it away with her bingo money!'

'No!'

'Admit it now, and save yourself all the grief. Jesus wept, Doug, you're neck-deep in shit. Come clean, and we'll put it in our report. With luck, the beak will take it all into consideration.'

Doug spent several moments considering the matter, licking his lips tantalizingly. 'You hate me, don't you, Davies?'

'I'm not very fond of any murderer, Doug.'

Jenkins put on his bravest sneer, waving an admonishing finger. Now he'd let the arrogant fuck have it! After all this time, all these years of suburban conformity, now was the moment to dip into the deposit account of life. Payback, with interest, thirty-odd years' worth. 'I know the fucking score, you know.'

'Score?'

'The caper.'

'Speak English, Doug.'

'Your poxy little game plan.' He shot a look at Mason. 'The two of you. You and your little pet monkey here . . .'

Mason bristled. 'Watch it, Jenkins.'

'Oh, like I'm really shitting myself.'

'Go on,' said Davies calmly. 'Tell us. I can't wait for this one.'

Doug grinned back, nodding slowly, running his tongue over stinking teeth. 'You don't remember, do you? But I do. I ain't never forgot, Frankie-boy.'

'Remind me.'

''Cause if you did remember, you'd never have nicked me and tried to pin a bloody murder on me. Not in a million fucking years.'

Mason stared quizzically at his boss. 'Shall I get an interpreter, Guv? Or maybe a higher chair? Don't know about you, but most of this rubbish is flying way above my head.'

Doug's eyes narrowed into hard little slits. 'That's because it don't concern you, dickhead. Before your time. This is . . . personal. Between me and the DCI.'

Frank sighed, fast becoming irritated by Doug's hijacking of the interview. 'Spit it out, then. Whatever it is. Then we can get back to the proper questions, eh?'

'So cool. So calm.'

'Doug, I'm getting . . .'

'In front of your little whipping boy? That how you want it, is it, Frank?' He lowered his voice to a whisper. 'You'd better be careful. I've had a lot of time to think this through. And once I start dropping my bombs, your reputation's going to be blown to fucking bits, Frank.'

The two CID men turned to each other, shaking their heads at the delay to proceedings. Davies nodded to Mason, who terminated the interview, then left the room, promising to return with coffee in five minutes.

'Off the record, then,' Doug smugly announced. 'Must be crapping yourself, Frank. Starting to come back, is it? The old memory slowly ticking over in that copper's brain of yours?'

Davies rubbed his weary face with both hands, rose from the chair, and tried to massage a little of the tension out of his neck. 'The tapes are off because DC Mason and myself suspect that whatever you've got to say is a personal matter which has no bearing on the current investigation. A note will be made on the transcript of your statement to the effect that . . .'

'If I go down for murder,' Doug interrupted, 'I'll fucking take you down with me.'

'You what?'

'You heard. The world'll get to hear about you and me. How you've always hated my guts because I was the one that managed what you didn't.'

'You're going to explain this, are you?'

'Maldon. The old days. You, the neatest little bluebottle in Essex, always after interfering with my operations.'

Frank laughed. 'That's what this is about? Because I nicked you a few times for thieving?'

'It was a vendetta,' Doug growled. 'Couldn't bear it, could you? Couldn't stand to watch us arm in arm on her days off. Fucked you proper, didn't it, to know she preferred mine to yours?'

'Jesus wept! What the bloody hell . . . ?'

'Ruth!'

'Ruth?'

'You hated me because I had her, and she chucked in the force to marry me.'

'Bollocks!'

'Useful thing, a ladder in them days.'

'What?'

'Ladder and a jemmy. My kit. When I wasn't giving Ruth a good seeing to, that is.'

Frank sat back down. What in God's name was the idiot waffling on about now? OK, so Doug might have been right about his feelings for Ruth, his disappointment in her romantic choices, but that was a long time buried. No longer relevant, surely? Times had moved on, any talk of a vendetta was ridiculous. Doug had been nicked because Davies honestly suspected he was the most likely suspect.

Doug beamed with satisfaction. This was it – thirty years in the making, time to play the one card he'd kept well hidden, even from Ruth. Besides, she'd never have believed it anyway. 'One afternoon,' he said casually, 'I'm giving a little terraced place the once-over, pretending to check the guttering, when I stumble across a most amusing scenario.'

'Oh?'

'Young couple. Having it away. Oblivious to the time of day.' He paused, studying Frank's face closely. It seemed unsure, withdrawn. He struck again. 'Policeman's uniform on the floor. Very intriguing, I think to myself, before lingering a little longer and getting a butcher's at the old slapper you were giving a . . .'

'Shut it!'

'Bad enough a married woman, Frank. But, you know, all that stuff that happened afterwards . . .'

'I said, shut it!' It couldn't be true, could it? Not after all this time? An image flew into the front of his mind. The room, bare floorboards, the way she smelled, laughter in his ear. And her request – her idea, to keep the curtains open. Shit! He'd seen. The thieving bastard had seen it, knew who she was!

Davies struggled to pitch some saliva into his rapidly drying throat. 'Whatever you may think you saw, Jenkins,' he croaked awkwardly, 'was a long time ago. There's no vendetta against you, by me, or any other member of this station. And I never, ever . . .'

'It was you,' Doug casually replied, enjoying every moment. 'Your little arse pumping up and down. I read your number on the lapels on the floor. 'Course, the full significance of . . . what you actually done, who she was, like, didn't really register until all that stuff in the papers . . .'

'You've got it all wrong . . .'

'You slept with a fucking murder suspect, Frank! You try to fit me up as one, when you used to screw one yourself. One that walked, Frank. One that fucking got away. And don't kid yourself that any of the locals believed all that bullshit in the papers, the kid an' that. Still, the copper's whore walked. Now, I wonder how that happened?'

Davies was beginning to feel nauseous. The small cell had seemingly shrunk to contain just him and Doug, the walls pushing the leering old con closer and closer into his own face. How was it possible? Had he actually seen anything? Up the ladder, peering in like he said? The curtains – her fucking stupid idea, keep them open, half the fun's in the thought that you might get caught. Fun? But he'd done it anyhow, going along, all the way, infatuated by a whole new world of forbidden sexual wisdom. And Doug had seen them. Dear God!

'What do you reckon the tabloids'll pay me for that lot, eh?' Doug sneered. 'Like I said, you've given me plenty of time to work it out. You charge me, and the whole fucking deal comes out in court.'

Davies felt suddenly light-headed. He fought to disguise his breathing, not wanting Doug to see his short, shallow breaths. 'I'll charge you because I suspect you of the murder of Mrs Ida Sharansky. All the rest is crap. Made-up bollocks.'

Doug shook his head. 'Tell you how the jury'll see it,' Doug replied cockily. 'DCI with love-grudge vendetta and twenty-eight-year-old secret to hide attempts to jail the one man who could ruin his reputation with a five-minute phone call to the press. I'll be out of there before my brief can say "massive compensation". Then I'll let the tabloids squabble over the story. Twenty-eight-year-old murder? Still a murder, isn't it, Frankie?'

Davies said nothing, wanting more than anything in the world to pulverize the grinning face before him with something hard and heavy. Wishing the arm-the-police lobby had had more success. One shot, straight between the eyes, and the complete joy of that single moment as his forefinger tightened and blew the bastard away.

Because he knew Jenkins would do exactly as he'd promised, understood full well what a skilled defence counsel would make of it, the implications that would be put before a shocked jury. Common sense told Davies to hand the investigation over to another officer, but then Jenkins would most likely tell the new man the same story. There'd almost certainly be some sort of internal investigation, which would discolour the whole case into the bargain. Either way, it was fast becoming a bloody awful mess.

How in God's name could he get out of this one? Denial, obviously – initially. But what if they looked a little deeper, further back? What if they found the bloody woman somewhere, and she confirmed the whole sorry episode . . . ?

But maybe, maybe there was a way out, light at the end

of this suddenly dark tunnel. More evidence, that was what was needed. Deal with the present, forget the past. Concrete evidence, inescapable proof that Doug had done for the old woman. Coupled with a full confession. After all, who would listen to the wild accusations of a man who killed old ladies for his beer money? Yes, that was it – the solution. Turn it all around, show Doug to be a callous, calculating lunatic. Guilty, Your Honour. Life sentence, throw away the key, all thoughts of whatever he muddied the court case with forgotten. Davies saw himself being congratulated by top brass for the arrest, dealing with the media pressure. More evidence – he could beat the bastard with more evidence.

Mason re-entered the cell, placing the tepid coffee on the table. 'You fellas finished your little chinwag about the old days, have you?' he asked brightly.

'We have,' Davies replied, tight-lipped, the rage growing with every moment he looked into Doug's triumphant face. It was easy, so easy to comprehend. Fortified by indignant fury, he now completely understood how one human being could cold-bloodedly murder another.

15

Ruth took a deep breath and knocked on the Portakabin door. A dog barked somewhere in the silent Sunday afternoon, a haunting sound echoing round the sparse industrial estate in Chelmsford's flat, characterless outskirts. To her left, three beaten-up saloon cars bore the tattered insignia of Whizzcabs, once one of Chelmsford's most flourishing taxi businesses.

She knocked again, resisting the urge to peer through the grubby window. Felix flapped gloveless hands round his rotund body in a futile attempt to keep warm.

'Are you sure this is such a good idea?' he asked.

'I have to know.'

'How do you even know she's going to be there? It's Sunday, for Christ's sake. No one . . .'

But before he could finish his plea to return to the warmth of the car, the Portakabin door opened. Margaret Simmons surveyed the pair of them, dishevelled, world-beaten, but far from surprised. 'Come mob-handed, have you, Ruth? What's it to be, handbags at twenty paces?'

'Can we talk?'

Margaret did her best to smile. 'You'd better enter my boudoir. Sorry it's such a mess, only I couldn't give a flying fuck about the place.'

'Woman after my own heart,' Felix mumbled as he followed Ruth inside to be greeted by a shabby desk, a large map of Chelmsford and an assortment of rubbish piled dangerously near a two-bar electric fire. The floor creaked ominously under their combined weight.

'Please,' Margaret offered, indicating two battered chairs. 'Make yourselves at home.'

Ruth sat, refusing a mug of red wine, and watching as Margaret poured herself another in a chipped cup ringed with dark brown stains.

'Don't suppose it's a cab you're after, Ruth?'

Ruth pursed her lips. 'You've already taken me for a big enough ride.'

Margaret nodded, acknowledging the accuracy of the shot. 'I knew this would happen, one day. Knew you'd be sat here, looking like you do.'

'So why the hell did you do it, Margaret?'

The blonde shook her head sadly. 'It just happened, Ruth. One of those things. God knows, I've sat here often enough asking myself the same thing. I don't know, Ruth. I just don't know.'

'And now you expect me to feel sorry for you, is that it? Poor, confused Margaret – all messed up with nowhere to go.'

'I don't expect anything. But I'm sorry, Ruth. I'm really sorry you got hurt.'

'You used to come to our house for supper, you and Harry. And all the time . . .'

'Christ's sake, Ruth!' Margaret snapped. 'I'm sorry! I'm sorry! I'm sorry! What else am I supposed to say?'

Ruth thought for a moment, attempting to pour cold logic on her boiling emotions. 'Does he know yet?'

'Harry? Police came looking for my cosmetics this morning. I'd given him a little of the story on Doug, but when the coppers walked into the bedroom and started rooting through my dressing table, well . . . I had to come clean.'

'Poor Harry. Another innocent.'

'Give it a rest, Ruth. He's chuffed to bits. He'll file for divorce on the grounds of my adultery, everyone will rally round, and I'll forever be painted the scarlet bloody woman.'

'Because you deserve it. Imagine my surprise when the police asked to search my house for your make-up. Level with me, Margaret. You're only wallowing in all this drunken pathos because you've been caught out. Be honest. How long would it have gone on for otherwise?'

Margaret startled to chuckle. 'For God's sake, Ruth, you don't get any of this, do you?'

'Explain,' Ruth demanded, growing rapidly tired of being betrayed, patronized and laughed at. How she wanted to smack the fat cow right across the chops. And what on earth was it about the woman that Doug could possibly have found even vaguely alluring? In preference to her? But maybe that summed him up, a man certain to make the most ridiculous choices, flattery's easiest victim.

'The whole reason, Ruth, that he got so bloody worked up that night was because I'd decided to end it. The job, him and me, the lot. I finished it, for God's sake. And you know Doug. Next I hear, he's been arrested, and the whisper is he's snapped and killed one of my customers. So what would you have preferred, Ruth? That I'd carried on shagging him, so the old woman might have lived?'

Felix sat, a silent third party, as the argument raged on. To him, it seemed that neither woman was prepared to acknowledge the depths of genuine hurt and remorse. Ruth refused to accept any form of apology, Margaret stubbornly resisted taking the blame. He felt it might be politic to try a little diversional therapy.

'That your answer-phone?' he suddenly interjected, the question hanging awkwardly in the tension-filled hut.

'What?' Margaret answered, unable to disguise her irritation at the interruption.

Felix walked to the answer-phone. 'It's flashing,' he said, pointing at the blinking light. 'Someone's left a message.'

Margaret stared at this stranger in total disbelief. 'So?'

'Don't you think you'd better answer it?'

'Now?'

Felix nodded, aware that every second's distraction served to defuse the stifling atmosphere between the two women. Besides, he'd decided he rather liked both of them. It would be a total disaster if they were to fall out over a matter so trivial as Doug's infidelity. The better outcome would surely be that Ruth and Margaret decided to up and off together, putting Chelmsford and their petty differences behind them. And what, he speculated, a delightful pair they'd make. 'Might be business,' he said. 'A rich Arab desperately in need of a cab to Stanstead.'

Margaret turned to Ruth. 'Is he taking the piss?'

'He's always been like that.'

'The phone?' Felix reminded them.

Margaret lit a Marlboro, and pointed it towards the answering machine. 'I'm not taking any calls, OK? The thing's only switched on because I can't be arsed to turn it off. It's been like that for days. The drivers get their own jobs on the street, especially at this time of year. They prefer it that way, all cash in hand with no commission to pay me. Satisfied?'

Felix thought it over. 'So what are you here for, then?'

'Like I said, I can't really go home now, can I? I give the drivers their regular jobs, then just sit here, making my plans.'

'Regular jobs?' Felix asked. 'Like the Sharansky woman?'

She nodded and turned back to Ruth, as Felix busied himself with the machine. 'I really am sorry, Ruth. Doug's a shit. You deserve better than him. Honestly.'

Ruth sighed, feeling the anger dissipate. So they had had an affair. So Doug had deceived her. Perhaps Margaret wasn't entirely to blame. Mostly, but not entirely. Maybe she too was after a little of what Margaret been in search of – adventure, a change to the old routine. Poor Margaret. It must have come as quite a blow to set out on an emotional journey of discovery with such a woefully inadequate travelling partner as Doug.

A series of pre-recorded voices burst from the corner of the room as Felix turned up the volume on the answer-phone. 'Something you said,' he announced by way of explanation. 'You've had this on for days.'

'So?' Margaret answered irritably. 'Are you obsessed with that bloody thing, or what?'

He kept one ear on the tape. 'It just occurred to me that maybe . . . Bingo!' He rewound the tape and hit 'play'. 'Friday night,' he said excitedly. 'The night Doug was supposed to have killed the old woman . . .'

'"Supposed" to? If you've listened to the telly . . .'

'Hush!' Felix ordered, amazing Ruth with his new-found authority. 'Just listen to this.'

All three sat in silence as a woman's voice issued from the

machine. An old woman's voice, a dead woman's voice, polite but faltering in the face of unfamiliar telephone technology.

'Hello, Whizzcabs? Is anyone there? Oh, I do hate these things. Can anyone hear me?' A pause, then: 'This is Ida Sharansky calling to cancel my usual taxi. I've someone coming round, you see, so I won't be going to bingo. I do hope you get this message. Thank you.'

An automatized voice cut in, recording the time of the message. Six fifteen on Friday the nineteenth of December.

16

The anger was still there, growing by the hour, raw fury eating at her insides. Agonizing in its intensity, unbearable in its white-hot demands for justice.

That man, that bastard, the local man the television had so casually informed her was helping police with their enquiries over the Ida Sharansky 'murder'.

Pretender! Parasite! Spoiler!

Murder, they still insisted on calling it? Murder?

Idiots! Every last one of them: police, newsmen, local gossips, and scurrying, frightened fools!

Good God, if they were going to apply that twisted logic to her life's work, then they might as well have told her she'd murdered her dear father! But they hadn't, had they? None had raised an admonishing finger in her direction.

Time and time again they'd told her she'd done nothing wrong, that she couldn't be blamed. And she still had the proof of it.

She'd hardly slept all Saturday night, listening with half a mind to the distant shouts and screams of drunks in the street outside, while relentlessly deliberating on a solution.

There was no other way. She needed to find another 'client'. It couldn't be avoided. She agonized over the decision, not because there weren't enough dispirited souls to choose from, even in a supposedly thriving surburban enclave like Chelmsford. No, the meat of the matter was the speed at which her next release would have to be carried out. She'd never worked to a deadline before, and the thought terrified her.

At four in the morning, exhausted by the ruminations, it

was still the only answer to her dilemma. Another poor wretch would be sent on their way, in order that Mrs Sharansky's sweet passing would be recognized for what it was. And the imposter, the one who'd taken the credit for her labours of love, would be spat out by the police authorities, to rot in the gutter where he belonged.

By five, her mind was made up. A plan had begun to take demented shape within her mind. There was some use to be gained from this. Maybe he'd been 'sent' to her, a tool to shape to her advantage. As dawn broke on Sunday morning, she suddenly felt recharged with vital energy. A new era was beckoning, and she was the unknown Messiah at its head.

It was time to go public.

'All You Can Eat For £3.95!' the poster had screamed, causing her mouth to water with warming saliva in the freezing street. It was lunch time, and Chelmsford's pedestrian precinct, which just twenty-four hours previously had teemed with shoppers in search of last-minute Christmas presents, now played host to the occasional window browser and an assortment of bored teenagers drinking cider and skateboarding aimlessly between the brick-built seats.

A pizza – she'd kill for a pizza. She loved pizza. Pizza and beans was her favourite, with ice cream after. And searching for the perfect client was hungry work. She must have walked ten miles at least, checking the parks for disenchanted alcoholics, the bus station for drug abusers, and endless streets for a suitable home crying out for the release of its lonely inhabitant.

Four hours' walking and nothing. She counted the last of her change to check that she had enough to qualify for the advertised feast, then pushed open the large glass door and walked into Pizza Hut.

An aroma of freshly cooked basil and tomatoes greeted her tired senses. The near-empty restaurant was warm, deliciously warm. A collision of mock Mediterranean fixtures and thick green tinsel ropes adorned the walls and ceiling. From unseen speakers, Bing Crosby's 'White Christmas' was piped around silent diners and bored staff. She was shown to a small corner table.

'Can I get you a drink before you order?'

She didn't bother to even look at the young waitress; her eyes were fixed on the little clear plastic tent-card repeating the unbeatable offer on the middle of the table. 'Is this true? All I can eat?'

'The salad bar's extra: £2.95 for a large bowl, £1.50 for small. The all-you-can-eat offer only applies to the pizza buffet by the window.'

Her mind was made up. 'Just the offer,' she said, glancing for the first time at the slim Asian-looking girl, her attention suddenly riveted by the sombre expression.

It was as if all her prayers had been answered in that one single instant. She felt like crying out loud, standing up and hugging the poor creature. Here she was, the next client, standing before her, pen poised!

'Anything to drink with your meal?'

Corporate script, she thought, but no amount of training could disguise the sadness hidden behind the dark brown eyes. 'Sulee Xang' read the lapel badge on the standard red T-shirt. It was all she needed. 'Japanese?' she asked.

'Vietnamese,' came the polite but slightly embarrassed reply.

'In Chelmsford?'

'I student. Not work here full-time.'

She made some small talk, pretending to understand the difficulties a stranger faced in a foreign land. The waitress nodded, biting her bottom lip.

She observed her throughout the meal, saw how her body language conveyed an inner pain. Occasionally she'd smile unthreateningly at the girl, knowing this had to be the one.

After paying, she waited in the Co-op doorway opposite, watching as new staff turned up to replace those who had worked the afternoon shift, praying silently that Sulee would leave on her own. Forty minutes later she was rewarded with the sight of the Vietnamese waitress making her way from the restaurant back up the precinct, head down against the biting winter chill.

She walked quickly to Sulee's side, immediately striking up

another conversation, letting her think that their meeting was an unexpected coincidence. To her joy, Sulee accepted her company, and the story unfolded in broken English.

It was Sulee's first ever time out of her native Vietnam. Her parents had slaved to provide her with an English university education. Reluctantly, she'd followed their wishes, ending up cold and alone in Chelmsford. She lived in the student residences in Rectory Lane, now near-deserted following the exodus of the majority back to welcoming homes for the Christmas holidays.

She nodded, commiserating and sympathizing, gently winning the girl over with a convincing tissue of lies designed to slide into Sulee's shattered confidence.

'It must be very hard for you.'

'I get by. New term start in three week. Others are back then. Some friends, maybe.'

Time to gamble. 'Those student places, quite new aren't they? I bet they're lovely inside.'

A hollow laugh. 'Come, I show you. Have tea with me.'

An attempt at refusal. 'I'm really not sure . . .'

Sulee brightening. 'Please. You see how nice they are.'

And that's all it took. Minutes later both women sat in an empty communal kitchen adorned with posters of the latest bands. Sulee apologized for the tea; money was tight. She mostly lived on fresh fruit and vegetables bought cheaply from the market. Powdered milk was one of her few luxuries.

She asked to see the girl's room, and was taken to a bare box-room containing a neatly made bed, a foldaway chair and a desk piled high with textbooks. Above, a single shelf housed photographs of smiling Asians, waving gaily in the Vietnamese sun.

She picked out a picture of a handsome young man sitting proudly on a moped, the boy Sulee had left behind, now prey to the attentions of other young girls. She complimented Sulee's choice, while commiserating with her dilemma. Then the tears began. Slowly at first, sad single drops running down over high cheekbones before falling from the young girl's delicate chin. Again the young student apologized, embarrassed at the scene. She told her not to worry, to let it all out. Sulee relented, saying she could take no more, she wanted to be back home with her family but simply couldn't afford the air fare. She missed them all so much, the pain was almost too great to bear. Powerful sobs racked the young body imprisoned by time and distance in an uncaring land.

Now, she decided. Now was the time to act.

She sat by the girl on the bed, stroking her thick black hair, offering words of gentle encouragement. This was going to be such a wonderful release, a real pleasure to instigate. She lifted the heavy hair with one slightly trembling hand, while placing the other on Sulee's shaking shoulder. Next, she drew back both thumbs and pressed her fingers delicately against the smooth skin of the girl's neck.

And began to squeeze.

Sulee struggled, panicking as the stranger tightened her grip, using her weight to force them both down on to the bed. She lashed out, terror flooding her mind. The woman was smiling, soothing her, as all the while her fingers fought to close her throat against the life-giving air. There could be no mistake. The woman wanted her dead.

The Angel of Mercy never saw the blow, a stunning impact of fist on face from nowhere. What was the stupid little bitch trying to do? Didn't she understand? Next, a knee struck home, then another stinging punch of light brown knuckles on her merciful face.

The pain was intolerable and her grip began to falter. Then she remembered the dogs in the surgery, snarling beasts that had snapped at her father as he plunged the dripping needle into their sweaty scruffs.

She struck back. Once, twice, three times, exchanging screams and blows with her reluctant client. Blood spurted from Sulee's nose, splattering the white walls as she shook her head in sheer panic.

Her grip was faltering. She straddled the girl, trying to pin the flailing arms down. Dear God! Now the woman was biting her! The ungrateful – fucking – bitch! The stupid – foreign – slut!

Be still! Just – die for me!

Jesus in heaven, sweet Jesus, can't you see what I'm trying to do for you, girl? Can't you understand the joy, the freedom I'm bringing you? Just – die!

This was insane, sheer struggling animal madness! How had it all gone so horribly wrong?

Sulee's blood-flecked teeth tore through flesh and ligaments in a sickening flash of pain. Her attacker screamed, ripping out great clumps of Sulee's hair, forcing the petrified student's sweating head to a hideous angle, adrenaline driving her on, ignoring the pain of Sulee's bony knees hammering into her back.

They fell to the floor. Something cracked under their combined weight. A rib? She felt no pain, it was Sulee who screamed. Heartened, she pressed on, reaching with her free hand, edging her fingers along the ground in a desperate search for something, anything to help her finish the job. They alighted on a steel pen.

Sulee continued to struggle violently to free herself, ignoring the pain, thrashing wildly, driven by adrenaline alone. No more screams came, as instinct concentrated every muscle in a vital struggle for life. Somehow she managed to roll on to her front, reaching for the pine bed leg in order to pull herself free of her silent, panting assailant. Then she felt her head being forced back, her hair held firmly in the other woman's grasp. Her throat seemed stretched to the point of tearing. Impossibly, she was now staring at the ceiling. From the corner of one eye, she glimpsed the brief flash of an arm, then felt the nauseous cut of cold metal tearing at her throat. Blood quickly filled her gasping mouth and she turned her eyes towards the shelf for the last time.

The proud Vietnamese family looked down and smiled in the midday sun as their beloved Sulee gave up her valiant fight for life.

17

Sunday afternoon, 4 p.m., darkness falling, streetlamps flickering from neon pink to cold orange.

Felix Pengelly blew into his freezing hands and waited patiently in the encroaching darkness outside Chelmsford police station.

A police car tore away at great speed, sirens blaring. That made two in the last ten minutes. Something was going down. He shivered, hating his proximity to whatever violence had occurred. Hating violence.

He deliberately hadn't joined Ruth and Margaret as they took Mrs Sharansky's tape-recorded message to Davies. It would have taken a team of highly trained arresting officers to force him back into any police station, and only then if they were armed. It was his hidden shame, his half-buried secret. Guns would always hold the power to terrify Felix Pengelly.

Suddenly it seemed such a very long time since he'd rushed to meet Ruth in the Sea Life Centre. He smiled at the morning's memory; better there amongst gaping, black-eyed sharks than in the foetid squalor of his flat. He loathed taking anyone there, and this didn't go unnoticed. One lady friend, of whom Felix had been particularly fond, had remarked that his reluctance was sadly symbolic of his life as a whole – he simply wouldn't let anyone into any part of it. Felix had merely nodded, before suggesting that they go back to her place as usual.

He wrapped his second-hand coat tighter against the December chill, thankful it was a Sunday. Any other day and he'd have missed *Oprah*, the highlight of many an afternoon. He began to stamp his feet to aid circulation, watching as another police car sped away. Three cars? This was serious.

He told himself to calm down. It was only another siren. Could mean anything. Anxious driver most probably bombing home with a takeaway. Or something.

He wondered how long the police would continue to hold Doug for, now Ruth had handed in the tape. Surely even Frank Davies would agree it was a fairly crucial piece of evidence. The old woman had cancelled the car because she was already expecting someone, a visitor. It had to be the murderer. Even Davies must see that, with or without his prejudices against Doug.

The hour spent debating the issue back in Whizzcab's office had proved rather pleasing to Felix. After coming to terms with the significance of the tape, Margaret had broken out another bottle of red, and he'd watched as the frost slowly melted between the two women. Ruth, for her part, was all set to burn the thing, seeing little point in doing anything to ease the suffering of her errant husband. However, no matter how much each woman loathed the man, neither had it in them to inflict him on a prison community for the next twenty-five years. And, on a more serious note, Ruth pointed out that if Doug went down for the crime when the real killer was in fact Mrs Sharansky's last visitor, the murderer would be free to kill again. Neither wanted such an awful possibility on their conscience.

They left for the station, Ruth's mind reeling. Again and again, she asked Felix what she was going to do with Doug if Davies released him. While he had been in custody, it wasn't a problem. Now, the real possibility that he could be back at the house in a few hours threw her into a panic. Felix had listened patiently, without pretending to offer any solutions of his own. People liked him for that, simply listening.

Two more cars left the station, unmarked, packed with grim, unsmiling men. CID.

He began to feel nauseous, recognizing the dread signs of another oncoming panic attack. He took deep breaths and searched for somewhere to sit. A bench – surely there had to be a bloody bench nearby? He told himself to calm down, let the feelings happen, roll with it as he'd done so many times before –

racing back to the flat, locking himself in against a ruined world increasingly riddled with crime and danger.

No bench. He sat down on the unforgiving steps, struggling to light a cigarette from a battered packet of ten. The image was back, taunting attempts to banish it from his fearful mind. A grinning, shotgun-wielding ghost from the past, both barrels levelled at his chest.

Twenty-one years on and he'd never forget that feeling, legs turning to water as it occurred to him that just the tiniest twitch, the merest contraction of the bandit's finger, would end it all in one explosive instant. And the youngster had merely laughed, relishing the moment, savouring his victim's fear, before running back into the night.

DC Pengelly resigned two months later, realizing that he could be a policeman all his life without making the slightest impact upon the world he had sworn to protect. A rising tide of broken communities ensured there'd always be thousands prepared to laugh in the faces of those they killed and maimed.

In the years that followed, he'd watched as his instincts were miserably borne out. Guns, drugs, prostitution and corruption – crime appeared to be winning, getting stronger, a sinister evil growing like some malignant cancer, strangling all dwindling supplies of good in its wake.

Felix was frightened. An ex-copper with five locks on his front door, hiding behind a carefully constructed uncaring facade. But still the villains came at night, stealing into his dreams to run riot with his paranoia.

He struggled back to his feet, the attack passing slowly, his breathing steadying on the cold night air. He thanked his lucky stars it had just been a mild one. His therapist had explained that panic attacks could be compared to thunder: some distant rumbles, others deafening booms, all completely unpredictable with no way of knowing when or where the next one would strike.

He wanted to go home. Where the hell was Ruth? Surely it shouldn't be taking this long? Something else had cropped up. The cars, their screaming sirens, the grim-faced men racing to some tragic incident. Calm down, man, think straight. Maybe Davies hadn't reached the same conclusion they'd done. What if Doug had confessed in the meantime? What if Doug had been the 'visitor' Mrs Sharansky was expecting? What if . . . ?

Footsteps approached from behind, and Felix turned, fully expecting to see Ruth, Margaret and Doug leaving the station. Something was wrong. Doug was missing. Margaret shrugged her shoulders and walked slowly back towards town. Ruth marched straight towards him, her face tight and strained.

'Waste of bloody time,' she said sharply, breath steaming. Without asking, she picked the half-smoked remains of his cigarette from his fingers and took a sudden, uninvited drag. 'We gave Frank the tape, then wasted half an hour talking about the relevance of it. Honestly, Felix, it was like trying to convince them the Pope's a Buddhist.'

Felix nodded sagely. 'I suppose he was bound to find it all a bit strange. You turning up with Doug's mistress, then handing him a tape to free the fellow.'

'That's no excuse! He's supposed to look at evidence objectively.'

Felix watched in slight surprise as she stamped angrily on the unfinished cigarette. 'So he won't accept it, then?'

'He'll have to now. While we were up there arguing the bloody toss about a tape his damn mob should've found in the first place, his sidekick stormed in in a terrible panic.' She was gabbling, panic, anger and excitement blurring the words. 'There's been another one, Felix.'

'Another one?'

'Murder. They all shot out and left me and Margaret standing there like a pair of bloody lemons.'

Felix shut his tired eyes. 'Are you sure?'

'We didn't catch all of it. But enough to know this time it's a student, found about twenty minutes ago by a warden or something. Apparently she had make-up left all over her face, too.'

'Oh, God,' he muttered weakly. Neither said anything for several moments, then Felix asked, 'What about Doug?'

'He's still in there, I suppose. They wouldn't let me see him.'

'They'll release him, surely. Especially now . . . in the light of . . . you know?'

Ruth shook her head. 'I managed to talk to the duty sergeant on the way out. Chances are, they'll charge him with stealing the old lady's wallet.'

'Remand job?'

'Police bail. He's still a vital witness. You know what an obstinate fool Doug can be. They lock him up and he could refuse to play ball later on.'

'So you can expect him home for Christmas, then?'

She began to walk slowly down the steps. 'God, I don't know. I just don't know any more.' She took his arm. 'Maybe I don't want him back, Felix. Maybe part of me wanted him to have murdered the old lady so I wouldn't have to take him back.'

'Ruthie, you don't mean that.'

'Maybe I'm just sick to bloody death of the man, and prison would've saved me the hassle of divorce.'

Felix put a comforting arm round her shoulder. 'You're too tired to think straight, is all.' His voice shook a little at the edges. 'It's been a strange old day. Maybe . . . maybe we should think about getting something to eat.'

'Eat? Now?'

'I'm hungry, Ruthie. Let's just spend a couple of hours shacked up in some restaurant stuffing our faces.'

'That'll make it all go away, will it?'

'Perhaps afterwards, we'll get back to your place and Doug will be there, and you can sort the whole crazy business out.'

She looked into his kind oval face and managed to return his half-smile. 'Mexican do you?'

'Olé!' he confirmed.

They walked quickly from the station, heading past the floodlit cathedral towards the deserted town centre. 'It hasn't been all bad,' Ruth reluctantly admitted. 'It's been nice having you around, Felix. Thanks.'

'Don't tell me, woman, feed me,' Felix instructed, hoping all thoughts of the murdered student would disappear the moment they entered the restaurant.

116

18

Davies leapt from the car, Mason by his side. 'What's the story?'

DC Hassloff struggled to read from his notes as he tried to keep pace. A mass of police activity surrounded them on all sides. 'Female. Foreign student. Alarm raised by duty warden twenty minutes ago. Bloody close to the same MO as the Sharansky woman.'

'Fuck! Fuck! Fuck!'

'Guv?'

'It's supposed to be bloody Christmas, isn't it?'

They marched briskly through the darkness into the paved and grassed quadrangle of the Rectory Lane Hall of Student Residences. Here and there one or two lights flickered, signalling the fatal emptiness of the place. 'Students home for holidays, are they?'

'Broke up two and a half weeks ago,' Hassloff replied. 'Just a handful of the overseas ones left.'

'Round 'em all up. I want every last one. Whatever they saw, whatever they heard.'

'On it right away.'

Davies ground his teeth, mind racing with procedural protocol. Another murder? Two in three days. In Chelmsford. And the thought that both might have been committed by the same hand, a hand at liberty while he'd toiled away with Jenkins. It beggared belief. They passed three police cars parked close to a lit entrance, their slowly rotating beacons sending lurid blue circling round the desolate collection of three-storey flats. 'Victim?'

'Name's Sulee Xang,' Hassloff read aloud. 'Vietnamese. Uniform have popped a few questions at the warden. He can't tell us much. Says he heard nothing. His office is at the other end of the block, and he was out doing the last of his Christmas shopping this afternoon.'

'On a Sunday?' Davies asked.

'Most of the stores are open, Guv.' Hassloff led them through a door guarded by two uniformed officers. Upstairs a throng of scene-of-crime officers in various guises went about their business in a blur of practised activity and urgent conversation.

Mason whispered in his Guvnor's ear. 'We've got a serial killer here, haven't we? We spend all this time chasing your man Jenkins's tail and —'

'Shut it, Sergeant!'

They stood at the entrance to Sulee's tiny box-bedroom, and, for once, even Mason was stunned into horrified silence. Blood covered all four walls and the window in wretched crimson arches, a gory tribute to the heroic struggle undertaken by the broken corpse at their feet. Beside it, the familiar figure of Dr Cloth, police pathologist, calmly carried out his public duty.

Davies cleared his gagging throat and forced himself to inspect the newly dead body. The throat had been hideously slashed. A gaping wound exposed torn ligaments and cartilage. The agonized Asian face had been clumsily made-over with lipstick. A large circle had been left on each cheek, and the open mouth was framed by an outsized clown's grin. 'What a bloody defiling mess,' he muttered.

Cloth said nothing, drawing Davies's attention to seven words scrawled in lipstick on the wall just to the left of the body. Streaks of blood ran through the message.

IDA RELEASED. SULEE RELEASED. NOW RELEASE IMPOSTER!

Davies sighed. 'I'm really not fucking ready for this.'

Cloth turned to the superior officer. 'Rumour has it', he said quietly, 'that you've spent the last forty-eight hours hounding the wrong man.'

'Rumours are dangerous things, Doctor.'

'Two-to-one it's the same brand of lipstick as used on the

Sharansky woman. Here –' he thrust an opaque polythene bag into Davies' hands. 'Hair samples. Medium-length, brown. Man or woman.'

'They match anything taken from the Nightingale Road scene?'

'Nothing that I've been given,' Cloth carefully replied. 'But in the light of this, I'd be tempted to search Ida Sharansky's place more thoroughly, Detective Chief Inspector. We get a match, then . . .'

Davies called Mason in. 'Who the fuck else knew about the make-up?'

Mason cleared his throat uncomfortably. No amount of television cop shows had prepared him for so much blood. 'I . . . I, er . . .'

'Get a grip, Sergeant.'

'Sorry, Guv. The make-up. On the old woman?'

Davies nodded.

'Just us. The lads on the squad. Jenkins, of course. And his missus. And the woman from the cab company. That's it.'

'No one else?'

Mason shook his head, turning greener by the second.

'Outside, Sergeant. Round up the remaining students, warden, the lot. Get 'em all down the nick for statements. Find out all you can about this kid . . .' He paused for a second. 'Family, friends, the bloody lot. Jobs she had, boyfriends, girlfriends, clubs, pubs she visited, the works. Every goddamned thing you can dig up. Then send a squad back up to Nightingale Road. Fingertip search of the place. I'm looking for hair samples to match those found here. See if any of the neighbours can think of any connection between this poor creature and Ida Sharansky. Maybe they were friends themselves, I don't know.'

'Very good, Guv.' Mason gratefully left the stinking room.

Davies turned back to the freshly slaughtered corpse, and the romantic-novel-reading pathologist dispassionately surveying it. 'Looks like she put up a hell of a fight. Any dabs around?'

'Not on the body as yet, Inspector,' Cloth replied. 'Though I'm inclined to agree with you, she struggled to the last. The blood patterning appears to come from one source, most probably the throat wound.'

'Knife?'

Cloth peered closer at the ugly wound. 'Wouldn't have said so, no. Screwdriver, maybe. See here? The skin's been stretched and torn around the thyroid cartilage. A knife would have simply sliced that in two.'

'Time of death?'

'Two, perhaps three hours ago. RM's only beginning to set in. I'd like her moved – ideally, before she's too stiff to fit through the door.'

'Give my crew twenty minutes to photograph the place. Then she's yours. Happy fucking Christmas.'

Cloth ignored the attempt at bravado. 'Got the beginnings of a big problem, Inspector.'

'Yeah? Tell me about it.'

'I'm serious.' He stepped away from the corpse and began to remove the blood-soaked surgical gloves and plastic apron. 'If we're looking at the work of the same person, then our killer has stepped up the violence significantly in the last forty-eight hours. If it continues to escalate . . .'

'If!' Davies barked. 'That's all it is. If!'

'The old woman wouldn't have struggled, of course, wouldn't have had this poor girl's strength.'

'So? Theories?'

'I need more time, Inspector.' He took a long look at the body.

'Just do it, quick. If I've screwed up over this, we've got a sicko wandering the streets picking on God knows who, God knows where; and furthermore, I'm out of a damn job.'

Cloth turned to the message on the wall. 'The imposter,' he said, reading aloud. 'I assume that's supposed to be your man. Your suspect. "Release the imposter."' He paused for a brief moment. 'It's almost as if they're rather upset not to have been considered a suspect themselves. Or maybe it's a threat: "Release the imposter, or I kill again."' He shook his head. 'Strange little planet, this, full of even stranger folk. At times I . . .'

But Davies had already left the room, spitting orders urgently to every member of his squad. Ten minutes later, he found

Mason outside, gently coaxing a dozen frightened foreign students on to a police minibus.

'Boot Sale!'

'Guv?' He ran over.

'I'm heading back to the station. The Super's going to want to hear it all.'

'All of it? Jenkins, this . . .' he shifted uncomfortably '. . . vendetta thing he's been bleating about?'

Davies looked back towards the guarded entrance. Flashbulbs popped rhythmically from Sulee's room above. 'I still can't believe Jenkins isn't our man, Boot Sale. He has to be in on this somewhere.'

'So. Maybe there's two of them on the job. One stiffs the old lady while Jenkins robs the place. The cabs woman, Mrs Simmons? She loves Jenkins really, and decides to kill the student in order to secure his release.'

Davies mulled it over. 'Lot of trouble for one wallet, Sergeant?'

Mason shrugged. 'Just a theory. I'm right with you, Guv. About Jenkins, you know. But if it ain't him, then . . . ?'

'We've got a nutter on the loose, Boot Sale. And it's frightening me to death. Check all the local nuthouses for runaways, crosscheck anything from any other force which compares. Any unsolveds with make-up, strangling, anything. And get the press in. Fast. But we control it. Limited press conference, public appeal for witnesses. I don't want to wake up to another one of these tomorrow morning.'

'Chelmsford's going to go up like a bloody tinderbox when this lot gets out, isn't it? Panic on the streets, the full monty.'

'Someone's got to know something. I don't think we have a lot of options left. Top brass are going to want the Serious Crimes Squad in, and I'm going to get the bollocking of a lifetime if we've screwed up with Jenkins.'

Mason could think of nothing to make his boss feel better. 'Good luck, Guv.'

Davies turned and walked quickly back to a waiting car, as a series of disturbing images fought for space within his cluttered mind. The foreign girl, throat slashed, murdered within the red-brick walls of this godforsaken place. How much of the blame could he take for that? How much of his ambition to nail Jenkins had blinded him to the obvious? That the dumb fool was telling the truth.

How much of Sulee Xang's death was down to his prejudices?

19

She lay neck-deep in tepid blue water, trembling with rage.

How could the damn girl have been so ungrateful? She had been the one who had sat crying her slitty yellow eyes out over her lost relatives and miserable life in England. But when push had come to shove, when offered the chance of a dream-ticket escape from it all, she'd lashed out, forcefully. Pure spite was what that was.

Bloody foreign girl. Probably believed in elephant deities and monkey gods, voodoo and the like. Probably didn't have the intelligence to understand the humane gesture of eternal peace being offered her.

What a dreadful release it had turned into. Completely undignified, little more than a westling match, debasing the ceremony of the purest act.

She checked her watch. She'd occupied the communal bathroom for nearly an hour, soothing her bruised, bitten body while listening to the distant wail of agitated police sirens. She pulled the plug, watching as a tiny whirlpool formed on the escaping water's surface, then began checking her body to make sure that all traces of the afternoon's work had been scrubbed away.

Leaving the halls of residence had proved an unforeseen problem. She was covered in blood. The girl's screams and protestations might well have alerted any number of people left in the building, so she'd had to work far faster than she'd wanted. Gone was the original plan to leave the girl beautifully reclined for the police to discover. Now the most important thing was to escape. Hours of work would be needed to cleanse the room and arrange the corpse with some semblance of dignity.

Instead, she had hastily tried her best on Sulee's face, but the result was more comical than dignified.

Trying to calm herself and think rationally, she'd hit upon the idea of leaving the police a message. The wall seemed the most obvious place, the lipstick her pen. Surely now there could be no question in their minds that a higher authority than their 'local man' was at work in the community.

Her latest client must have been some sort of keep-fit enthusiast, for her tiny wardrobe boasted several tracksuits and pairs of trainers. She'd changed, putting her own soiled clothes into a bin bag, before leaving at the double. To her relief, no one gave a second glance to the middle-aged jogger who passed by carrying a plastic bag, clearly breathless from the effort. She thanked the heavens for the long dark winter's night. During the cruel light of day, someone might well have noticed her flat court shoes slapping on the frosted pavement. Sulee's trainers were simply far too small to complete the deception.

It took the best part of an hour to reach her bedsit, fear and anger driving her through throat-burning pain. As she saw it, there were two people to blame for the shambles. The girl herself, for turning the ethereal experience into an unholy mess, and the bastard pretender. Without him and his undoubted lies, none of it would have been necessary in the first place. Not a single punch, not a single kick, just a firm pressure as with dear Ida – a sweet passage into the next world and all the peace it promised.

He'd sentenced the girl the moment he'd opened his mouth. After all, he must not have denied the charge, otherwise the police fatheads would have released him, and according to local news bulletins that morning, he was still in custody. He simply had to have confessed, turning her good work into the sordid murder investigation the TV, radio and papers were full of.

She may well have been Sulee's reluctant executioner, but he'd signed the death sentence.

The last of the bathwater drained away and she began to towel herself dry. The house was deathly quiet save for the distant moaning and groaning from a pornographic video somewhere downstairs. Another lonely soul, she mused, seeking private satisfaction from an electronic box. She sat listening to the muted sounds of synthetic passion, hoping it wasn't one of the grubby cinematic ventures she'd once had to undertake. Life hadn't been easy, and she'd gone to great lengths to ensure the anonymity afforded by a cash-in-hand lifestyle.

Thank the good, forgiving Lord for men, and their obsession with putting their things into ladies. Their things had allowed her to continue the good work. Even if it did sometimes make her feel sick to have them in her mouth.

Yet it had to be this way if she was to bring mercy to the lonely and dispossessed. False names and addresses, untraceable references, the constant struggle for the next fifty pounds to pay the rent. Her whole existence a sacrifice to easing the pains and woes of others.

She dressed, smelling her hair for smoke. The first thing she'd had to do upon returning was to burn both sets of clothes in her bedroom grate. Now all that remained of Sulee's release were a few purple bruises, some deep scratches, three bite marks and the dreadful memory of it all.

But at least the ungrateful little bitch would be happy now, safe amidst bosom of her spiritual family. She wondered if her own father would have been there to welcome Sulee and explain the reasons for her sudden passing. He had such a gift for rationalizing the unacceptable. Their chats in the surgery were as clear in her mind now as those far away days when he'd sat her on his lap and explained the merciful reasons for his 'sleeping machine'.

She made ready to leave, swilling the bath and collecting her soap and shampoo. The local news would be on in just a matter of minutes, and would hopefully provide a more satisfying end to the day. Surely those dim-witted fools at the police station must have released the imposter by now?

And if they had, she'd find him, track him down, use him. Yes, the 'local man' figured very heavily in her plans. Very heavily indeed.

Upstairs, in her attic room, she turned on the black-and-white portable. Cartoons! She loved cartoons! This was excellent. She watched agog, as Sylvester made yet another dismal attempt to swallow the big-headed yellow canary. She began to laugh, happy to be transported from the cruel, misunderstanding reality of the world outside, to the monochrome-toned lunacy of the cartoon.

Then she suddenly felt it, a tightening. Something was missing, something was wrong! Panic threatened to overwhelm her. She couldn't breathe. Her heart thumped inside her heaving chest as it sent her blood racing through her body.

The blue handkerchief! Where was her handkerchief?

20

Chief Superintendent Neil Butler struggled to keep his temper. The more he heard, the worse it got.

'Frank,' he said quickly. 'Are you telling me that the man you've virtually charged with the Ida Sharansky murder may now be the wrong man? Is that it?'

Davies nodded, hating every moment spent in the superintendent's office. 'I just don't know. I feel he should be connected in some way, but . . . I just don't know. In the light of this afternoon's –'

'I know all that, man!' Butler roared. 'Stop bloody repeating yourself!'

'Sorry, sir, I just . . .'

'Just what?'

Davies bowed his throbbing head and pinched the bridge of his nose between forefinger and thumb. Two hours had passed since he'd returned to the station, a whirlwind of frantic meetings, squad briefings, discussions with the CPS – and now this, the expected carpeting from the boss. 'We're doing all we can. The whole of CID's on it; Uniform are conducting house-to-house –'

'Bit bloody late for that now, isn't it?' Butler countered angrily. 'I've had the duty solicitor in here twice trying to fathom your obsession with this Jenkins character.'

'Not an obsession, sir . . .'

'What the hell were you playing at, Frank? Jesus Christ, man, weren't there any other suspects?'

'Like I said, he fitted the charge. He's got so much previous . . .'

Butler flicked contemptuously through Doug's photocopied

criminal record. 'Nothing about murder in here, Frank. Couple of stretches for breaking and entering nigh on thirty years ago. Parking violations. Speeding tickets. Nothing to turn him into a murderer.'

'He was on the bloody premises! He doesn't deny it! He stole her purse, for God's sake.'

It was Butler's turn to massage a little life into his world-weary face. 'As far as I can gather, the situation's this: the CPS tell me we can go for charges on robbing the old woman's pension. Then we'll ask for police bail.'

Frank was aghast. 'So he walks?'

'For Christ's sake, Frank, don't have a go at me! Whose cock-up is this? Jenkins isn't going to give us any more unless we let him go. He's sitting down there smiling like a baby, spouting all sorts about shouting his mouth off to the papers the first chance he gets. Police harassment, Frank – and you know how they love that sort of thing.' He gave Davies his sternest look. 'Anyway, while you've been fannying around playing catch-up with whoever's running amok in the community, we've struck a deal with Mr Jenkins.'

'You what?'

'Don't come the wide-eyed innocent, Frank. You knew it would happen. Jenkins has agreed to "forget" his petty vendetta, and co-operate fully with further enquiries, provided he walks from the magistrate's court.'

Davies felt his heart begin to pound in his chest. His shirt was too tight, constricting his anger, sending it coursing to his shaking fingertips. 'You don't deal with a shit like Jenkins!'

'I just have.'

'For fuck's sake!'

'Watch your mouth, Frank. Someone had to do something. It was becoming a bloody farce. This way, your name and this station's is kept out of the papers, and he plays good-boy when we need him.'

Davies shook his head. 'You can't trust him.'

'We have to. It's done. He's up before the magistrates tomorrow morning, and out of our hair. Just don't fuck up like this again, Frank. I've covered your arse. Remember that.'

Davies stood to leave.

'Sit down! There's more.'

He sat, completely deflated.

'The Regional Crime Squad wants in. Two murders in three days, linking factors. It's too big.'

'Like I said, sir, I've got everyone on it.'

'Well, now you've got some extra help. Philippa Rand, forensic psychiatrist, joins us tomorrow. Send all you have over to headquarters so she can swot up overnight.'

Davies bristled at the thought. 'A bloody shrink nosing around?'

'It's the way it's done, these days. And frankly,' he paused for greater sarcastic emphasis, 'you need whatever help they've got. Brief the rest of their team when they arrive.' Butler checked his watch. 'Now, we've got an hour before the press conference at eight. Get your squad together in five minutes so we can figure out what the hell we're going to say.'

Davies sat in the function room of Chelmsford's County Hotel and watched gloomily as the smooth-talking press liaison officer rose to his feet at the other end of the long table.

Maybe calling the press conference at short notice hadn't been such a good idea. What the hell had they to say? What could they show them? No photographs of the latest victim could be released without relatives' permission, and the Vietnamese Embassy in London didn't hold out much hope of making contact for at least two or three days. Nevertheless, Butler had managed to persuade everyone it was a grand idea, the perfect forum for casting the investigative net far out into the public domain.

As expected, the evening conference had attracted a scrum of eager journalists and camera crews anxious to make the front page with their own exclusive angle. Davies knew what would happen – the moment they learned that the two killings were connected, they wouldn't leave town, cluttering the investigation with inept theories and foolish imaginings.

To his immediate right, Chief Superintendent Butler stared stoically ahead, buttons specially polished for the big media event. Next to him, two of Ida Sharansky's neighbours had already given carefully coached testimonials under a barrage of endlessly clicking cameras and popping flash guns.

The press officer cleared his throat, smiling benignly. 'Ladies and gentlemen,' he began confidently; a veteran of polite, relevant, smothered communication. The training college would have been justifiably proud. 'I shall now read a prepared statement on behalf of the Essex Police, concerning today's events. After which, there will be a brief opportunity to question Chief Superintendent Butler and Detective Chief Inspector Davies.'

All at once a battery of hand-held microcassette-recorders pointed towards the long table. Davies felt like the condemned man facing death by technological firing squad.

'Following an emergency call made to Chelmsford police station at three fifty this afternoon, investigating officers were called to the Anglia Polytechnic University student residences on Rectory Lane. Here, they discovered the body of an overseas student, later identified as Miss Sulee Xang. Detectives are now treating this as a murder enquiry.'

Frank averted his gaze from the frantically scribbling hacks a few feet away on the other side of the table. He wondered how long it would be before the first tabloid journalist asked whether the crime was sexually motivated.

The press officer continued. 'At this early stage in the investigation we are appealing for help from members of the public, other students, relatives, associates and friends who may be able to give us any background concerning Miss Xang. Anglia Polytechnic authorities disclosed earlier this evening that she was a promising student, who unfortunately couldn't return to Vietnam this Christmas.'

He paused, clearing his throat in a serious but unsensational way. Charm personified, and a difficult line to tread. Help was needed, and fast. But stressing any urgency would send shock waves surging into the nervous community. 'It may be possible that the deaths of Ida Sharansky and Miss Xang are linked in some way. While we are reluctant to release any details which would jeopardize the investigation . . .'

He went on, stepping gingerly on the thin ice of the grim truth. But the hacks saw right through it. There was a serial killer in town! An excellent result, suburban slaughter exclusive on an otherwise dull news week.

Davies adjusted his tie, preparing himself for the squawking

130

cacophony of questions from the floor which would inevitably follow. They had it all figured, had it sussed, these journos, he thought. Practically salivating with excitement. That would be a sure-fire way to sell papers: each tabloid with its own sponsored psychopath, dressed in a T-shirt bearing the paper's blood-red logo – they were all blood-red, he mused – striking without mercy whenever domestic and international world events went a bit slack. Palestinian peace conference collapses in tatters for the tenth time? No sweat – send our boy over to Brighton with the cleaver. I want a front-page lead on a family of four slaughtered as they ate sandwiches on the beach. Send him to Brighton.

Or Bognor, Hastings, Clacton, Southend . . . Chelmsford?

'. . . and so, in conclusion, we are asking members of the public to be extra vigilant this Christmas. Especially those who may be on their own. Don't admit visitors or strangers without adequate identification, and should you know of someone living on their own, why not pay them a call to make sure they're all right?' The press officer turned to Davies and Butler. 'The Chief Superintendent and DCI Davies will now answer a few questions.'

The mêlée started. Dozens of hands shot instantly into the air, together with a mass braying of eager voices. Butler nodded to a young woman at the front.

'Mia Stevens,' she announced. 'The *Sun*. Didn't you lead us to believe that you were already holding a suspect for the murder of Mrs Sharansky?'

Butler nodded coolly.

'The wrong man, obviously.'

'Not necessarily.'

'But you say these murders are linked?'

'There are certain similarities.'

'What similarities?'

'Giving details of this kind would only serve to prejudice the enquiry.' He addressed the entire room with booming confidence. 'An enquiry, I might add, which currently employs the full resources of the Serious Crime Squad.'

'So whatever's happened, it's very serious?'

'We're treating it that way.'

131

'And you held the wrong man to start with?'

A dreadful pause. Butler was beginning to flail. He looked to Davies to save him.

Davies reluctantly obliged, a trickle of sweat running down his back. 'While we don't wish to alarm members of the public . . .'

Another voice from the throng. 'There's a serial killer at work in Chelmsford, Inspector! Come on, what's the story with the original man helping you with your enquiries? Is he part of it? Is it a gang thing?'

'Look . . . it's complicated. But really, what we want is for the public to –'

Another voice. 'The Asian girl. Was she naked?'

Another. 'Was Mrs Sharansky sexually interfered with?'

'Serial killer or not?'

'Two murders in three days – why couldn't you have stopped it?'

'Is there a monster in this community?'

'Was she young, attractive?'

'Where will the killer strike next?'

It was spiralling out of control. Davies, teeth-grinding temper bubbling over, jumped to his feet. 'That's enough!'

The room came to an abrubt silence, voices replaced by speeding camera motordrives and a constant strobe of flash guns.

Davies's hands remained splayed on the desk like a sprinter on the blocks. His face, too, radiated athletic determination – a man one gunshot from physical explosion. One question, one more photograph.

He spoke quietly, trying to find the press officer's reasoning tones. 'In the light of this afternoon's events, we have taken advice from the CPS and have agreed to drop initial charges made against our chief suspect for the murder of Ida Sharansky. However, a charge of theft will be levelled against him. He will still be available to help us with further enquiries.'

'So he's not the Christmas Killer, then?' a lone voice ventured from the backlit gloom.

'Please. There is no need for any tabloid hysteria.'

'Two bodies in three days would make me pretty bloody hysterical, Detective Chief Inspector. Especially if I had the

132

misfortune to live in a town where the police seemed incapable of catching the right man.'

'Look you stupid piece of sh–'

The press officer was straight back on his feet. 'Conference concluded, ladies and gentlemen. I'm sure you'll all appreciate we have a vital investigation to pursue.'

A chorus of disapproval. 'You've told us nothing!'

'Give us names!'

'Details!'

'The public has a right to know!'

Butler and Davies made for the exit, heads bowed, waving questions aside.

'What the fuck did you think you were playing at, Frank?' Butler hissed when they were both outside. 'You don't piss these people off, for Christ's sake!'

Frank turned to him slowly. 'Why not, sir? Why the hell not? I mean, what did that achieve? We can't tell them anything, because we don't bloody know anything ourselves! All that's going to do is put the fear of God into little old ladies looking forward to Christmas. Those bloody journalists will be all over us now, prodding and poking, nailing us to the fucking wall. And meantime, half the damn town will side with them, and swallow whatever crap they come up with to sell their goddamned papers!'

'And whose fault is that, Frank? Who fucked up big time pulling in an old adversary when he should've been considering all the fucking options?'

Davies stared into the fuming face for a few seconds, then turned quickly and walked straight back to the police station.

21

'. . . Well, you're just not safe in your bed at night, are you? Especially us senior citizens. Easy targets, aren't we? I mean, there's dozens of them come knocking at our door: double glazing this, electric meter that. Could be any number of murderers after interfering with us in a sexual manner before making off with our savings. Young kids. Mark my words, it'll be a gang of them. You wait and see if I'm not right. Course, different in our day. National Service, doing your bit for King and country. Taught us respect, you see. And the noose. Wouldn't dare think about robbing senior citizens for fear of a last visit from Mr Pierrepoint carrying his table of weights and measures for the drop. Country's too slack on them, in my opinion . . .'

Jude Farrow tried her utmost to resist the overwhelming urge to drive the silver cake-slice straight into Mrs Wilson's neck. For Pete's sake, why wouldn't the bloody woman shut up? When would she shut up? As usual, the old motormouth from number twenty-six had succeeded into turning their annual pre-Christmas sherry foursome into a continuous wittering monologue.

Maybe not simply the cake-slice; maybe the remains of the Black Forest gateau first, then the slice, followed by a broken sherry glass rammed brutally into the creamy, gasping face. Rammed beautifully brutally.

'. . . and the police. Oh, my word. Well, we all saw it, didn't we? Not half an hour ago. Incompetents in uniform. I mean, Mrs Farrow, tell me what we pay our council tax for? Two murders in three days, and they don't have a clue where to start? May as well release a dozen lunatics on to the streets with names and addresses of all us senior citizens, for all the good they're doing. Totally disgraceful. And what's more . . .'

More, more, more. Jude looked across at Mr Wilson, asleep in the armchair, grateful someone else was providing an audience for his wife's infinite ramblings. Probably looked forward to this for months, she thought bitterly; probably his one night off in a year of being completely bored out of whatever remained inside his skull.

In the kitchen, William Farrow washed up, attending to squeaking plates and filo-crumbed baking trays, out of earshot, out of the vocal firing line.

The same every year, year on year. Except this time . . .

Jude finished her sherry before pouring herself another large one. It was him, she was certain of it. Years had passed, events had spun dizzyingly by, but it was him. Beamed into her living room, embarrassed, but unknowingly closer to the awful truth. The plainclothes man, the Detective Chief Inspector, Melanie's man in uniform, rising to the bait as the questions avalanched him in a protest of outraged fury.

They had all been watching, even Mrs Wilson, silent for once as news of the second murder broke. Jude, William, their two duty guests, all glued to the fifteen-year-old colour set, shaking their heads and sipping sorrowfully at their sherry.

And afterwards sleep overcame Mr Wilson, and William wandered silently to the sanctuary of his kitchen, leaving Jude alone with the vitriolic 'senior citizen'.

'. . . who's next, that's what they asked, didn't they? And the police couldn't answer, could they? Had no idea. Next to useless in my opinion. I mean, it's all very well getting their helicopter into the sky now, but it's too blooming late for some, isn't it? There's a brutal murderer at large, and they don't have a clue! I mean . . .'

'Chelmsford,' said Jude eventually, barely a distracted whisper.

'Chelmsford?'

Jude stared at the golden balls hanging from the imitation tree. So quiet, so silent, so festive. Yet deadly. Constructed from the thinnest, sharpest glass. Like so many other wonderful things, a dangerous potential lurked within the shiny orbs. Just like children. Little girls. 'It's all happened in Chelmsford,' she said quietly. 'Ten miles away.'

Mrs Wilson wasn't to be swayed. 'That's no comfort, is it? I mean, it's twenty minutes in a car. And they all have cars, you know, these young gangs. Won't take them long to realize they've got to move on.'

'She doesn't drive.'

'Beg your pardon, Mrs Farrow?'

Jude jumped in sudden shock. 'I'm sorry . . . I'm miles away.' What the hell had she said? It was the drink, numbing her mind, loosening her tongue. Not now, not after all these years. Tread carefully, Jude; very, very carefully.

'Not far enough, though, are we? That's my point.'

Jude began to relax. The moment had passed. The silly old bag hadn't picked up on it, too obsessed with her own righteous thread. But it had been close. Too close.

The police, the face from the past, his face, little sister's lover boy. So eager, so overflowing with lustful energy, so keen to fertilize her new beginning. How much longer would it take them? The first suspect had been cleared, so they were looking for another. Another killer performing random acts of motiveless violence. Possibly living in the Chelmsford area.

They'd come for her soon, she was sure of it. They probably knew already. Had to, didn't they? Had to know the whole damn story. Very likely used the news as a complete set-up, knowing she would be watching. Maybe they had a van outside, a black one – yes it would be black, stacked to its metal ceiling with modern machines sending laser beams into her home, reading her pulse, heartbeat, the agonies of her frightened mind.

Jude's hand took a fierce grip on the narrow sherry glass. A rush of white noise began pounding inside her temples. Mrs Wilson appeared to blur at the edges. Maybe she was one! A highly trained policewoman in an elaborate disguise planted many years ago with specific orders to open Jude up, prise the forbidden knowledge she held so tightly in the deepest recesses of her conscience.

The old bitch had nearly succeeded just now, hadn't she? Nearly started a dreadful tumbling of wicked truths. The woman was bugged, she was sure of it; a hidden microphone wired into her bra, relaying every word. Cameras in her eyes, sending Jude's cracking facade back to a smoky room full of grinning police. And him, of course, standing at the back, nodding to his colleagues, reminding them whose hunch it was.

'. . . and of course, Mrs Jones from number six was telling me just the other day that she'd found a beer can in her window box. Imagine that! Can't think what the country's coming to . . .'

The pressure was building, intolerably. A thousand irrational thoughts struggled to be heard inside Jude's roaring brain. They knew. They had to. They were watching, listening . . . laughing at her.

'. . . and Mr Fletcher, he went over to this group of youngsters by the bus stop and . . .'

'Shut up!' Jude yelled, causing Mr Wilson to wake with a start. 'What the hell do you want from me? Shut up! Bloody shut up!'

Mrs Wilson's mouth hung half-open in shock. William Farrow hurried in from the kitchen to his wife's side, placing two damp hands on her shaking shoulders. 'Jude, please . . .'

'Leave me alone! All of you!'

'Jude, please, it's late. You're tired.' He gently took the glass from her trembling hand. 'Time for bed, eh?'

She stared dumbly back, bottom lip quivering.

'I think', said Mr Wilson awkwardly, 'perhaps it's time to leave. Come on, Ruby. Coats on.'

Mrs Wilson stood slowly. 'It's the drink,' she said cautiously. 'Must've had at least half a dozen large ones.'

'Sorry.' William apologized on his wife's behalf. 'Like I say, late night for all of us.'

Jude had begun to moan, resting her head against her husband's aproned midriff. He stroked the back of her silvered head reassuringly.

'Well, happy Christmas, one and all,' Mr Wilson offered gallantly. 'Must do it again. This time next year?'

William shook the outstretched hand. 'Of course,' he replied, leaving his weeping wife as he showed their two embarrassed guests to the door.

The bells of Chelmsford Cathedral struck midnight as Ruth and Felix finally arrived back at her little terraced house.

Swaying slightly, she rooted for her keys, angling her handbag towards the streetlight for extra illumination.

Felix stamped his feet in a futile attempt to ward off the bitter chill. 'That's another thing they've got wrong,' he panted. 'Global warming. Give me a subtropical Christmas climate any time.'

'Another thing?'

He shifted uneasily, noticing how attractive the pale orange light made her, bathing her in burnt sienna to rub away time's ravages, restoring the plucky young policewoman of thirty years ago. 'Well, I meant . . . you know, the Doug business. Got that all wrong, didn't they? Seems people get stuff wrong all the time.'

She found her keys. 'And what have you got wrong, Felix?'

He sighed and smiled. 'Another time, maybe. It's late. My stinking bedsit will be pining for me to reinfest it with my unnatural bodily odours.'

'You have someone waiting for you?'

'Sophie.'

'Ah.'

'You'd like her. Petite, big green eyes, gorgeous black hair. Costs a fortune in cat food, though.'

Ruth opened the front door. 'Coffee?'

'Better not, Ruth.'

'Sure?'

He looked up at the stars. 'Nice night for a drive. Besides, Doug might be back and he'd kill me.' He instantly regretted the expression. 'Not that I really mean that, Ruthie. More a figure of –'

She kissed his freezing cheek. 'Shut up, Felix. And go home.'

'You don't want me to check inside, first? Just in case . . .' But words failed him.

'I'll be fine. If he's in there, he'll be pissed on the sofa, and that's where he'll stay. Thanks, Felix, for everything.'

'Hey, it's been . . . different, honestly. Next time your old man's up on a murder rap, give me a call.'

She laughed softly, then watched with a vague twinge of regret as he walked towards the dilapidated Austin Morris. She stepped inside, unwilling to face waving goodbye as he drove away. Must be the wine, she thought, and the cold. Better off in the warm.

There were three messages on the answering machine. She took off her coat, kicked off her shoes and settled on the sofa, enjoying the darkness. At least Doug wasn't home. And what a joy it had been to spend a pleasant evening stuffing her face and listening to semi-intelligent company for a change. A brief, warming respite from the labours of the day, Doug, Margaret, the affair, the stolen purse, the cab company closing, and the ever present anxiety of what lay ahead in the unforgiving chill of another New Year.

Yes, Felix was a trusted friend. She had at least one. Maybe that's all she would need, all anyone ever needed. One good friend simply to be there.

She reached over in the gloom and fumbled with the answerphone. There was a click before a familiar voice invaded Ruth's contented darkness.

'Mum, it's Marie. Got your message. What on earth's going on? Dad's in some kind of trouble? What's happening? Please ring me back – any time. I can be over in thirty minutes. Please, please ring back.'

Ruth sighed, putting it off until the morning. The answerphone threw out the second message.

'Mrs Jenkins, I've been informed of the . . . change in your domestic circumstances by one of my staff. The message you left was . . . incomplete, to say the least. However, I still feel there is much to be gained from your spending time with Rene this Christmas, and I do hope you will reconsider. She really is most confused and upset by watching some of the other residents leave with their families. Please call me as soon as you can. Thank you.'

She groaned, pressing a cushion over her face. That bloody Watkins woman!

'Jumped-up little Hitler!' Ruth complained from behind the cushion. But she'd have to ring in the morning, she knew that. Have to accept their 'arrangements', with or without Doug. After all, this was her mother, even if it was blackmail of the most despicable, buck-passing order.

She sat up, slightly deflated, recognizing the first angry throbbings of an impending hangover.

The machine clicked a second time.

'S'Doug. Calling from the nick.' The voice was oddly calm, composed.

'Shit,' she said out loud, reaching for her bag, fumbling for a cigarette.

'Looks like it turned up trumps for your old man, Ruth. Fella what done for the old lady has topped a student this afternoon. But I guess you know all that by now. Plod's got more egg on his face than an explosion in an omelette factory. Especially your old buddy, Franky Wanky Davies.'

Ruth lit up with a shaking hand.

Doug's voice turned bitter. 'Did me a little deal, they did. Let me have a few privileges. Like this call. And the bail. Yeah, that's right. Guess who's out for Christmas, Ruth? Don't worry about it, I won't be coming back home. Couldn't live with a woman who thinks I'm some kind of murderer, could I?'

Ruth exhaled. 'For Christ's sake!'

'Gonna make myself a star tomorrow, Ruth. This whole business has blown up nicely in my favour. Gonna act the tit in court, then the papers'll be dying for a few choice words. And when they hear about my wrongful arrest and Frank's twenty-eight-year vendetta against me, they're going to want to pay big bucks for that. Rumour has it in here, he's already screwed up some press conference, so my story's going to be the final nail in his coffin, ain't it?'

'Grow up, Doug,' Ruth moaned at the machine.

'So, all I'm saying is, if you know what's good for you, be out tomorrow. 'Cause when I walk from court, I'm coming round to get a suitcase of stuff, then fuck off round one of me mates. Least they don't think I'm a murderer! I ain't coming home, Ruth. Not until you take that back, every bloody word of it. Thirty years I've been straight, thirty years, and where has it . . .'

Ruth turned off the machine, and sat meditating as she finished her cigarette in the fluctuations of glowing red in the darkened room. Had she ever really known Doug at all? Had the last twenty-six years been an incredible blunder? The gamble which hadn't paid off? How much of it was her fault – changing him, locking him into a system which had ground him down?

Ground her down. Down to an office cleaner living with an unemployed adulterer.

She lit another cigarette.

'Frankly, my dear Douglas,' she said softly, 'I don't give a damn.'

22

'Guv?'

Davies raised his head slowly from the pool of saliva on his paper-strewn desk. 'Boot Sale?'

'Wakey, wakey.'

'Oh, Jesus.'

Mason picked up the empty half-bottle of whisky and tutted. 'Best hide this before the Super sees it.'

'What time is it?'

'Just gone eight.'

'Date?'

'Monday, twenty-second.'

'I'm in the nick, aren't I?' He struggled to open both eyes and focus.

'Large as life, Guv. Well, death, in your case.'

Outside in the main squad room a few dispirited CID officers wandered in to replace yawning colleagues who had worked the night shift.

Davies tried ineptly to rub some life into his aching face. It was still dark outside. 'Feel like shit.'

'I'll get you a coffee. Any news on last night?'

Davies shut both eyes once more, recalling the pathetic haul the press conference had reeled in. He yawned, hating the feeling of having slept in his suit, cold sweat stickily lining his clammy armpits and tingling feet. 'Pizza Hut confirmed that the girl had been working for them for the last four weeks. Kept herself to herself. One or two fellow students rang in. Pretty much the same story. No one in Nightingale Road can recall anyone calling on Mrs Sharansky on the night she died.'

'Apart from Jenkins?'

'Apart from Jenkins.'

'So we're no further forward, then?'

Davies opened his eyes a second time, squinting to adjust to the harsh striplighting. 'On the contrary, Sergeant,' he said sarcastically. 'We had six confessions within an hour of the television news. Two arrived in person to surrender themselves to the forces of law and order. One was, I'm reliably told, dressed as Santa Claus and carrying a meat cleaver.'

'Fucking hell.'

'That's the press for you, Boot Sale. Give them a murder, they'll think up a nickname. Give the sad old sickos a nickname, and you give them a concrete reason for aspiring to it. The Christmas Killer is alive and well, thanks to the bloody press.'

'I'll get you that coffee.'

'Appreciate it.'

Mason hovered by the door. 'Talking of the press, Guv: thought you might like to have a butcher's at these. Congratulations. You made the front page.' He walked over and dropped three tabloids on to the desk. 'My missus reckons you look quite handsome.'

'She only has you for comparison, Sergeant.'

Mason left, leaving Davies to wearily inspect all three papers.

NEIN! NEIN! NEIN! POLICE ADMIT BUNGLE IN
CHRISTMAS KILLER SLAYINGS!
BAD TIDINGS WE BRING! CHRISTMAS KILLER STRIKES
WHILE POLICE INTERVIEW WRONG MAN.

The final headline, while being the shortest of the three, was also probably the most succinct expression of the mood the previous evening.

FORCE – OR FARCE?

Each headline was accompanied by an equally unflattering variation of Davies's exasperated face, cunningly cropped to support the weight of the story, together with an inset photograph of

143

Ida Sharansky – supplied no doubt by a cash-strapped relative – and a hastily conceived artist's impression of Sulee Xang.

Mason returned with the coffee. 'Where do they get off, these bloody paper people? I mean, what's their gripe? Why blame us?'

Davies sighed heavily. 'Probably goes back to when our boys sent them the bill for policing the Wapping riots.'

'Some thanks for securing their bleedin' jobs.'

Davies took a tentative sip, grimacing as the lukewarm, muddy slop made contact with his whisky-furred tongue.

'So what now, Guv?'

Davies stood and stretched, immediately regretting it. The headache was colossal. 'First I ring my wife and try to explain that I haven't been raving it up all night on some massive Christmas bender.'

'Best of luck.'

'Thanks. Secondly, we drive over to police headquarters to see a . . .' he rummaged painfully through the disordered desk, before squinting to read from a yellow Post-it note '. . . Philippa Rand at the OPU.'

Mason blinked uncomprehendingly. 'OPU?'

'Offender Profiling Unit.'

'Ah. Psychobabble now, is it? Forensic psychiatrist steps in to save the day?'

'It's not my idea, Boot Sale. But that's how it's done these days, apparently.'

'Waste of fucking time.'

Davies considered the point. God, he wanted to go home and sleep. A visit to HQ following this morning's revelations would surely be inviting every joker there to take the piss. 'Granted, Boot Sale. But at the moment, we haven't got an awful lot else, have we?'

Essex Police Headquarters was in most eventualities a five-minute drive from the station. A vast concrete complex, home to the many specialist services offered to the region's undermanned outposts. The police helicopter lived there, tactical weapons units, and the driving school – complete with oil-pumping skid pan and extensive repair bays.

And, of course, the OPU.

'Pop the noise on, Boot Sale,' Davies instructed as they waited for traffic lights.

'Emergency, is it?'

Davies swallowed twice. 'Put it this way: if I'm not in HQ's toilets in the next minute, I'm going to puke in this car.'

'Jesus Christ!' Mason flicked the siren switch and floored the accelerator, parting curious traffic as they sped up Springfield Road past the prison, then turned right into headquarters.

Davies ran from the car at the first opportunity, dashing into the building, hand over his gagging mouth. Mason switched off the engine and ambled inside, chuckling to himself. Whisky – always did it for the Guvnor. Never learned.

'Come to see Philippa Rand,' he informed the startled receptionist. 'Sergeant Mason, DCI Davies.'

'Was that . . . ?' she pointed towards the still swinging door.

Mason nodded. 'My Guvnor. S'been a long night.'

A familiar figure walked into reception. DCI Keith Knowles, drinking buddy of Mason's before he'd made the move to headquarters. 'Boot Sale!'

'Keith,' Mason warily acknowledged. It had been two years since the two of them had 'gone for the gallon' during one of their legendary pub crawls. The move had changed all that. Promotion meant Knowles was too busy for the binges. 'Been given a chance to really hit the big time,' he'd told Mason, on one of the rare occasions he'd answered the thirsty sergeant's calls. 'Don't want to blow it, know what I mean?' Mason knew. Knowles was a fair-weather friend, their bar-room comradeship an embarrassing memory for the rank-climbing DCI. 'Howzit going?'

Knowles nodded. 'That your Guvnor doing the Linford Christie impression down the corridor?'

'Needed the bogs.'

Knowles nodded knowingly. 'Got the shits has he? Seen the papers and crapped his trousers on the way down here?'

'Just feeling dicky, that's all.'

'Chewed him up, didn't they, the press boys? I mean, what was he thinking for Christ's sake –'

A rogue hand plopped unseen on to Knowles' shoulder. A restored DCI Davies stood behind him. 'I was thinking, Keith,'

145

he said slowly. 'Shouldn't you have your head up someone's arse, instead of wasting valuable brown-nosing time delaying an investigation?' Davies had little time for Knowles, either.

The startled man flushed scarlet. 'Sorry, Frank. You know how it is. Got to expect it, really. Front page and all that . . .'

'I was expecting', Davies coldly replied, 'to see a young lady from the OPU. Now.'

'Philippa Rand? She's upstairs. Waiting for you.' He led the way, Davies following, Mason at the back making an obscene gesture with a practised hand.

They entered a small room off the first-floor corridor. First to strike Davies was the electric hum of an impressive computer, then the bobbed-cut blonde working over it. Philippa Rand stood as the visitors crammed into her office.

Knowles did the introductions.

Davies sighed and sat next to the neat, bespectacled woman as Mason and Knowles leaned against the wall behind. He looked at the young face, flatteringly lit by the VDU, placing her in her early thirties and deciding she'd have been better suited selling cosmetics at Debenhams. The manner, too, was officious, slave to the new technology, operator of its preprogrammed conclusions. But at least it wasn't so bright in here. His pulsing head thanked him for the chance to beat the worst of the whisky's nauseating aftermath. Never again, he reminded himself to tell himself. Not today, anyway.

'So, Miss Rand. What have you got for us?' The unenthusiasm flooded the claustrophobic room. He had heard of offender profiling, of course, even attended a two-day seminar at headquarters on the selfsame subject, sitting in a lecture theatre with thirty-one similarly disinterested senior officers from the region, as an eager young buck with a flip-chart and an overhead projector had tried unsuccessfully to sell them on the merits of the great American idea. Davies had spent most of the first day swallowing a ceaseless parade of yawns – and the second speculating on the sexuality of their astronomically keen instructor.

'Bearing in mind I've only had access to the files since yesterday afternoon,' Philippa began hesitantly, 'and that OPU is merely intended to glean a cross section of possible suspects from the community as a whole . . .'

146

'Bugger all?'

'Come on, Frank,' Knowles urged from behind. 'Give the girl a chance. She's come up with some interesting stuff.'

Davies turned away from the screen. 'You already know about this?'

'Frank, most of us in the building are working on this case. For Christ's sake, what did you think? That we were all going to wait until you showed up before we went ahead?'

Davies turned back, silently admitting the inevitable. The case had become HQ's. The Regional Serious Crime Squad's. All his team would be used for from now on was information gathering. Sent out, under orders from this mob to pull suspects, grasses, and to doorstep possible witnesses. He'd lost it. Why? He didn't want to face it, but Jenkins had been the innocent catalyst. An old lag, and a hunch that went badly wrong. Fatally wrong. Although, in some respects, at least the second killing had thwarted Jenkins's hopes of a full-scale media dissection of Davies's past lapses with a certain married woman. What tabloid could possibly be interested in his claims now? They'd crucified Doug, just as surely as they'd hung the DCI out to dry. Now all the press wanted was the killer's identity. But not half as badly as Davies.

He turned to the nervous woman. 'Sorry, Miss Rand. Please, do go on.'

Her fingers went to practised work on the keyboard, bringing up a scanned photograph of the writing found on Sulee Xang's bedroom wall. Once again Davies was faced with the seven career-shattering words.

IDA RELEASED. SULEE RELEASED.
NOW RELEASE IMPOSTER!

'I started with this,' she said timidly. 'The only real communication we've had with the killer so far. Notice the word "release". It gives us our first real pointer.'

Davies raised a sceptical eyebrow, suddenly absorbed in the quiet professionalism. He wondered what it had taken to persuade Miss Rand to pursue such a career, locked in a darkened room, dispassionately analysing demented messages from

147

twisted minds. He allowed her to continue, intrigued to discover just how far she could run with this.

'Release. It's a very empowering choice of word. Used three times, it clearly forms the basis of the killer's logic for the crimes, Detective Chief Inspector.'

'Frank, please.'

The first hint of a smile. 'Again, the choice of the word "imposter", with relevance to the timing of the second murder, leads us to speculate firstly that the killer works alone and is therefore suffering from damaged pride that another could be accused of the crime. And, as I've since been told, Frank, you were holding the wrong –'

'And secondly?' Davies was in no mood to have past mistakes reanalysed by all and sundry.

'They're most probably angry that it had been considered a crime at all.'

'How so?'

'They "release" them. They're on first-name terms with their victims, and, as in the case of Ida Sharansky with the answerphone message from the cab company, she was expecting a visitor.'

Davies chewed his bottom lip. She'd sure done her homework. 'Possibly the killer, but it could have been anyone stopping by for a chat.'

Philippa was becoming more animated. 'But your files indicated that, prior to last Friday, Mrs Sharansky had always gone to bingo once a month on that date. The statements from neighbours confirm this. She was an old woman, a lady of precise routine. But here she was cancelling all because she expected "someone" round. Someone who had most probably befriended her fairly recently.'

'Then killed her? Why?'

'Released her,' Philippa repeated. 'That's the crucial difference. Liberated her.'

'From what?' came Mason's confused voice. 'A night down the town on the bingo?'

She ignored the remark, pressing on. 'Both victims could technically be termed loners. Very few real friends or concerned relatives close by. Bear in mind, the killer probably has quite a different perspective on the murders. Now, somehow, most probably via the news, they hear that the Ida Sharansky case has turned into a murder hunt. Furthermore, a suspect is held. They don't have much time. The important thing is to find another victim as soon as possible in order that the "imposter" be released.'

'So they find the nearest unattached person and do away with them?'

'Befriending them first. Gaining their confidence. I'd say it was fairly certain the Vietnamese girl allowed the killer into her room. Maybe even invited them there.'

'But the scenes were so different. The old lady was dolled up in the armchair – the other was like an abattoir. Same killer?'

Philippa nodded. 'They simply had a good deal less time to gain the victim's confidence.'

'Tell you what worries me,' Frank slowly announced to the room. 'We held Jenkins. About to charge him for it. Surely whoever's doing this would've been chuffed to buggery some other poor sod was going to take the drop for it?'

'Like the lady said,' Knowles chipped in, 'pride. Killer wants the credit for themselves.'

'Since when have you been a bleedin' expert?' Mason hissed.

Knowles turned to Davies, brushing aside his former drinking buddy's barbed remark. 'We're trawling through our own data banks, looking for matches on the same MO. Tricky task, though, given that these two cases are so different apart from the use of make-up.'

'You're sure, then, are you?' Davies replied. 'Ruled out all the copycat stuff? I mean, I was there, Keith, both scenes. In one the old girl's been made over to look like she's posing for the last family portrait; the other poor kid looks like she's auditioning for a bit part in the latest Jack the Ripper movie.'

Philippa said, 'It's the psychological motive that binds the two killings together, Frank. Same town, same time-frame, same victim profile. Sad, lonely, vulnerable, easy to befriend.'

Davies mulled it over. 'And the records, MO matches? I mean, what the hell are you actually looking for?'

Knowles cleared his throat. 'It's actually something we thought you might be able to help us with, Frank.'

'Oh yeah?'

'It's an enormous task. We've got fifteen years' worth of unsolveds and coroners' open verdicts pouring in from every force in the country. Thousands of them, and . . .'

'You thought those idle bastards back at New Street would do all the bloody donkey-work for you?' Davies found he was talking through gritted teeth. 'Like we've got nothing fucking better to do?'

Knowles shifted uncomfortably. 'Superintendent Butler promised your squad's full co-operation on the project.'

Davies nodded slowly. What else would he have expected? Relegation confirmed by Knowles. A political slap for screwing up the press conference. 'Yeah,' he said slowly. 'I bet he did.'

Philippa broke the uneasy silence. 'The most important thing,' she said, attempting to bring the conversation back round to her researches, 'is that the killer wants you to know that they're "releasing" them. It appears to be the only motive that I can identify. Maybe even sees this act of release as some sort of mission, chosen role. And the efficacy of the Ida Sharansky killing could well imply there's a long list of previously "released" victims.'

'Released to where, for God's sake?' Davies asked, rapidly tiring of the theorizing. It was all guessing games, after all. When faced with the reality of it, what did any of them actually have? Just two dead bodies in a quiet provincial town, and tenuous links between them. Now it felt as if the whole investigation was wandering into cosy computer graduate theories a million miles from the actual crimes. Maybe Mason was right – sheer psychobabble.

She smiled. 'Where do we go when we die?'

He thought for a second, face contorting into a creased mask of disbelief. 'Heaven?'

'Some people still believe in it.'

'Come on! This nutter's sending them to heaven?'

'Or any other sort of afterlife they happen to believe in. Heaven fits the "release" theme. Remember, there are no obvious signs of hate in either killing. No sexual molestation. Just the deaths of two sad and lonely individuals. And in the Ida Sharansky case, maybe an attempt at dignifying the corpse.

150

Probably had the same intention with the second victim. But there was no time for a makeover. This was hurried. Violent.'

'Religious nutter, then, is he, our man?' Mason scoffed. 'Defrocked vicar with a penchant for lipstick? Pervert, transvestite type? Reads the Bible, hangs around the cosmetic counter at Boots, then nails himself to a cross every Easter, made up like the Virgin Mary?'

Philippa turned to the smirking sergeant. 'Who said anything about it being a man?' she coldly replied.

23

Just two days before Christmas and Chelmsford buzzed with news of the murders. The public's fear and their enthusiasm to dutifully respond to appeals for help and possible sightings gathered at a frightening pace, and soon the police station was flooded with calls from frightened OAPs demanding reassurance, mental defectives gleefully confessing to the crimes, and a steady flow of anonymous callers eagerly promising to reveal the Christmas Killer's identity in exchange for the much vaunted Community Action Trust rewards on macabre offer.

The town itself was swiftly invaded by an outside army of fired-up journalists, hungry for useful titbits to fill their four-page spreads. The police presence was high profile: uniformed officers patrolling the streets, the all-seeing helicopter constantly hovering overhead, traffic officers re-routing traffic from both the Nightingale Road and Rectory Lane murder scenes.

And ever present, the main fear, the unanswered question. Where will the Christmas Killer strike next? Who's next on the list? Chelmsford had somehow woken to a nightmare spiralling out of control – there was a lunatic at large, and police were powerless to do anything.

Ruth stifled a yawn as she sat in Chelmsford's packed magistrates' court, watching Doug standing defiantly before the three sitting JPs.

Doug's imminent release from police custody had attracted a considerable crowd anxious to glimpse the local man who had now openly admitted to stealing Ida Sharansky's purse. Ruth could feel the hostility towards the petty thief who once

152

stole her heart coursing like a shock wave through the crowded judicial building.

Many, she assumed, were eager reporters. To her left, an earnest young woman sat making a pastel sketch of Doug's arrogant features, an unsettling cross between a serious portrait and a crude caricature.

As he'd been led in by two uniformed officers, Ruth had been surprised to see her husband wearing an Essex Police tracksuit, looking for all the world as if he'd jogged from the nearby police station. Then it dawned on her that his clothes were most probably still undergoing forensic testing.

Equally unexpected, she felt no real sympathy for his predicament, despite the many sleepless hours she'd spent trying to make some sort of sense from the madness. She wasn't to blame, she reassured herself. Doug had simply done what he'd done for his own reasons, as he'd always done, drunk or sober, bitter or greedy, angry or pained. He'd crept in and stolen a dead woman's purse after his mistress had informed him that he was out of a job. He'd flipped, got blind drunk and landed himself in a whole heap of trouble. His trouble – not hers.

And, in truth, Doug's affair made it so much easier for Ruth to sit and join the rest of the onlookers in prejudiced judgement over the offence. She was almost thankful to him for that. Because if she'd really cared for the man, she would have been ruined by grief. Any sense of despair had been swiftly cut down by the rage of betrayal.

The senior JP peered with distaste at the grinning man before him. 'Douglas Anthony Jenkins,' he intoned, 'you stand before us today accused of a crime which you openly admit your guilt to. It appals this court to think that any member of our community could sink so low as to steal the belongings of a dead woman . . .'

Ruth studied Doug's face, recognizing the cocky youngster she'd first seen many years ago. She remembered it all vividly: standing alongside Felix, resplendent in her uniform, giving evidence from a notebook against the cheeky young villain she was eventually to marry. Then there was the wink, given to her just before he had been taken down to enjoy three months at Her Majesty's pleasure for house-breaking. Don't worry love, it seemed to say. You was only doing your job, after all.

So, what in God's name had happened? How had time changed the once handsome rogue who robbed flowers from gardens and left them at the police station during the first stages of their courtship? Maybe the others were right, the dissenting voices – Frank, the senior officers – warning her that Doug would always be a villain and nothing would change that. And wasn't that one of the truths Ruth had always run from, that she'd taken Doug on more as a challenge than a husband – to break him, re-sculpt him, prove her judgement right? To prove that a few months under her profound influence would bleed the lawlessness from him? A bloody-minded marriage – a bloody mistake.

For the inescapable reality was that once Doug had reluctantly agreed to go straight, he had lost ninety per cent of his criminal allure. The challenge was over – too soon. Ruth was out of a job, pregnant, and living with someone she'd never really known. Doug had, she was forced to concede, not done anything wrong – he'd simply not done anything. The new law-abiding Doug was boringly predictable. Straight – it was such an appropriate word for his unexciting personality.

And now this episode. This explosion of the unexpected, after all this time. The affair, the arrest, whatever he was supposed to have done to the old woman, the whole courtroom scene. She looked at Doug and knew that suddenly he felt transformed by the buzz of notoriety, returning to his roots, shaking off her matrimonial chains. Doug Jenkins was off the leash, but ill-equipped for a triumphant return to villainy. The years spent in Ruth's righteous captivity had dulled the edge. Bravado became misplaced stupidity.

'It is with some regret', the JP continued, 'that I am forced to accept investigating officers' claims that you might still be of some use as a material witness in the ongoing investigation into the death of Mrs Ida Sharansky. In such instances, my hand is forced to comply with their request that you be granted police bail until this case can be heard in Chelmsford Crown Court, where I'm certain, Mr Jenkins, you will receive no further leniency for your distasteful crime.' He paused, consulting the two other Justices. 'Do you have anything to say before bail conditions are imposed?'

Doug turned to the crowded court. His moment had come. 'S'matter of fact, I have.'

Ruth held her breath.

'I want a formal apology from the Old Bill for the murder charge. I ain't pretending to be no saint; I done a bit of bird in my time, petty thieving an' that. But that was nigh on thirty years back. It's like they never give up on you . . .'

'Enough, Mr Jenkins,' the JP replied. 'From what I gather, the officers who brought the charge had very good reasons for doing so. Almost overwhelming, in my view.' His two colleagues nodded in support.

Doug paid them no heed. 'They tried to fit me up for something I never done! Birmingham Six, Guildford Four – it's the same all over this country –'

'Mr Jenkins! I will not have this courtroom used as a cheap political platform! One more outburst and –'

'Yeah, I robbed the old dear's wallet. What the hell was she going to do with the money? Brown bread, for Christ's sake!'

The whole court erupted into chaos, as Doug stood defiantly in the eye of the storm, staring at the bench. Ruth shook her head sadly, watching the frantic shorthand of excited reporters trying to capture the mayhem. Boos and jeers erupted from all sides. What in God's name was the fool playing at? Then she realized, saw it in a millisecond – the wink again, but not at her, at Wapping's finest. Doug had set out to court the tabloids this time. It was just as he'd warned her on the phone. Money, it was all about money. Playing the wronged old lag slotted up by the local constabulary. He'd planned it all, every contentious word, stirring up the hate, the interest, the intrigue, to have those journalists' chequebooks flapping in anticipation.

It took well over three minutes to restore any semblance of judicial order. Doug was duly fined for contempt, taking it with a cocky shrug. What was a lousy two hundred quid fine when he must have a couple of grand in the bin by now? Expenses, he mused. Monies incurred during the procurement of more monies. He'd put up a good show. The journos must be gagging for a four-page exclusive by now. Then he'd welcome his own

155

finest hour. Davies would be named as the scumbag he was. Harassing an innocent man – resignation issue, surely? Plus the little matter of knocking off that married woman all those years ago. No question, Davies was finished. Career over. Vindication through public opinion. Jesus, life was wonderful, sometimes.

'Moving on,' the JP growled. 'The conditions of your bail are thus. That you reside at your home address . . .'

'Nah,' Doug shot back. 'I'm dossing down at me mate's. The cops . . . police have all the details.' His appointed solicitor rose and confirmed the arrangement.

'Very well, Mr Jenkins. You are bailed to appear twice daily at Chelmsford police station at eight a.m. and three p.m. Failure to do so will result in immediate arrest and detention.' Details of a night-time curfew followed, together with the request to make himself constantly available for further questioning.

'And I must warn you, Mr Jenkins,' the JP concluded, trying without success to conceal the contempt in his voice, 'I am well aware that you might think that your antics here this morning may have somehow endeared you to certain members of the popular press.'

Doug winked again at the public gallery, a horribly clumsy gesture which made Ruth prickle with embarrassment. How could he be so blind and stupid? Hadn't he seen it coming?

'I would remind you that it is a serious offence to talk to anyone about matters concerning this case, and the ongoing murder investigation. Do I make myself clear, Mr Jenkins? I do not wish to see your face staring out from any of the morning's papers.'

He shrugged. It wasn't a major blow. He could wait, find a way through. A kind of deposit deal, maybe. One grand cash upfront secures the whole deal when it's safe to talk. Yeah, a grand plan.

After all, they couldn't possibly refuse now, could they? Be falling over themselves to give him the cash.

Wouldn't they?

24

'A woman?' DC Hassloff said slowly, pointing to the gruesome black-and-whites of Sulee Xang's mutilated corpse pinned to the squadroom walls. 'A woman did that?'

Davies nodded, scanning the unbelieving faces. They were back at New Street police station, debriefing the squad on the morning visit to headquarters. 'According to the boffins down the road.'

'Jesus. Where they get that from?'

Davies couldn't blame them for questioning the logic. The very idea had seemed just as appalling to him. 'They figure', he went on, 'she wouldn't have let a man into her flat. She had no boyfriends and, from what we've been told, she was shy, quiet and apparently lonely. Kept herself very much to herself. Simply stuck to the task of getting on with life. Coping, existing. Same with Ida Sharansky. Easier for a woman to gain her confidence. Besides, the Vietnamese student wasn't exactly built like a brick. They reckon a man intent on killing her could've strangled her quite easily, without the mess. The autopsy reveals the body was covered in bruises. Poor kid struggled to the last – most probably, they conclude, with someone of a similar strength to herself. Plus, no indications of sexual interference in either case.'

A female officer begged to differ. They were all tired, and this latest revelation would take some beating. 'Begging your pardon, sir. But no woman I know would've made such a botch job of the old lady's make-up. And, I mean, why bother with it in the first place? Why not simply do the deed and run? Surely we were closer with the Jenkins thing – the killer tries to disguise the murder by covering the bruises?'

Some of the squad turned to the head-and-shoulders shot of Ida Sharansky, her face a tragic mask of basic cosmetic ineptitude. Then on to Sulee's hurried death mask, like a cheap imported children's doll.

Mason opened his notebook. 'Got a theory for that as well.' He struggled for an instant to read his own writing. 'Call it . . . post traumatic . . . neurological stunting.'

Davies picked up the thread, sensing the growing apathy in the room. It was hard for them, working all hours, only to have the case snatched away by the silicon-chip resources and terminal theorizers up the road. But at least they seemed to be siding with him, still doggedly clinging on to Jenkins's original involvement as a decisive factor. After the morning's trip out, however, he himself was not so sure any more.

He sat on the edge of a desk. 'If we accept that Jenkins is out of the frame, and ignore his opportunistic pilfering of the old girl's purse, then nothing appears to have been stolen from either scene. The killer simply kills, makes some sort of attempt to tidy the victim up with cosmetics, then disappears again. To our way of thinking, anyway. To her, if it is a woman – and let's face it, it could well be . . .'

'Or a dwarf,' said one dissenting voice.

'Or a kid,' said another.

'Or a weedy bloke. Homo or something?' added a third.

Davies nodded, acknowledging all three. 'Whoever. They believe they are "releasing" these people. That appears to be the only motive. The killer chooses lonely targets, possibly spends a little time befriending them, then kills them. Who knows, maybe the victims ask to be killed. Maybe it's a two-way thing.'

'Assisted suicide?' said Hassloff sceptically. 'Looking for unhinged woman GP, with this neurological stunting whatnot, are we?'

'What is all that bollocks, anyway, Guv?' came a weary voice from the back. 'New term for a fucking looney?'

Davies held up a silencing hand, waiting politely for the derisive laughter to die down. 'It comes back to the make-up. They're looking at it as the work of a child.'

Hassloff shook his head. 'No. I'm losing this. A kid now, is it? Killing for kicks? Come on, Guv. Two motiveless deaths in less than a week. It's a psycho we're after, not a flaming kid.'

Mason, still reading from his notebook, said, 'They don't disagree. What they reckon is, because her logic's all fucked up, she's somehow stunted. Acting like a kid. Doesn't see death as the end but a sort of new beginning. Kills these poor sods as a favour – in her mind.'

'Bullshit,' said a tired voice from the back of the room. 'Let's check the local nut-houses again. Probably a fucking runaway.'

Davies stood. 'We've done that God knows how many times. Every mental patient in the community is accounted for. Besides, none fits the description given by the profiling unit. None has her particular . . . diagnosis.' He was losing them, could see the scepticism glazing each tired face. 'Look,' he tried, 'all it is is a theory. Fuck it, I know how bloody ludicrous it sounds. But what else have we got?' He let the silence settle momentarily over the deflated room before continuing. 'The forensic psychiatrists reckon they've come across this sort of thing before. They call it a mental protection mechanism. Certain areas of the brain stop developing following a specifically traumatic incident. It means the person won't ever have to face it rationally as a grown adult. It leaves you mentally the same age, at least in some respects, as when the event occurred.'

Hassloff took the role of squad spokesman. 'Which is why the old lady's face looks like it's been made over by a kid?'

'According to them. Possibly.'

'So, where does it leave us?'

'Searching the crime files and public records, Detective. Going over them like a dozen bent accountants looking for a tax loophole.'

'For what?'

Davies swallowed hard. Why was it all beginning to sound so implausible? He wished he had Miss Rand by his side, her cool, confident tones impressing the shit out of them. Like he'd been impressed. Eventually. But now that the gloss had worn off, maybe it was all psychobabble, pie-in-the-sky rubbish. 'Headquarters seem to agree that we're most likely looking for a woman who may have suffered some distressing death encounter as a child. For instance, her family may have been wiped out in a car crash, and she was told they were all safe in heaven, or something.'

'Or something?' Hassloff echoed.

Davies looked at him accusingly. 'What the hell's the matter with you? It's just an example, for Christ's sake!'

'Sorry, Guv.'

'Forget it. Where was I?'

'Car crashes,' Mason prompted.

'Right. Yes. Thank you.' God, he wanted a drink. 'So this kid's mind hangs on to that thought. Doesn't allow it to mature any further, and recognize the fact that Mummy, Daddy and little brother Brian are really rotting in the local cemetery. Its notions of death are all twisted round, arse about face. Possibly even sees it as a good thing, depending on what they've been told by others as a kid.' He sat back down on the desk, sighing heavily. 'Anyway, it sort of made sense to me at the time. I don't know now.'

There were one or two half-hearted murmurings of understanding, but Davies knew full well what they were – team spirit, the squad not wanting the guvnor to know that they thought the whole thing was the biggest crock of shit they'd heard in their lives.

'The bottom line is', he concluded, 'we plough through the records, chasing up anything that might fit. Wandering orphans, car crashes, childhood tragedies, unsolveds, coroners' open verdicts – the lot.'

'And meantime, what's headquarters up to?' a despairing voice asked.

Mason replied, 'They're running all the way to the end with this. Ploughing through all the suicides on record, 'cause they reckon their suspect is homing in on lonely, vulnerable types, then dispatching 'em according to the profile. They're co-ordinating all the house-to-house stuff, checking on all the pensioners. And get this for clutching at straws: they've even got two undercover officers miked up and dressed as dossers, 'cause they reckon this nutter might be homing in on all sorts of waifs and strays to find the next victim. Fucking crackers, if you ask me.'

Now for the bad news. 'And if anyone's thinking of three days off for Christmas, forget it,' Davies informed them. 'Eight-hour shifts, twenty-four hours until this business is settled.'

A voice from the front, Sergeant Jones, the squad's Welsh wag. 'Headquarters dressing their boys as dossers, are they? Bloody typecasting, innit?'

And for the first time in seventy-two hours, the first hint of a smile played on Davies's cracked lips.

25

Christmas Killer?

Christmas Killer!

Christmas Killer!!!

She held the trembling tabloid in one hand; the other balled into a white-knuckled straining fist.

Couldn't they see it, even when the writing was right under their stupid noses? Left on the wall for the world to see? She hadn't 'killed' anyone!

She flung down the lying paper and returned to the bubbling saucepan. Never mind them. Never mind their stupidity, it was ravioli today. She had the dollies out specially. Her three favourites sat on the bed, arms outstretched, waiting for the orange meat-and-pasta wallets to be rubbed over their plastic chins.

And that man. That awful man. Making people laugh in the courtroom. A horrible man. But she knew what he'd want. One look at him had told her.

She would use the wig, the one they all liked when their things got bigger, poking like grilled sausages from the front of their piss-stained trousers. They all liked the blonde wig, these silent, shambling men, paying their money to hammer between her thighs. But then so did she, enjoying its silken weight over her pinned hair, revelling in the character changes it wrought. The wig made it easy to be the sort of lady they wanted, distancing her inner self from the revolting things they asked her to do. Yes, she'd definitely wear the wig for him.

Money – they loved that, too. He loved it, that Douglas Jenkins – she could tell, known too many like him, however fleetingly.

She'd had to be so very careful, sitting in the crowded court, blending in. But it had been worth the pounding fear of discovery, just to see the sad pretender in the pock-marked flesh. And, of course, the address. His 'dossing down at me mate's' address. Very useful.

He had reminded her for all the world of the wicked man in the Bible – the Judas man. So clearly had this come to her that it was difficult to concentrate on what was going on. Douglas Judas Iscariot Jenkins. History repeating itself, an ignorant unbeliever selling his soul for the journalist's thirty pieces of silver. Oh, she'd seen all that, the photos and the hubbub afterwards, Judas penned in by cameras and paper people. A cardboard man surrounded by paper people. A useless, leering man, destined for far greater things than his sad little mind could ever entertain. Far, far greater things.

She was very angry with Judas, and it really didn't do to make her angry. But he'd find that out soon enough.

She had the will, the conviction, and the way. The dollies were always telling her so, urging her on; even little Ida, quite jolly in her grey-painted hair.

And a gun. She'd always had a gun.

Dear Mr Fabian's service revolver would trigger a whole new respect for her. But she needed time to work it all out. Mustn't rush a job as important as this. Just a few days would suffice.

Why couldn't anyone see it as clearly as she did? It all seemed so blindingly obvious. Every town, every village, every group and tribe of *Homo sapiens* since the dawn of time had professed to believe in the afterlife. Here in Chelmsford, not less than sixty yards from the magistrates' court, the splendid cathedral stood as a monument to her convictions. God was good. Heaven was good. Suffer the little children to come unto me . . . so why wait, why drift on in your own personal hell, day after day, when the angels could minister to all your pains and woes right now?

She couldn't be wrong. After all, if heaven didn't exist, then there'd be no churches, no vicars, no priests, no bishops – nothing but a biological life with no meaning save to generate more empty shells, starved of all godliness.

The man Jenkins would help. These shitty, twisted, wretched papers would help. TV, radio, every modern medium would broadcast her Christmas message of hope to an increasingly desperate world. She would provide the perfect escape from the madness, with all the skill and compassion of a fireman leading screaming children to safety from a blazing room. She knew. She'd been in a fire.

She ate the ravioli, having first fed each doll in turn and acknowledged their loving thanks. Jesus had died to save our sins. But that was far too long ago. Now it was time for another to make a similar gesture.

She smothered a grin, wondering if people would soon be wearing golden service revolvers round their necks instead of crucifixes. Times were about to change, after all.

26

Ruth's phone rang four times.

'Ruth?'

'Uhuh?'

'S'Frank.'

'Oh.'

'Look, Ruth . . . I just wanted to say . . . I'm sorry. Really sorry for what's happened.'

'Guess you've done that, then.' What the bloody hell did he want?

'And the other day . . . Well, I never meant it to come out like that.'

'Like what?'

'Doug and . . . the woman at his cab company.'

She tried to be cool about it. 'S'pose it would've done, sooner or later. Same old cliché, though, isn't it? Wife's always the last poor sap to know.'

'If it's any consolation . . .'

'Frank, it's Christmas Eve. My senile mother's watching a Sooty video in the lounge, my adulterous husband's buggered off, and I don't know what the hell I'm going to do for money next year. There aren't any consolations.'

'Look. I'm . . .'

'You any closer?'

'Closer?'

'To catching this Christmas Killer?'

'Not really my case any more. Headquarters and the Serious Crimes Squad are calling the shots. You know how it is, they piss about with computers and whatever theory fits, we do all

165

the paperwork.'

'You must have been chuffed to begin with, though, eh? Finding out that Doug had been to the old lady's house? Never liked him, did you? Never gave us a real chance.'

'Now come on Ruth, you know that's not . . .'

'Couldn't wait to pin it on him, could you?'

A sigh. 'It wasn't personal, Ruth. He fitted the facts, that's all.' Another pause. 'But when all's said . . . Well, you could've done a lot better than him, Ruth.'

'No. I could've done a lot better with him, Frank. That's the difference.'

'Right. So I just wondered . . . Has he . . . spoken to you at all?'

She thought about this. 'You want to know if he's rung up to brag about talking to the papers? That's it, isn't it? He's got plans, Frank, I'll tell you that much. Left me a message on the answerphone. Doug sees this as his shot at the big time.'

'You know what the papers are like. They'll print any old rubbish.'

'So what the hell's the story, anyway? How's he got you in this state?'

'You know Doug. Going off half-cocked all the time. Puts his arrest down to some nonexistent vendetta I've got against him. Lunacy.'

'Then why worry? I've read the papers. There's nothing in there, at least about you and him. Just a whole lot of stuff about what an idiot he is. Made quite a prat of himself in court yesterday. Besides, the JP gagged him from talking.'

'For now.'

'Meaning?'

'They sometimes save stuff like Doug's for later. You know, a big spread after the case is solved. I just wondered if he'd . . .'

'I came back late from court yesterday and he'd already been back, grabbed some clothes and gone. We're not exactly on speaking terms, in case it's slipped your notice. Sorry, I can't help you.' But she was glad she couldn't help him.

A long silence, then: 'I don't suppose you could have a word with Doug – if he rings – and ask him to call me, could you?'

'For God's sake, Frank. You know where he is. Just pull him

166

in for questioning.' But she knew he would never risk it again. A private word was what she suspected Frank wanted, a little chat somewhere discreet, a chance to iron out their differences before Doug tried to sell whatever story he had, grease his sweating palm with hush money. 'Easy enough for a senior officer like you, surely?' she teased.

'Well, anyway. Can't chat all day.'

'Christmas Killers to catch.'

'Exactly.'

'And I'd better join Sooty and my mother.'

'Bye then, Ruth.'

'Bye.'

She replaced the phone feeling twice as good as before. Someone else felt as rotten as she had. Frank, for all his rank, money and career success, was sitting in an office just two miles away, sweating on an unknown murderer's intentions and her husband's lust for cash. She was still none the wiser as to whatever was causing Frank to fret so openly, but, then again, his concerns seemed the least of her problems.

Ruth wandered into the lounge where her mother watched an orange glove-pupped squirt a miniature water pistol into its playfully outraged operator's face. God, she thought, there's money for old rope.

Her mother stared at the screen intently, watching the favourite video so considerately left by nursing staff when they'd delivered her two hours previously. Ruth was under instructions to show the video immediately, apparently allowing Rene to 'untraumatically acclimatize to the new and potentially confusing environment'. This was the third time through; the rolling credits had twice so far triggered a flood of tears lasting the duration of the tape's rewinding until the appearance of the puppet hero again, ready to unleash himself into the same infantile capers once more.

And now for a third time. 'OK, Mum,' Ruth wearily replied, reaching for the remote, and watching the screen fizz to grey as the video's internal spools powered backwards. 'Be on again in a minute. Don't cry. Hang on.'

She wasn't so much being wound up as rewound. How many more times?

'You hungry yet, Mum?'

Just more tears. Perhaps it was time to ring the home, have her taken back into the professional care of those who washed, wiped and fed without really caring at all. Those who did it mostly for the money; keeping the elderly alive as long as possible until death arrived to cheat them of their weekly income. Ruth sighed. Why in God's name was she so damned cynical all the time?

Sooty made his now familiar wave to his crumbling fan. Rene brightened, waving back, choreographed by many repeated viewings to respond with all the apathetic enthusiasm of a condemned man at his last prison pantomime.

Ruth left her to it, wondering if there wasn't a shop open where she could buy one of the little orange bears for herself as a manual aid for the days to come. Too late. Far too late. It was Christmas Eve, and the last thing she fancied was a trip around town, wheeling her weeping mother in a fruitless search for Sooty.

She needed to call someone. Had too much on her mind. She sat by the phone, lit up, then punched in a ten-digit number.

'Felix?'

'Ruthie?' His voice was soft and croaky from sleep.

'Not disturbing you, I hope?'

'On the contrary.' A yawn. 'Saved me.'

'Saved you?'

'Must've fallen asleep watching the film. Would've missed the best bit if you hadn't rung. Look, here it comes. Go for it, Stevie boy! Power the thing up! You can make it! Wheelie it, Steve, pull her up!'

'Felix. You're watching *The Great Escape*, aren't you?'

'Shhhh.'

The line went quiet, save for the distant doomed attempt of a long-dead Hollywood superstar to leap the barbed wire.

'Oh, bollocks!'

'Felix, he never makes it.'

'One day, Ruthie. One day.'

'Why are men like that? What makes you want to sit down and watch the same old rubbish time and time again? Doug's the same. Any old Bogart stuff, Edward G. Robinson . . .'

'How is he?'

'Doug? Not a word. Nothing.'

'I read the papers. What the hell's he playing at? Didn't he realize he'd be splashed all over the front page like public enemy number one?'

Ruth exhaled into the mouthpiece. She wanted Felix with her, not a disembodied voice issuing from a cold piece of plastic in her hand. 'If I know Doug – and I used to think I did – he probably thought that any coverage he got would up his price.'

'Price?'

She sighed. 'He's got some damn fool idea about selling his story: Davies, the murder charge, the old days – something like that.'

Felix chuckled. 'So Frank's starting to sweat over a harassment charge, is he?'

'Felix?'

'Yes?'

'What am I going to do?'

'I don't know, Ruthie.'

'I don't want to be alone.'

'Not so bad, after a while.'

'I went wrong with Doug, didn't I? Expected too much, maybe. Set impossible standards. Wanted him to be dark and dangerous . . . decent and law-abiding. I had this image of him, reformed. And I was part of that. Somehow he'd met me and given up all the bad stuff, but . . .'

'Like they say in all the corniest movies, shit happens, Ruthie. You just have to deal with it. You want him back or don't you?'

She felt the first salty heaviness of tears, suddenly flooding her smoke-stung eyes. 'I don't know,' she croaked. 'I just don't know. He's out there somewhere, and I hate him. But I want to know where he is. I can't just forget about thirty years overnight. But he has. And it's killing me to think that he can.'

Felix let her weep for a while. 'You want me to come over?'

She sniffed. 'No . . . I'll be all right. I'm just . . .'

'Tired.'

'Yeah.' A long silence before she added, 'Thanks, Felix. Again.'

'S'okay, Ruthie. Know what my advice is?'

169

'What's that?'

'Keep watching and hoping. One day we might all make it over the wire.'

She smiled and replaced the phone.

27

Ruth woke early on Christmas morning, determined to enjoy the day. She washed quickly in cold water, humming carols and savouring the drifting aroma of roasting turkey which had filled the house overnight. Downstairs she could hear her mother calling, but like all the recent troubles and complications, she chose to ignore the persistent whine cajoling her to pack her homework and be ready for school. No event, no person, not even an act of God himself would ruin her Christmas. Today was her time out from the insanity, a brief respite from the madness of the past week. She piled on the make-up, applying a vivid mask of gloss and rouge to ward away any of Fate's evil spirits which might lurk unseen in the tiny terraced home. Satisfied, she took two deep breaths, smoothed down her bright red dress, turned from the mirror and marched downstairs.

Rene waited on the bottom step, grey hair hanging limply over a face swollen by medication. 'Mr McNeil will tan your backside if you're late again, Ruth Golden.'

'Mother . . .' Ruth was patient and informative, refusing to be budged from her self-imposed happiness, 'Mr McNeil died over twenty years ago. I'm forty-seven years old. It's Christmas Day, and I won't, repeat, won't be going to school.'

'Holidays is it?' Rene replied. 'When does term start? You'll be needing new buttons on all those blouses.'

Ruth smiled, still unfazed by her mother's senile ramblings. 'Let's get you dressed, eh?' She led her shuffling into the darkened front room, unpegged the purple woollen blanket from the window, folded away the camp bed so thoughtfully provided by the nursing home, and set about dressing the bewildered old woman as she'd been shown by bored nursing staff just two days previously.

The phone rang. Her daughter, Maria, concern seeping through the crystal clear connection from Bury St Edmunds.

'Mum.'

'Marie, how are you? Happy Christmas. How are my beautiful grandchildren?'

'What's going on?'

'That rather depends on what paper you read.'

'So it is Dad, then?'

'It's your father.'

'In court? For stealing a dead woman's wallet?'

'The very same.'

'And saying all those things? I can't believe it. Simply can't. Why in God's name didn't you call me about this? I've been waiting and waiting, worried out of my mind. Dad was on a murder charge, and you didn't even phone me?'

Ruth smiled, glad nature had its own way of redressing the balance of family worry. She recalled the many nights she'd lain awake into the small hours, ears desperately straining for the sound of teenage footsteps tiptoeing quietly to bed. 'Can you ring me back in about twenty minutes, love. Only I'm trying to finish dressing your grandmother and she's rather a handful.'

A silence as the penny dropped. 'Granny Rene's with you?'

'Large as life and mad as a March hare.'

'Mum! You mustn't! Can I speak to Dad?'

'He's not here, Marie.'

'Not there?'

'He's staying with a friend until . . . this all blows over.'

'Not there. For Christmas?'

'Marie, I really have to see to . . .'

'We're coming over. Right away.'

'Don't do that, Marie. I can manage. Besides, it's probably better I'm left on my own for a while.'

'What's going on, Mum?'

'Life, I suppose.'

It went on for another five minutes, Ruth determined her daughter should stay away at least until Boxing Day, Marie struggling to make sense out of a situation which seemed to get stranger by the minute. At length, they compromised, Ruth promising to ring back later.

She replaced the phone, jumping as it instantly began ringing again. A journalist, this time. How on earth did they track her down – and on Christmas Day? But then she supposed it was a fair bet that they'd find her at home. He mumbled an apology, then offered her three hundred in cash to meet in a hotel of her choice to spend an hour giving 'her side of things'.

It wasn't as if she couldn't do with the money. Cleaners didn't get a healthy Christmas bonus, a fact she had discovered when she wheeled her mother round to the cleaning agency to collect her December pay packet. There was an extra £7.20 in it, the result of several staff whip-rounds in the offices she cleaned. Her employer looked almost embarrassed as he explained that it had had to be shared amongst eleven of them.

But to actually, willingly, meet this man, sit down and coldly discuss the failings of her marriage . . . she was tempted, very tempted. That is, until the reporter went on to ask her to bring 'something split and low-cut for the photos'. She kissed the money goodbye. Doug had made enough of a fool of himself; she had no desire to join him. Twenty grand, maybe, but three lousy hundred? She hung up, unplugging the phone from its box by the skirting board.

She returned to dressing her mother.

'What you got me, then, for Christmas?' Rene asked as Ruth brushed the thinning hair over her balding pate.

'Later, Mother; we haven't eaten yet.'

The old woman's eyes twinkled. 'Got you the best. You and that young villain of yours.'

'Very good, Mum.'

'Where is he, then? Out robbing old folk, I'll bet.'

'Don't, Mum. Please.'

'Saw him last night,' Rene whispered confidentially. 'Behind the telly.'

'That's yesterday's paper, Mum.'

'He lives there.'

'It's a photograph.' She crossed the room and picked out the mauled tabloid, turning to the relevant page. 'See? Look what

173

it says, "Worse Than Scum! Christmas Killer Suspect Admits to Robbing Corpse."'

She sighed and tossed the paper into a bin, then switched on the television. Rene's eyes slowly wandered to the illuminated screen, eventually alighting on a particularly bad cartoon version of *Treasure Island*. Ruth watched with some sadness, shocked at how easily her once fiery, lively mother could be totally absorbed in such wretched nonsense.

She left the room, humming 'Good King Wenceslas' all the way into the kitchen, determined to recapture her early-morning mood. The wine helped considerably, two glasses of the stuff as she prepared far too many vegetables.

Then another glass.

Then another.

Later, much later – two bottles of red wine, one dismally silent burnt Christmas dinner, three octogenarian toiletings, four repeats of the infernal Sooty video, half a box of violet creams, several inane phone calls and the inevitable no-longer-funny Morecambe and Wise repeat later – Ruth sat alone with her mother in the front room, pouring what she promised herself would be her last glass for the evening.

'Get me my bag, would you, love?'

Ruth slowly obeyed, passing Rene her black patent leather handbag. She watched as the old lady fumbled inside before passing her an envelope.

'Didn't have time to wrap it. Fingers couldn't have managed, anyhow. Little girl at the home helped.' Rene's eyes twinkled in gentle anticipation. 'Didn't want to. Said I was mad to think of it. But I know how you could do with the money.'

'Mum. You shouldn't have,' Ruth replied, torn between politely returning the envelope, or ripping open its contents. Money – please let it be cash.

'See,' Rene pointed to the green tissue-paper hat barely perching on her head. 'Not crackers all the time, am I?'

Ruth opened the envelope. A collection of lottery receipts spilled on to her lap. 'Oh,' she said quietly.

'Two hundred of them, in there,' Rene grinned. 'All for you. Same numbers on each one.'

'Same numbers?'

Rene winked. 'Got to thinking, didn't I? Got to thinking, if you could win a million with just one ticket – gives you two hundred million with these.'

'You spent two hundred pounds on lottery tickets?' Ruth's mind span with the insanity. 'They let you do this?'

'Like I say. Didn't want me to. Had to keep it hush-hush. Secret stuff.'

Ruth carefully refilled the envelope with its useless contents and slipped it unseen into the black handbag. 'Very kind of you,' was all she could think of. 'Thanks.'

'Pleasure's mine. Set for life, you are now.'

'Right.' She went and kissed Rene before the tears began again.

The old lady suddenly held her tight, drawing Ruth's face down to her flabby cheek. 'Help me, love,' she whispered urgently. 'I want to go.'

Ruth drew back. Not the toilet again? Why, it couldn't have been more than an hour since . . . But Rene's eyes signalled otherwise. Ruth could only guess, but she supposed the old dear wanted the familiar surroundings of the twilight home. 'Can't, Mum. You're here for another few days. It'll be nice. We'll . . .'

'Not that. I want to go. On.'

'On?'

'I want to join your dad.'

Ruth's heart began to pound. 'Don't talk silly, Mum.'

'Ruth,' Rene pleaded. 'Me brain's all wrong. I can feel it sometimes. Like waking up out of a bad dream. I want to go, Ruth.'

Ruth turned from her. 'Just feeling bad, that's all. It'll pass.'

'I've had me time. Sorted you for more money than you'll ever need. I'm ready, Ruth. Do it, now. Before I change my mind.'

'Do it?' Ruth whispered.

'Send me over, love. I can feel your father. He's waiting for me, wants me. Wants his Rene . . .'

'Please,' Ruth begged. 'Let's just go to bed, eh?'

'Wants his Rene.'

'Mother!'

175

'Kill me, Ruth.'

'Shut up!'

'I'm done here.'

'No!'

'Your Christmas present to your old mum. Don't let me end up like all the rest. I know how it's going to be, Ruth. I see them every day . . .'

'How about some more Sooty?' Ruth attempted, tears streaming down both cheeks. Her body began to shake as an urge grew inexplicably inside her. A wicked urge. Rene's rantings feeding it word by twisted word. How she wanted to do it! Just grab the nearest blunt instrument and bring it crashing down on to that pathetic head, end the sound of that pleading voice.

'Don't want the bear, Ruth. Not any more.'

Ruth's fingers fought to jam the reluctant tape into the machine. 'Let's just see what Sooty's got to say about all this, shall we?'

'Wouldn't ask,' the voice continued, 'but I'm too weak to do it myself. Pillow would do, Ruth. Please.' Rene made a grab for her daughter's wrist.

Ruth's head felt as if it was about to explode. 'Shut up!' she screamed, twisting away from the leprous touch. 'For God's sake, shut up!'

Red wine caused Ruth's world to slip and slide, as if she stood in an invisible churning sea in the slowly spinning front room. She began to sing, insane lyrics appearing from nowhere, filling the space with irrelevant noise.

'Please, Ruth!' Rene made a sudden pathetic lunge towards her daughter. They collapsed together, Ruth smothered under all eight stones of her mother's feeble life-tired weight.

And Ruth screamed.

She kicked out, arms and legs pushing the heaving woman from her, as if wriggling out from under some gigantic spider pinning her to the floor. A lock of her mother's hair had fallen into her open mouth. 'Get away from me! Leave me alone!'

Then she was up on her feet, leaving it all behind, running out of the house, sprinting up the frosted street, lungs burning from the unfamiliar effort as the freezing black night tore into her wine-ravaged throat.

Within seconds, she was fifty yards from the house, dashing for the deserted town centre, passing silent streets cluttered with parked cars, front windows twinkling with tiny lights strewn over artificial trees.

And the further she ran, the angrier she became. How could her mother do that to her? What right had she to suggest such a thing? To her daughter – flesh and blood turned executioner?

That was the point of the home, for Christ's sake! That was its very reason for being. She had gone there to die! To save everyone the effort of watching and waiting for the rotting inevitable. That was what they paid the money for, sold her house for, cashed in the insurance plans for – waved bye-bye to any inheritance for – so she could die on someone else's carpet. In their space; sanitized, bleached, specifically staffed for the bloody purpose!

But not her house! Not her hands! Not her pillows! Theirs: let them earn the last of her father's money, let them be the ones to drop the pennies over her pleading-spaniel eyes!

Ruth's pace slowed, and she gripped her sides in agony, breath billowing in great gasps. She'd stopped before a parade of shops she knew well. A pub, several specialist stores, two charity shops, a Chinese restaurant and a pet shop.

A pet shop: Paws for Thought.

It was like an instruction. She paused, before walking unsteadily towards the large plate-glass window and peering through into the blue gloom beyond. One or two tiny pin pricks stared back at her, nervously flashing and flitting at her presence. She nodded, then waved at the captive inhabitants, feeling a distant chuckle rising from deep behind her still-heaving lungs, begging to be heard in the icy desolation of the empty street.

Forty-seven years of near-normal life had been unravelled in less than a week. A thought was crystallizing, begging to be heard, slowly overpowering the alcohol-addled recesses of her shattered mind.

And it went, 'Fuck it!'

So she did.

28

'Kind of stunt I'd expect your old man to pull.'

Ruth struggled to open one eye, a sixth sense telling her not to even attempt raising her head to identify the owner of the vaguely familiar voice. 'Pardon?' she half sighed.

'The old "brick through the shop window" caper. Smash and grab. Course, your old fella wouldn't have chosen a bleedin' pet shop. Off-licence'd be more his style.'

'Sergeant Mason?' Ruth enquired, squinting and turning her head very slowly. She couldn't for the life of her work out why Davies's partner was standing in her bedroom doorway. Or why the walls had closed in during the night, crushing wardrobes and flimsy furniture to leave a fair impression of a police cell. A damned accurate impression of a police cell.

The pet shop. He'd said pet shop. She groaned, seeing the half-brick leave her hand, heading in an ungraceful tumble towards the vulnerable glass. Did she really do that?

'Gave us all quite a giggle, Mrs J, believe me. Just sorry the guv'nor wasn't in to see it. Don't worry, though, I'll give him a copy of the tape as a late Christmas present.'

'Tape?'

'CCTV, Mrs J. Closed-Circuit Television, installed at a cost of hundreds of thousands by the average, honest community-charge paying Chelmsford citizen for the purposes of protecting the town and its immediate environs from late-night trouble-makers and brick-lobbing hoodlums like yourself.'

She collapsed back on to the hard bench, staring at the pink ceiling, now acting as a kind of screen for flashing memories from the night before. The brick . . . the explosion . . . the alarm

. . . the squad car . . . the police station . . . the charge of wilful damage and disorderly behaviour . . . the fingerprinting . . . the phone call . . . the cell door slamming. 'My mother,' she said softly, closing her eyes to it all.

'Don't you worry about her, Mrs J,' Mason replied jovially. 'Social Services shovelled her up last night after a complaint from your neighbours.'

'Complaint?'

'Seems the poor old dear was intent on burying herself in your front garden. Uniform turned up to find her naked with a spade, digging her own grave.' He took a noisy slurp from a cracked coffee mug. 'Mud up to her knees, she had. Frankly, I'm surprised she didn't die from hypothermia. Apparently, they were putting bets on in the ambulance.'

'Please, Sergeant. I've got a terrible hangover. There's only so much I can cope with.'

'Not concerned for your mum, then?'

She raised herself painfully on to one elbow, smarting from the myriad of scratches crisscrossing her hands and wrists. Her late-night encounter with the brick and the window had left her lower arms looking like she'd hand-fed a pride of hungry lion cubs. 'I assume from your provocative manner, Sergeant, that my mother is alive and well somewhere, most probably Broomfield Hospital. And I'm doubly sure that if anything untoward had happened to her, you'd be charging me with murder.' She looked the smug detective straight in the eye. 'That seems to be the form round here, after all.'

He lifted his cup at her and smiled, enjoying the banter. 'Give it a rest, Mrs J. Your old man's no angel, you know that. He was giving that friend of yours a seeing to, wasn't he? Could have done a lot of things, couldn't he, eh?'

Ruth swung her feet to the floor without attempting to raise her torso. 'Can I go now?'

Mason considered the request, nodding sagely. 'In a minute. You've got some fat geezer hanging round in reception, prepared to vouch bail for you. Sweating like a pig, he is. Got a thing about cop shops. Ring any bells?'

'Felix,' she groaned, snatches of the previous evening's phone call from the custody desk bounding into her bruised mind.

179

'Another one of the guvnor's old mates, apparently,' Mason replied, finishing his coffee. 'Stick together like fucking glue, don't you?'

She sat up, white streaks flashing before her eyes, turning her vision into a badly scratched film. 'It's been a strange week.'

'You like pizza?'

The question caught her unawares. 'Not for breakfast.'

'The Pizza Hut, in the High Street. Go there often?'

'You're not about to ask me out, are you?'

'I prefer the younger birds myself.'

'The body but not the brains. It figures.'

Mason nodded unashamedly. 'Woman with brains is a dangerous thing,' he said, motioning her to the door. 'A very dangerous animal indeed. All that guile and cunning, mixed with a portion of sex appeal. Can make a man do some very strange things, Mrs J.'

'I'll take your word for it.'

'Would you mind following me, Mrs Jenkins?' The tone had switched to official; playtime over.

'Would you mind if I threw up over your shoes? I need the bathroom.'

He led her out of the holding cells, down a maze of corridors, up a flight of steps, then, via the ladies', into a large open-plan office. A dozen plainclothes detectives were hard at work, poring over maps and answering phones. 'Welcome,' he said, 'to the nerve centre.' They headed towards an office at the far end of the room, its darkened windows overlooking the empty street below. A clock on the wall told her it was eight.

Eight o'clock in the morning – Jesus Christ! No wonder she felt bloody awful! And Felix, waiting downstairs – what time had he had to get up to come over here?

She slumped into a chair, watching Mason do likewise opposite. The desk between them housed several photos of Frank Davies and the kids. 'Frank's office, right?'

Mason nodded. He walked over and closed the door before sitting back down. 'I've got a lot of time for my guv'nor.'

'Is this a confession?' She really, desperately wanted a coffee.

'Top brass reckon he made a bit of an arse of himself over the Sharansky affair.'

180

'He did,' Ruth replied. 'He arrested the wrong man.'

'Your husband.'

'The wrong man,' Ruth repeated, wondering where all this was leading.

Mason leaned back in the black leather chair and placed both hands on his head. 'Quite a week, you said.'

'I'm sorry?'

'Just now, in the cell downstairs. You said you'd had quite a week.'

'I don't think anyone would deny that, Sergeant.' A coffee and a cigarette. She'd kill for a hot drink and a fag.

He gestured towards the outer office. 'Not a sight I ever thought I'd see. Whole damn squad in on Boxing Day.'

'Guess they need the overtime.'

'It's got nothing to do with money,' Mason replied, a hint of anger in his voice. 'Pride.'

'Is this going to take long, only . . . ?'

'Guv'nor's been pulled off the case. They reckon the big boys over at HQ can handle the hunt for the killer. We've been relegated to a team of researchers, really.'

'Seems fair, from what I know.'

Mason nodded sarcastically and stood, walking to a wall covered in black-and-white photographs of the corpses of Ida Sharansky and Sulee Xang, taken from varying distances and angles. 'Two murders, Mrs Jenkins. Two murders in one week-end in a town whose most serious incident is normally the annual bottle fight between pissed-up youths in the Rat and Parrot car park.'

Ruth forced herself to look at the dreadful images. A brandy and a cigarette. Forget the coffee.

Mason continued. 'I'm not a brilliant copper, Mrs Jenkins, but I'm no dickhead, either. And I look for links, just like the textbook tells me to.'

'I'm sure you do.'

He sniffed and wiped his nose with the back of his hand. 'And I'm looking at one right now.'

'Me?'

'You, Mrs Jenkins.'

She stared blankly back.

'You see,' Mason explained, 'I thought to myself, not "who" but "why"? Why did the student have to die? What's the score? Who comes up trumps?'

'Me?' Ruth repeated, feeling suddenly nauseous again.

'Very convenient for you, wasn't it? The moment Sulee Xang died, we were more or less obliged to let your old man off the hook for Ida Sharansky's murder.'

Ruth shook her head, trying to make some sort of sense of the accusation.

'The young girl would've been very easy to kill. She worked at Pizza Hut. A quick conversation some time, an invitation to see her place at the near-empty halls of residence. You already knew details of the Sharansky killing unavailable to members of the public . . .'

'You think that I . . .' Words failed her, eyes rooted to the photographs showing the savage gore of Sulee's butchered corpse.

He lowered his voice. 'Confidentially, Mrs J, the techno-buffs and nutter-shrinks up at HQ are working on a very strange hypothesis. Fucking far-fetched is the term I'd use.'

'Can I go home now?'

Mason ignored this. 'But I've been going over one or two things while the guvnor's been putting his feet up.'

'Please? I need to see my mother.'

'Things like this,' he said, reaching into a black box behind him and dropping a sodden see-through plastic bag on the desk. 'We found it in the student's bedroom. Familiar, at all?'

Ruth looked blankly from the desk into his accusing eyes.

'Let me help.' He smiled. 'I ran a check on you last night. Put you through the computer. Couldn't figure how a decent, respectable citizen like yourself could start tossing bricks through windows. Set me thinking. Set me searching.'

'Like I said,' Ruth replied through gritted teeth, 'it's been a duff week. I just had too much to drink and . . .'

'And what, Mrs Jenkins?'

She paused, biting her bottom lip. 'Just . . . lost it a bit, I suppose.'

'Right. You "lost it a bit". I like that. I really do.'

'Now can I go home?'

Mason ignored her a second time, pulling on a pair of pink latex gloves before picking up the polythene bag. 'Couldn't really figure this out at first. We assumed it was hers – the student's.' He began cautiously to open the bag, pulling out a faded blue square of cloth splattered with rust-brown stains.

He looked up at Ruth and smiled. 'Just an old handkerchief, Mrs J.' He unfolded it and neatly flattened it on the desk. 'Forensics have finished with it and sent it back to us to file under evidence. Needed blood samples from it, you see.'

Ruth stared in horror at the wretched material, realizing the Vietnamese origins of the innocent-looking brown stains. The poor struggling girl's blood.

Mason continued. 'And as I'm running you through the system last night, I happen upon a very . . .' he searched for the word with all the theatrical ability of a bad amateur, '. . . interesting discovery.' He paused to milk the moment.

'Sergeant, unless you're arresting me, I really have to go . . .'

'Ruth Golden. WPC Ruth Golden, according to the records. Did a short stint of duty with my guv'nor down Maldon way in the sixties. Yes?'

'So?' Something unsavoury was beginning to flash at the corners of her memory. Something connected.

Mason turned over the hankerchief with a magician's flourish, and pointed to the bottom left-hand corner.

Ruth felt as if she'd been punched violently in the stomach. There, faded, almost threadbare, but clearly visible in her mother's own embroidered hand: R.G. 1969.

'See where I'm heading, Mrs J?' Mason sneered. 'R.G. Ruth Golden. You.'

Ruth struggled to form any sort of defence. It was hers. Her handkerchief, lying inches away from her like a suddenly remembered treasure from the past. It all came rushing back; her mother slipping the starched cloth into her new uniform as she set off for the graduation at Hendon. But how in God's name had it ended up . . . ? She found herself hypnotically drawn to the images of the slashed student pinned to the walls. How had it ended up in that place of death?

'You do recognize it, don't you, Mrs J?'

'I . . . er . . . no. Of course not.' Gaining confidence now, adrenaline kicking in. Thank Christ they didn't have her wired to a bloody polygraph. 'Never seen it before in my life. I mean, it could be anyone's . . . Roger Green's, Richard Grantham's . . . Rita . . .'

'Ruth Golden's?'

'No! Now I need to go home.'

Mason hissed, 'Your handkerchief, found at the murder scene. A murder which resulted in your old man walking free. Could be, couldn't it? And I say that you could be in deep, deep shit, Mrs Jenkins.'

'This is ridiculous,' Ruth protested. A face shot from nowhere, a drifting snapshot from the past. A death's head, taunting her with its innocent smile – challenging her to find its relevance. Small, ovoid, crying. 'It's bloody madness! A ludicrous thing! For Christ's sake, I've got a cast-iron alibi for Sunday afternoon. Ask Felix Pengelly. Ask Margaret Simmons. I spent it with them. Ask them, see for yourself!'

'Oh, I will, Mrs J. You can be sure of that. When you've got two bodies and very few links, you just keep hammering away.'

'Look, I swear to you . . .'

Mason smiled and walked to the door. 'I trust you can find your own way down to the front desk. I'd escort you, but I've got rather a lot to be getting along with.'

Ruth stayed put, determined to snuff out Mason's nonsense then and there. 'Listen, what the bloody hell would I have to gain by killing the girl? To get my stupid husband back – is that what you think? The man who screwed his boss while I cooked his bloody dinner? You really think I'd risk so much as a parking ticket for him?'

Mason stood by the door. 'I'm not going to pretend to understand relationships, Mrs Jenkins. But let me tell you this. If you'd stuck with the force instead of marrying that lowlife, you'd have witnessed some pretty strange shit yourself. Call me jaundiced, if you like, but nothing surprises me any more.'

Ruth stood, frantically trying to control her anger. 'I'd call it clichéd, narrow-minded and bloody stupid,' she snapped. She walked to the door, turning her back on the photographs. 'No wonder your bosses are calling in the specialists. You couldn't investigate a mugging in a kindergarten.'

Mason smiled, refusing to rise to the bait. 'Until we meet again, Mrs Jenkins.' He held out his hand.

'Sod off,' Ruth replied through gritted teeth, pushing past his sweating bulk.

29

'Ruthie,' Felix tried diplomatically, 'it's just a damn handker-chief. How can you be so sure it's yours?'

'Because I recognized the bloody thing, Felix. And it was there, in that poor girl's room.'

'You're certain of this?'

She nodded. 'And now Mason's coming up with all kinds of stuff. Like I said, he was almost implying that I killed her myself.'

'Well, that'll never stick.'

She sighed heavily. 'Just when I thought I was out of all this, just when I thought the nightmare was ending, that bloody handkerchief turns up, and suddenly I'm back in it again.' She turned to him. 'And all I can think is "How?" How on earth did it get there?'

He took her arm and they began walking over the grey-green frosted grass. It had been a long morning. After leaving the station, they had checked on her mother's progess at Broomfield Hospital, then made the forty-minute drive to the rest home in Shenfield where she had apologized to tight-lipped staff for the previous evening's debacle.

A long morning, a very long morning, thought Felix.

And now this, this curious handkerchief business. Ruth's continued insistence that the bloody, bloodied thing was hers, over and over.

It had been his idea that they go somewhere quiet in order to try to rationalize matters. Ruth had muttered brief directions to Hylands, a beautiful country park, home to a lovingly renovated eighteenth-century mansion just three miles from Chelmsford.

Now they walked arm in arm across the wide lawns, joining young families and dog walkers out enjoying their annual Boxing Day stroll.

'Okay,' he said, willing to accept her bizarre hypothesis for the moment. 'Maybe it is yours, maybe you're right. It could be just a fluke coincidence. Somehow the Vietnamese girl happened upon it, and that's all there is to it.'

'How?'

He thought for an instant. 'Boot sale, perhaps. Jumble sale. Students are always going to those.'

She turned to him, face worn with worry. 'Aren't you missing the point, Felix? Suppose it wasn't hers? Suppose it belonged to the killer? That's what Mason's implying.'

'Comes to the same thing,' he replied. 'Anything could've happened to it in the last thirty years. I mean, you say your mother gave it to you when you graduated from Hendon. That's over thirty years ago, Ruth. You could've dropped it, mislaid it, had it pinched, given it to a friend, lost it . . .'

They stopped at a bench overlooking the mansion and the rolling grounds, and for a moment neither said another word, each lost in their own separate confusions, reluctant to accept the word of the other.

'Let's try it this way,' said Felix eventually, taking her cold hand in his. 'When was the last time you can remember seeing it?'

'Two hours ago,' she said miserably. 'Eighteen inches below my nose.'

'Before that, Ruthie.'

'I don't know.' Another flash, a lightning glimpse of something heroically keen, comfortably right. That face again.

'You used to take it out on the beat with you in Maldon?'

'I suppose so.' Now a weight on her lap. Wriggling, upset; distant voices shouting. One voice protesting, accusing. Soft hair under her chin. 'I think . . .'

'What?'

But it had gone, hiding, teasing her, concealing itself somewhere deep inside. Chuckling, shivering. Asking for a lollipop. 'Something happened,' she said quietly. 'Back then.'

'Maldon?'

187

She nodded. 'A child, maybe.'

'Child?'

She let go of his hand, stood up, then sat back down. Then stood up again.

'Boy or girl?' he prodded.

She turned to his expectant face, suddenly seeing him much younger, bursting with the naïve optimism of youth. 'You were there.'

'Where?'

The wriggling weight on her lap, soft brown hair statically clinging to her police smock. The smell of a newly laundered nightie. 'It was a girl,' she said. 'I gave it to a young girl.'

'Excellent!'

'Excellent?'

'You gave it away. It began its journey from the moment you gave it to someone else. Don't you see? You needn't worry about it any more.' Now Felix stood, rubbing his hands and stamping his feet. 'All we have to do is tell this Mason fellow who you gave it to, and leave him to find out how it ended up where it did.' He placed an arm over her shoulders. 'Then we can go and get some lunch, eh?'

'She was crying,' Ruth said softly.

'Gets better all the time,' Felix replied jovially, failing to pick up on Ruth's ominous tones.

'You were there, too.' Her mind's eye replayed the gradually clearing details like a mental projector refocusing in the darkened cinema of her memory. 'Something to do with an accident.'

'Scene of an accident? Little girl knocked down by a bus? You mopping the blood off her knees?'

'Tears.' She saw the face quite clearly now: anxious, determined, not frightened of the police, but someone else – the shouting voice from another room. A female voice. Her mother's voice. 'I gave it to a little girl in the station. She was crying, confused.'

'And I was there?'

'We all were. You, me, Frank . . .'

'Frank? You sure?'

Ruth nodded.

Felix frowned, trawling his own collection of faded memories. 'An accident, you said?'

'Something to do with this girl's mother . . . and the girl . . . she'd . . .'

'Killed her father.'

A wave of sudden pain surged through her, the rush of the distant past racing to be remembered. 'Yes. Yes.' Those little damp cheeks, the imploring face, the uneasy silence in the crowded room. 'Yes. You remember? That girl, Felix. That terrible thing.'

'The Websters,' said Felix sadly. 'Poor kid killed her own father.' He thought some more. 'Injected him. He was a doctor . . .'

'Vet,' Ruth corrected, her heart beginning to pound with the confusion of long-forgotten sensations and images. 'She was so worried, so . . .'

'She put him to sleep, I think. Something about . . .'

'Being in heaven. Daddy's all right now.'

'The Websters' little girl. Jesus Christ, I'd forgotten all about it.' He paused, watching a greying labrador limp half-heartedly after a bleached white stick, instinct driving its rheumatic limbs through the obvious pain of retrieval – just to have it thrown out again by a bored owner. 'And you gave your handkerchief to her?'

'Positive.'

Somehow, he didn't feel as hungry any more. 'So what now?'

'We find her,' Ruth replied quickly, beginning the long walk back towards the car.

'We?'

She turned, an isolated figure in the unforgiving winter landscape. 'Please, Felix.'

'What for? All you do is tell that Mason fellow . . .'

She took his arm once more. 'What was her name, Felix? The little girl?'

'God knows.'

She began walking him reluctantly back towards the distant speck of his pastel-blue Austin Morris. 'Think, Felix, think!'

'I don't know, for God's sake.'

'Please.'

'Why? Why is it so important? It'll all be on police records, somewhere. Maldon, most likely. They'll tell you all you need to know. Name, address, the lot.'

'Could you take me there, Felix?'

'Now?' She was practically jogging him towards the car.

'If I know who she was, maybe I can find out if she remembers what she did with the handkerchief. Find out how the hell it ended up where it did.'

'I'm hungry, Ruth. And will you slow down, I'm going to slip and bloody break something!'

'We'll eat later,' she said, adding to their speed in her excitement. 'On me, I promise. Please, please help.'

Felix was beginning to pant. He'd had enough, reached the end of it with Ruthie. Been phoned up at eleven on Christmas night, had to listen to a drunken request from an old friend begging for bail after she'd gone berserk with a brick and a shop window. Had to travel – without breakfast – thirty miles to collect her first thing that morning. Then had to suffer the progressively stranger machinations of her mind while acting as unpaid chauffeur as she set about smoothing the many ruffled feathers generated by the pet-shop fiasco. And now, finally – on top of all this – the ultimate camel's back-breaker: she was running him at breakneck speed across iced grass while insisting that he donate the rest of his day in following her every whim!

Then, just as he was about to let rip with a self-righteous cannonade of wholly justified objections . . . he slipped and fell on to the frozen ground.

'Felix! Are you all right?'

He ground his teeth. 'It's you I'm worried about.' He got up gingerly, instantly aware of the slowly seeping damp patch on the seat of his trousers. 'It's bloody Boxing Day, for God's sake! A day of rest. A day for putting feet up in front of the telly, cold turkey sandwiches, six-packs of cheap lager, the occasional cigar . . .'

'Felix, I'm sorry . . .'

'No! I'm sorry, Ruthie! Sorry I ever got mixed up in all this. I'll tell you what,' he was panting and grimacing at the same time. 'How about I just run you home, then you call the station at Maldon. They'll tell you what this bloody girl's name was. Then you can call Frank, tell him what you know, and he'll put his sergeant straight. And if the bloody handkerchief is at all important to their investigation, then they'll have a pretty good idea where to start, won't they?'

Ruth looked into the puffing, puce face, and felt genuinely sorry. She was surprised; she hadn't felt that way in a long time. True, she'd felt guilty about abandoning her mother the night before, and there had been a degree of shame after smashing the shop window – but this was real remorse, and she couldn't for the life of her work out why she felt it so deeply. This soft, damp-buttocked friend had somehow wheedled in beneath her stout matrimonially constructed defences and unwittingly elicited a real response. It disturbed her, silenced her, made her suddenly find a point of unsurpassed interest in the frosted banality of the grass by her feet.

'OK,' she said quietly. 'Probably the best way.' Why was he so anxious to go home, his own home? Who waited for him there, besides the wretched cat? 'I just thought if we went now . . .'

'Now?'

'. . . then we'd strike while the iron was hot, so to speak.'

'To Maldon? Now?'

She took a step towards him, resisting the peculiar urge to wrap both arms round him and blend herself into his good flesh. 'I want to finish this, Felix. I want to find out what happened to the handkerchief. I need to know that girl's name.'

'Why?'

'So that I can be sure I had nothing to do with any of this.'

'Of course you haven't, Ruthie.'

'I don't know, Felix, I really don't. The longer this goes on, the more it seems to . . . involve me.' She took his arm once more, gently coaxing him to walk by her side. 'First there's Doug, then the affair, then the old lady dying, and him stealing her purse. Next, one of my old handkerchiefs turns up at another murder scene, and the police are quite rightly getting rather suspicious about my involvement in all of it.'

'Like I say, have a word with Frank . . .'

'All Frank's concerned with', she responded bitterly, 'is Doug keeping his mouth shut. No, I can't trust the police. What

191

will they think when I suddenly come back three hours later, changing my entire story and . . .'

'Changing your story?' Felix stopped dead in his dew-dampened tracks.

Ruth searched the bright grey sky, hoping to reduce her next statement to an unimportant quip. 'I told them I'd never seen the handkerchief before.'

'Oh my God.'

'Felix, I was shocked, confused, didn't know what to –'

'Why didn't you tell me this before?'

'Because I knew you'd probably react like this.'

'You didn't tell them it was yours?' Felix reluctantly thought the business through. 'So now you can't go back there and say it is. Right?'

'Right.'

'For Christ's sake!'

'I'm sorry, Felix.'

'I just want to go home, Ruthie. I'm very tired of all this.'

'Felix.' She looked straight into his eyes, searching out what remained of his patience. 'Please help me. If I can just find out what happened, then I can clear myself in my own mind. That's all I want to do. I simply want to know. For certain.'

He remained silent.

'I've had the worst week in history,' she continued. 'God knows I've lost just about everything – maybe even my marbles. And I don't want to lose you as a friend. But I need your help, Felix. I want your help. You were there. With me and the girl. The Webster girl. Maldon, the old days. As soon as I find out who she was, where she is . . . maybe she knows what happened to the handkerchief. Please, Felix. Help me out of all this mess.'

Felix studied her face for a long time.

30

Five hundred quid?

Who did they think they were fucking kidding?

Five hundred for the year's biggest exclusive? Bloody cowboys!

Doug slammed down the phone for the thirteenth time that morning. A short distance away, his sleeping host lay slumped in a wobbling armchair. Empty beer cans littered the fetid front room, together with occasional plates of half-eaten, dried-up food, a stomach-churning testimony to the unusual culinary Christmas the two had shared.

For his part, Doug had felt that Steve's long-winded, rambling monologue on the wondrously liberating life of the divorcé was somewhat flawed. Even after seven cans of Stella, half a bottle of vodka and two litre-bottles of cider, it seemed to him a rather lonely way to spend your days. And, perhaps more worryingly, a grim foretaste of what to expect in his own long wilderness years ahead.

Unless he managed to get back with Ruth. Or another woman. Any other woman. Who needed Ruth, the woman who had more or less sided with the filth in calling him a murderer? No, any woman would do. He wouldn't end up like Steve, broken by marriage, putting a brave face on the wretchedly crushed heart.

But first, he had the complex problem of managing his new-found celebrity status. Things hadn't gone exactly as planned. Sure enough, he'd made the papers following the show trial at the magistrates' court, but there it appeared to end. Despite swapping phone numbers with up to twenty eager journalists, not one seemed willing to commit themselves to paying realistic money for his version of events. Even Doug could understand the crux of the problem – he was demanding cash upfront, they wanted a sampler of what he was so keen to sell. Which, of course, meant giving away much of the plot. Instead, he stuck to resolutely ringing the hacks who'd never called, repeatedly teasing them with "a fucking corking story about the copper who screwed up in the Christmas Killer case", which seemed to whet their voracious appetites . . . until he gave his name.

'Doug Jenkins?' they replied. 'The bloody grave-robber? Sod off, you're history, pal.'

Which didn't bode well for Doug. Thirteen calls this Boxing Day morning alone, and still the highest bid for his exclusive stood at a meagre five hundred quid. Bollocks to that, he thought. This thing can wait. That nutter, that Christmas Killer, was bound to pop another soon enough, then the asking price would go up with the body count. Two grand at least.

Then, he'd start on the autobiography, maybe when he was inside for nicking the purse. He was almost certain to get three months for that. Time enough to attend a creative writing course, sketch an outline from the privacy of his own cell.

He'd win all right; Doug Jenkins would get there in the end. The public would know of his struggle to conform against overwhelming cynicism from his wife and the police – a shocking exposé of trust hammered to pieces by prejudice.

He wandered to the fridge, staring forlornly at its mouldy contents. Jesus, when was the last time Steve went shopping? It seemed the only way food could qualify for entry was to be at least six weeks past the sell-by date. He made do with a butter sandwich. Again.

He was about to make his fourteenth phone call while the phone's owner remained unsuspectingly asleep, when the doorbell rang.

Bollocks! Who the hell could that be?

Sighing heavily, Doug trod a delicate path through the festive debris and slowly opened the door to peer out at a smart young woman standing on the doorstep.

Well, hello. Luck's changing already. Blonde – class, bit of style.

One of his dozing mate's minicab conquests? A late-night passenger, lipstick smudged by over-priced cocktail juices, short of the fare, and drunkenly agreeing to a body-doubling fumble in exchange for the ride? Now popping back for more of the same? Not that it had ever happened to Doug, this piece of cabby folklore. Always the other lads on the rank, but never him. He'd had to make do with that old hag Margaret, for God's sake . . .

'Well?'

'Douglas Jenkins?'

'Who wants to know?'

31

It took Felix the best part of an hour back at Ruth's to convince her that Maldon police station wasn't altogether the best place to begin her redemptive search for the little girl. Much of the sixty minutes was consumed with the act of consumption itself: three cups of coffee, two cold turkey sandwiches and an unnaturally large slab of Sainsbury's Christmas cake. Ruth made do with three tangerines.

'Let's face it,' he said between mouthfuls, 'it's going to look a bit strange, isn't it? Asking for information about a case that happened nearly thirty years ago? Even if we are old coppers ourselves. They're going to want to know why, and then we're stuck for answers. We certainly can't mention the handkerchief. Every copper in Essex'll be chasing this Christmas Killer thing.'

Ruth nodded reluctantly. 'What else? Newspapers? The local library? There must be a report of the case somewhere. At least that'll give us a name.'

'Ruthie,' Felix replied patiently, 'it is a bank holiday. What's going to be open?'

She chewed on her bottom lip. 'I've got to do something, Felix. Sitting here watching you stuff your face is getting me nowhere.'

'Can I ask you something?'

She raised an eyebrow.

'What did it feel like?'

'What?'

'Smashing all that glass.'

The smallest of smiles appeared. 'Great.'

'Thought it might.'

'They've charged me, you know? I'll be up in court next month.'

He took her hand and winked. 'And I'll pay every penny of your fine, Ruthie. I'm impressed, I really am. I'm a big fan of working-class anarchy.'

'You're teasing me.'

'Maybe. But I meant what I said. Every penny. I call it value for money.'

Ruth lit up. 'Yeah, well don't make too much of it, OK? I was drunk as a lord and out of control.' She held his admiring gaze. 'And it's not the sort of thing I want to specialize in.'

'Of course, Ruthie. Say no more. But nice to have done it once in a lifetime, eh?'

She watched an accidental smoke ring drift lazily to the ceiling. 'Yeah. Once in a lifetime.'

'Moving on. Where's your phone book?'

'Sorry?'

'BT's door-stopper. That great floppy volume they shove through the letterbox once every few years and make so completely unreadable that you feel compelled to use their pay-through-the-nose directory enquiry service instead. Where is it?'

'I'm not sure . . .'

'Find it, Ruthie.' He wiped the last few currants and crumbs of fruitcake from his lips, before rubbing both hands together in a businesslike fashion. He felt restored and invigorated, fortified by food and having traded his damp trousers for a pair of Doug's. 'The phone book gives us what the recorded operator can't. Addresses. We start with all the Websters in the Maldon area.'

Ruth set off in search of the directory. 'Then we call them, right? See if any of them are related to the little girl . . . can give us a name?'

'Exactly. It's a start, isn't it?'

She returned with the dusty, curled volume of names, numbers and addresses, quickly flicking through to the 'W's. 'Then we go round and see them, possibly?'

'Well, I don't know about that, Ruthie,' Felix replied hesitantly, still fairly confident that the whole venture would end

197

in a reassuring trail of dead-ends, more tea, cake, and a chance to catch last orders. 'Let's just see how we get on, eh?'

An hour and a quarter later, a pastel blue Austin Morris containing a disenchanted driver and an excitable female passenger approached the outskirts of a small Essex town famed for the salt crystals collected from its muddy river estuary. After an absence of twenty-six years, PCs Golden and Pengelly were back on patrol in Maldon.

'Boxing Day,' said Felix. 'I can't believe anyone'd agree to see a pair of complete strangers on Boxing Day.'

'She's old,' Ruth replied, recalling the frail voice on the end of the line. 'Probably lonely. They like to talk.'

She'd spent ages, receiver in one hand, pencil in the other, phoning each of the Websters in the Maldon area. If Ruth could find a surviving family member who recalled what had happened to the little girl after the tragedy, then she might be able to trace the path of the handkerchief.

Might.

After forty minutes, twelve phone calls and four Marlboro Lights, she hit pay dirt. A Miss Enid Webster guardedly admitted to being related to a Richard Webster – Cousin Dicky, she'd called him – who'd been a vet many years ago, before – and here the old woman's voice had dropped almost to a whisper – there had been an accident such as Ruth was describing. Ruth's spirits began to soar. A name, did she have a name?

Of course she did. You don't forget flesh and blood. Chloe. Dear Chloe.

Chloe Webster.

They'd left immediately.

Felix pulled up outside a large ivy-clad house set on a steep hill overlooking Hythe Quay, with its splendid arrangement of sprit-sail barges wedged firmly in the dark mud of low tide. One or two families wandered the breezy promenade, hats, scarves and gloves battling against the chill winter wind.

Ruth made straight for the front door, pressing a faded brass bell. Several moments later, a kindly old face peered out from behind the woefully inadequate security chain.

'Miss Webster? We spoke on the phone. About Chloe?'

The face smiled, the door closed momentarily, then reopened to allow Felix and Ruth inside.

'Can't be too careful. Could've been those poll-tax people after me pension.'

'I think even they have the occasional day off, Miss Webster.'

'Don't you believe it. Bastards and parasites, they are.'

Ruth flushed slightly, always uncomfortable when the older generation swore. Somehow she imagined foul language to be something one grew out of, a habit abandoned by the elderly as 'not quite right'.

'Couldn't agree more,' Felix announced, stepping forward and offering a hand. He liked her. 'Whole lot of them should be shot before dawn.'

'Aye. With rusty bullets.'

'And us pulling the triggers.'

'You are . . . ?'

'Felix. Felix Pengelly.'

'Wasn't expecting two of you.'

'I'll blend into whatever background you have.'

She smiled, rather liking Felix in return. 'Come through,' she said, leading her two guests into a large sitting room, an immaculate temple to the furniture and tastes of the forties. A ginger cat sat contentedly on an inviting sofa, licking its paw and surveying the new arrivals with feline contempt. Felix sat down beside it and attempted a stroke. Flinching at the cold hand, the cat glared menacingly, forbidding any further contact.

Ruth sat on a high-backed dining chair, looking at the sad display of Christmas cards adorning the mantelpiece over a large fireplace, home to a noisy fan heater. The whole house seemed to be silently screaming, 'I'm too big for her, she can't manage me any more. Too old. We both are.'

Enid Webster appeared with a tray of tea and biscuits, smiling at the pair of them. Ruth was suddenly consumed with the urge to smoke, sensing, quite accurately, that it was the very fact that she most probably wouldn't be able to that made her want to. It was always the same, regardless of her age; faced with anyone over sixty-five, Ruth initially felt like an inadequate teenager, and twice as tongue-tied.

Fortunately, Enid broke the embarrassing silence. 'On the phone, Mrs Jenkins, you said Chloe had something of yours?'

'That's right. I'm keen to trace it.'

'Good friend, is she?' Miss Webster asked hopefully.

'We knew each other a long time ago.' It wasn't a lie, and Ruth was keen to protect the sweet old woman from the true purpose of the visit.

'Ah.'

Ruth took the proffered cup and saucer, desperately hoping she wouldn't drop the lot on her lap. 'Is there a problem, Miss Webster?'

The old woman sat down opposite, as a flicker of guilt and sadness briefly crossed her wrinkled face. 'When you said you wanted to find her, I . . .' She looked at Felix for forgiveness. 'I might have misled you a little.'

He smiled back reassuringly.

'I had it in mind, you see,' she continued, 'that you might know a good deal more about dear Chloe than I did. I thought that if I could talk to you, then . . .'

Ruth felt the embarrassment acutely. 'We'd be able to help you find her?'

Miss Webster nodded. 'I suppose I've wasted your time.'

Ruth glanced at Felix, who returned her bemused expression. She took a sip of tea, determined to make something of the visit. 'When did you last see Chloe, Miss Webster?'

'I have wasted your time, haven't I?'

'Maybe,' Ruth gently replied. 'But if we all put our heads together, we might be able to come up with something.'

This seemed to soothe Miss Webster, who nodded slowly. 'Dickie was my cousin,' she said. 'Richard Webster. He was a vet . . . Chloe's father, the one she . . . You know about the accident?'

'Awful tragedy for the whole family, Miss Webster,' Felix replied, secretly relieved that the door to Chloe Webster seemed to be shutting by the second. With a little luck and a following wind, he'd be back home for the Bond film.

'I never married, Mr Pengelly. This is my parents' place. Was. Mine now. Far too big. I just can't bear to give it up.'

'Must be a constant struggle.'

She smiled politely. 'I thought about marriage, but after what happened to Dickie, I just couldn't face it.'

'The accident?' Ruth prompted.

Enid shook her head sadly. 'The marriage itself. They argued, Dickie and Melanie. All night and all day. Should've been a match made in heaven – and for a while it was. Then it just seemed to go bad. It was like she wasn't satisfied or something. Restless, she was, keeping on at him to move up to London.' She appealed to the whole room. 'Well he was happy where he was. A little vet's practice in Great Totham, a few miles up the road from here, from his family. He didn't want any of that flash London living. And then it happened. Out of the blue. He wasn't there any more. So none of it mattered.'

'And Chloe,' Ruth pressed. 'What happened to her after . . . her father died?'

Enid looked slightly ashamed once more. 'They took her. Melanie's side of the family. She had a sister who kept an old folk's home in Danbury.' Her eyes misted over slightly. 'It was different in those days. The mother had more rights. Her sister was godmother to Chloe, so she got her.'

Ruth fought to assimilate the information, a frown crossing her face. 'Melanie Webster gave her daughter away?'

Enid nodded. 'What could we do about it? There weren't millions of these useless social workers like you have nowadays. If you didn't want your kid, and found someone else who did, you took it to a judge to decide.'

'What happened to Chloe's mum, Miss Webster?' Felix asked, trying to prevent digestive crumbs from cascading into his lap.

There was undisguised bitterness in the answer. 'She was happy as Larry, wasn't she? Took off up to London as she'd always wanted. No husband, no child to tie her down. As far as I remember, she married a bookmaker from Leytonstone. Got married, had another kid, and wound up in a tower block in Stratford. Fags got her in the end. Died of cancer several years back.' She stared at Ruth. 'So much for the good life, eh?'

Ruth looked into the grey eyes, sensing that Miss Webster interpreted as righteous justice the fact that Melanie Webster's dreams had fallen apart as completely as if she'd hurled them from the skyscraping flat to the disinterested pavement below. 'And Chloe?' she asked softly.

Enid blinked, drawn suddenly back to the question. 'Like I say,' she sighed, 'once Melanie had managed to convince the authorities that she couldn't stand to live with the child who had killed her husband, and would even put it up for adoption, Chloe's aunty stepped in, and the poor kid was bundled off to the old people's home.'

'You think Melanie Webster lied to the authorities?' Felix asked.

'She wanted rid of Chloe. It didn't fit the image of a carefree girl around town to have a little kid tugging at her skirts.'

'So she went to live with Melanie's sister.'

Enid nodded. 'Jude Farrow. The Maltings, an old people's home in Danbury.'

'And then?'

She shrugged her shoulders. 'The visits just dried up. We used to go across, in the beginning, a big group of us, all the Maldon Websters, out to see Cousin Dickie's child. And it didn't seem right to any of us.'

'Right?' Ruth asked.

'To have a child grow up in and amongst all that . . . death, you know. All those old folk, and very few friends of her own.' Enid smiled at the memory. 'Lovely little girl she was, always bright and cheerful. Oblivious, almost, to what she'd done. Like she'd blocked it out, somehow.'

'Did you talk much about the accident?'

'None of us knew how to.' She paused and refilled Ruth's cup. 'Course, by then, Jude Farrow was getting a bit of a reputation as a lush. Accidents were happening, people were dying in there before their time, so to speak. It came as no surprise to us that the place burned down to the ground. I think nearly twenty died in the fire.'

Ruth felt a sudden surge of tremendous disappointment, assuming Chloe had perished in the blazing building. Then logic took over, reminding her that Enid Webster seemed just as keen to find Chloe as she was. So she was alive!

'And then?'

'Are you a vindictive woman, Mrs Jenkins?'

The question ambushed Ruth. 'I don't think . . .'

'I am. When it comes to family.' Enid stood and left the room, leaving Ruth, Felix and the cat glancing curiously at each other in total silence.

A minute later she returned, clutching an A4 envelope. 'Burglars could come in here and take all this stuff –' she announced, flicking her arm at the ancient bric-a-brac trying its best to lighten the room. 'I wouldn't give a monkey's.'

'As long as they didn't take that, right?' Ruth pre-empted, pointing to the brown envelope now lying on the table between them.

'Exactly.' Enid placed a hand on it, almost caressing the worn grain. 'This, to me,' she said in hallowed tones, 'is justice. Proof that the Lord our God, while he may be making a right cobblers of most of it, occasionally gets it right.' She slid the envelope over to Ruth expectantly.

Ruth opened the ungummed envelope and reached inside, pulling out a carefully clipped newspaper article, seemingly about plans to extend local fishing perimeters.

'Other side,' said Felix helpfully.

She turned the faded paper over in her hands, revealing a complete article, accompanied by a photograph of an elderly couple holding hands and trying their best to look blissfully content in front of a bungalow.

Under the headline 'Caring Couple Finally Come Home', the copy did a fairly routine job of promoting 'brand new retirement bungalows for the over sixties'.

The third paragraph explained the reason for the article's preservation.

Pictured above are Mr and Mrs William and Jude Farrow, two of Oakwood Park's newest and most satisfied customers. The Farrows, who opted for the rheumatic-suppressing 'Chandler' home style are no strangers to post-retirement care, having run a rest-home for many years of their working lives.

'This home gives us the independence we want, together with a range of labour-saving fixtures and fittings to help us lead a normal, active lifestyle,' said Jude Farrow yesterday.

Ruth stopped reading as the copywriter dashed straight into the hard sell.

'Kept that eight years, I have. They got what they deserved, to my mind,' Enid Webster explained. 'Living in one of them crappy retirement complexes. Used to carry on like lady muck, she did. Her and her sister. Where are they now, eh? One's six feet under, the other's rotting away in a centrally heated cardboard box with no upstairs. Like I say – justice.'

Ruth passed Felix the article. 'After the home burned down, what happened to Chloe?'

'They moved away. The Farrows and Chloe. She would've been about twelve or thirteen by then. That was that. We found them, tried writing, telephoning to arrange another visit – they just wouldn't answer. Chloe sent us the occasional postcard, and we'd always write back begging her to drop in and see us, any time. But she never did. Once Dickie's parents had died, well, I suppose we all sort of gave up on her. She never came to either of the funerals, you see.'

'Perhaps no one told her about them?' Ruth offered, vaguely wondering why she was springing to the defence of someone she'd only once met briefly, so many years ago.

Enid sighed. 'When you rang this morning, Mrs Jenkins, I thought you'd be able to tell me more about Chloe's later years.'

Ruth shook her head. 'I knew her just after her father died,' she said truthfully. 'I've not seen her since.'

'Then what was it you gave her, that's so important to you?'

Ruth hesitated before answering. 'Some peace of mind, perhaps.' And before Enid could even try to unravel the answer, she was sliding the article back into its envelope, and motioning to Felix that it was time to go. 'Thank you, Mrs Webster. You've been so kind.'

Enid was confused. 'I'm not sure how I could've been. Peace of mind, you say?'

Felix stood by her side. 'A piece of mined Uranium gold,' he said confidently. 'Priceless.'

'Gosh. Chloe never mentioned it.'

He winked at her. 'Would you, Miss Webster? Would you?'

The old cheeks coloured slightly. She turned to Ruth. 'If you find her, would you . . .'

'Of course,' Ruth replied, feeling quite sorry for the self-confessed vindictive woman, who now had nothing but the occasional spark of hope to remind her of the little girl the family forgot. 'I'll tell her to get in touch.'

'If she doesn't want to see me, tell her to write. I'll understand.'

'If I find her, Miss Webster, I'll tell her.'

32

'Jayne Styles, Mr Jenkins.'

Doug felt suddenly foolish. Had he actually said that? 'Who wants to know?' Shit! Who the hell didn't know Doug Jenkins in this town, now that the bloody papers had done such a job on him? Practically the whole of Chelmsford knew who he was, thanks to the front-page balls-up.

His face flushed. 'Look, if you've come to have a pop at me, darling, then I feel sorry for you. It's bloody Boxing Day, in case you haven't . . .'

'Pop, Mr Jenkins?'

'A go. You know, venting your spleen . . .'

'I've come to make you rich, Mr Jenkins.'

But he hadn't heard. 'You'll have to join the fucking queue, love. I got misquoted, that's all. Now I don't know what damn group you're from, probably the bloody church or something, but like I say . . .'

'Very rich, Mr Jenkins.'

'You what?'

'Money. That's what you want, isn't it?'

His eyes narrowed slightly. 'I'm not sure I . . . ?'

'I'm a journalist, Mr Jenkins.'

Another hack. So that was the game. But she had mentioned money. 'And? Miss . . .'

'Styles. Jayne Styles.' She proffered a black-gloved hand. 'You've been getting a rather rough ride these past few days, Mr Jenkins. Quite the chump of the month.'

'Only 'cause your mates stitched me up. Quoted me out of context.'

She nodded. 'Staffers, Mr Jenkins. Staff journalists. You've been shooting your mouth off to the wrong people.'

'Eh?'

'They don't care what they say, as long as they sell papers.'

He couldn't disagree with that. But she'd mentioned money, hadn't she? Folding stuff. Moolah. Readies, lovely readies. He was intrigued enough not to slam the door in her face. 'How did you find me, anyhow?'

'Your bail address was given in court, Mr Jenkins. It wasn't difficult.'

'Right.' His face flushed a second time. This woman was smart, or at least a good deal smarter than him. And Doug didn't really appreciate the merits of a clever female brain. Margaret, Ruth – they'd been fancy, and look where that had left him. Most of all, he wasn't about to let this chick take the piss much longer. 'Congratulations, Sherlock, you found me. If it's a quote you're looking for, how about this: Mr Jenkins wishes it to be known that when the truth finally emerges, he'll be taking a one-way trip to Rio on the proceeds, and saying "Thank you and goodnight" to the world who didn't believe him.'

She didn't hesitate for a second. 'Five thousand, Mr Jenkins. For your story.'

'Five grand?'

'Cash.'

Holy shit, what was going on?

She read the crumpled confusion. 'I'm freelance, Mr Jenkins. Only interested in the truth. Your truth. I figure it takes a lot to drive a man to do what you did, say what you said. It's human interest stuff, after all. Don't disappoint me, Mr Jenkins. Tell me there's a four-page exclusive locked somewhere inside the misery of all this: your arrest, the old lady's purse, the student's murder. Don't you see? You're the innocent swirling vortex slap bang in the middle of all this.'

Now she was really speaking his language. Or seemed to be. He had no idea what an 'innocent swirling vortex' actually was, but it sounded the business. Sounded as if she had the inside line on his predicament. And, of course, the promise of money. More money than he'd spent the best part of the morning trying to extract from the phone. Ten times as much. No – couldn't be right. It had to be some kind of a wind-up. Mate of Ruth's, maybe, on a mission to take the piss. And now he looked a little closer, was that really her own hair? 'Five grand, you say?'

'You tell me what really happened, I make you a rich man.'

He studied the face for several seconds. It was a gamble, and he had to jump. What if she was straight? What if he closed the door, and missed the chance of big money? How often would he kick himself for that? Five thousand times, maybe. Fuck it, go for it. 'When?'

'Now's as good as time as any, Mr Jenkins. Give me your story, then I can begin negotiations to sell it to the media, playing them all off, getting the highest bidder.'

'But they hate me, think I'm a right dick for saying what I did.'

She smiled. 'Believe me, the only people the papers hate is each other. One will say you're a . . . dick – the next will pay big money to prove otherwise. Think about it, Mr Jenkins. It's a tabloid war out there. The *Sun* says two free goes on the lottery, the *Mirror* counters with three.' She paused, letting the message sink in. 'But they all listen to Jayne Styles.'

And Doug listened, his mind processing a myriad of imminent spending opportunities as she unfolded her plan. He saw himself in Vegas, the last of the high rollers, dolly bird on each arm, Havana cigar in his mouth, glass of Jim Beam waiting on the velvet baize of the roulette table as his chips finally came rolling home . . . He wanted to kiss her, this Christmas angel, knocking at his door bearing tidings of joy. Five fucking grand – and the chance of vindication! This was sweet, so sweet.

'It's a hell of a story,' he nodded eagerly, all caution expired. 'I've been hounded, you know. All my life. Tarred by the police for being a bit of a wide boy in my youth. Married one of their own, didn't I? Rest of 'em hated the idea. Fella who nicked me – bloke called Davies – he . . .'

'Not on the doorstep, Mr Jenkins.'

'Right. Course. Sorry, love . . . I mean, Miss Styles. Just that I'm not used to all this high-powered stuff. Bit slow, sometimes, you know.' He bit at his bottom lip. 'Five big ones? Cash?'

'On the nail. Two hours' work, at the most. Come with me. I have a room in town, and a photographer waiting with the money. We'll get some suitably poignant shots of you after you've finished telling me your side of things. Then the money's yours. Simple as that.'

'I just can't believe it. This is fucking unreal!'

'Believe it, Mr Jenkins. You're about to be forgiven by the misinformed people of this land. Do you have a coat?'

'Coat?'

'It's a ten-minute walk from here, Mr Jenkins.'

'Oh, right, I see. Yeah. Let's do it.'

'No time like the present.'

Two minutes later, Doug walked by her side.

Three minutes later he began to wonder why this fast-talking journalist didn't have a car.

Five minutes later he suspected he saw a stray brown hair protruding from beneath her blonde wig.

He said nothing, the money powering him on, beating down any faint objections raised by his cash-crushed common sense. And, that body of hers, she was fit. Maybe, when he had the readies, after he'd fed her the sob story, just maybe she'd fancy a week in Vegas too. Smart piece by his side, he could do a lot worse.

Seven minutes later, she showed him into a darkened hallway, past a rusting bicycle and up a creaking staircase. She went first, hips swaying seductively. What a body! He just knew, just knew there was a terrific arse under all that winter clothing, waiting for his . . .

Twelve seconds later he was in the room.

Where the fuck was the photog–

Two seconds later it all flashed white.

Then black.

To unconsciousness.

33

'What I'm saying is,' Felix tried diplomatically to explain, as the Morris stalled for the fourth time in ten minutes, 'do we really have to do this now? Like today, this very instant? It's cold, the car's beginning to seize, and so will I if we don't stop off for a pint at least.' It was an inane request, and he knew it. Finding any pub open after three o'clock on Boxing Day was going to be as difficult as tracing the thirty-year voyage of a wandering blue handkerchief.

'Please,' Ruth persisted. 'Just another ten minutes. It has to be round here somewhere.'

They'd been driving for the best part of an hour, mostly crawling along Danbury's many quiet avenues, hoping for a glimpse of Oakwood Park, home to Mr and Mrs William Farrow, and as Ruth explained to an ever more thirsty Felix, the next port of call. But as the minutes ticked by, she knew she was swiftly emptying her moaning friend's reserve of goodwill. He was right. He deserved a pint at least. So did she, if she allowed herself to think about it. Enid Webster had given them a concrete lead as to Chloe's adolescent years after her father's death. Maybe it wasn't necessary to track the Farrows down right that instant. But something spurred her on. Something dark, swelling with distant, dreadful possibilities she'd rather not face, or discuss out loud. But she herself had said it earlier. If it was her handkerchief that had been found in the student's bedroom – and she was as sure as she'd ever been that it was – then there were two stark choices. It belonged to the victim, or the killer. And if it were the latter, then . . .

'It was our first, wasn't it?' Felix suddenly asked, pulling

Ruth's meandering mind back into the cramped comfort of the ageing car.

'Sorry?'

'The little girl – Chloe Webster. It was our first real . . . killing, I suppose.'

'I notice you didn't say murder.'

He shook his head, eyes trained on the road, maintaining a steady, whining twenty-five. 'Accidental Death, I suppose I meant. Been so long since I wore uniform, I've forgotten most of the jargon. S'all the same, though, isn't it? Accident, murder, death by misadventure, suicide – all comes down to killing, doesn't it?'

'What's brought all this on, Felix? I don't like you depressed.' She tried her best smile – and lost.

'She injected him, didn't she? Thought he was dying of flu or something ridiculous.'

'Put him to sleep,' Ruth replied, hoping his mood would lighten. 'A horrible accident, that's all.'

'I made mistakes, Ruthie.'

'What?'

'Back then. With the Webster girl. I screwed up.'

She studied the usually cheerful face, searching for any telltale signs that it was about to break into the most enormous 'fooled you!' grin. Nothing happened. 'It was a long time ago, Felix,' she offered tactfully. 'Like you say, it was our first . . .'

'Killing.'

'Felix?'

'First or last, it makes no difference. I had my ear to the ground in those days. Ran the beat, hunted down the gossip. I went there, Ruth. To the Websters' – had to drop a dog or cat off there late one night after the surgery closed. And that's what they were like. Him and his wife. Arguing like cat and bloody dog. Jesus, what a row. Anyway, it all went quiet after they spotted me. He put the animal down, or whatever, and I left.'

'Felix,' Ruth insisted, 'you can't blame yourself if theirs wasn't the marriage made in heaven. From what Enid Webster told us this morning it was common knowledge they didn't get on.'

'The wife,' Felix said softly. 'Melanie Webster. She had a lover.'

211

Ruth paused to take it in.

'Couple of the local lads in the pub knew about it.' His eyes met hers for a fleeting second. 'See what I'm saying, Ruthie?'

'No . . . not really . . .'

'I knew. I knew all this when the girl was brought in on the night her father died. The mother was there, too, remember?'

Ruth nodded, the desperate screams of the brand new widow echoing cruelly down the police station's cold brick corridors. 'So what are you saying, Felix? That because Melanie Webster had a lover, that gave her a motive to kill her husband?'

He shook his head sadly. 'All I'm saying is that I should've told someone. I mean, we all took the word of the little girl as gospel, didn't we? Just accepted that she'd upped and killed her dad. But ask yourself this, Ruthie. Who had the biggest motive for killing him, eh? The daughter – to put him to sleep because of a concept she couldn't understand – or the wife, to rid herself of the husband who wasn't going places fast enough for her?'

Ruth shook her head. 'I don't know, Felix. You're crowding me out with all this. I'm sorry, but it's too much to take in. You're asking me for motives when all I'm trying to do is find out how my handkerchief ended up in that poor girl's bedroom. Whatever happened, happened.' She glanced over, but saw he was far from convinced. She tried again. 'Look, Felix. All you had was gossip, for God's sake.'

'They were reliable sources,' he replied grimly.

'So?'

'What?'

'The lover? Who was he? The bookmaker she ran off with?'

'Maybe. Maybe not. No one really knew. Word was she was seeing someone else, and that was all I was told –' He braked suddenly, throwing Ruth forward in the passenger seat. 'There!' he pointed.

She followed his gaze, turning to see a small wall-mounted sign at the beginning of a neat road running away to their left:

JAMES DRIVE (leading to Crowthorpe Gardens and Oakwood Park)

They'd already twice driven past it.

'You really think they're going to want visitors?' Felix asked.

'I'd like to try, Felix.'

'And if no one's home?'

'Then I'll try again tomorrow.' She turned to his world-weary face. 'Don't worry. I'll take the bus.'

'It really means that much to you?'

'Yes, Felix. It does.' And not for the first time that day, she found herself wondering what meant more. To discover the handkerchief's possible pathway to the murder scene, or simply to have someone who believed in her enough to indulge her unrealistic whim? One thing was blindingly certain – Doug would have told her to sod off long ago.

They drove the last few yards in silence, pulling up in front of a crescent-shaped development of two dozen bungalows looking out on to a frost-carpeted lawn abundant with harshly pruned rose bushes.

One quick enquiry to a helpful neighbour pointed Ruth and Felix in the direction of the Farrows' bungalow, a clone of all the others: featureless, unthreatening, corporately designed to provide that 'perfect retirement opportunity' Enid Webster's treasured article had so lovingly described.

'God. You only need a couple of tumbleweeds blowing about the place and you've got a bloody ghost town.'

'Shhh, Felix.'

'What do you mean, "Shhh"? I want to make some noise. This place needs noise. Like a morgue.'

They stood on the doorstep, Ruth taking a deep breath before ringing the bell. 'Come on, come on,' she muttered, feeling the chill after the warmth of the car.

Felix waited four seconds. 'They're not in. Let's go.'

Ruth waited another three. Then another five, before finally making out the heart-warming sound of footsteps from the other side.

The door opened, and a tall, fragile-looking elderly man peered out.

'Mr Farrow? William Farrow?' Ruth asked. Jesus, she sounded like a policewoman again. What was happening? She went with it, trusting the long lost manner had a purpose, most probably to cover her embarrassment at the entire predicament.

The old man said nothing, simply squinting slightly under the glare of the setting sun. His face flushed orange under the cold red light, and Ruth was suddenly struck by how ill he looked. Deep sunken eyes lay enfolded in tired fleshy lids, hollow cheeks hung heavily over the greying jawline, and she wondered if it all hadn't been some dreadful mistake. The poor man was obviously suffering. She chastised herself, wishing she was anywhere else in the world but this broken being's doorstep.

But she had to be sure. Had to try.

'Look,' she said, 'I know this is going to sound rather strange, but . . .'

'Strange?' he repeated softly. Ruth noticed for the first time that he was barefoot, and seemed to be wearing pyjama trousers.

Felix cleared his throat, anxious to excuse himself from the awkwardness. 'If this is a difficult time, Mr Farrow, then . . .'

William Farrow searched both faces slowly. 'She said you'd come. I just wasn't expecting . . . so soon.'

'Like I say,' Felix continued, taking Ruth's arm, 'perhaps another time . . .'

A woman appeared by the bewildered man's side, her face alert, eyes bright with life. He turned to her. 'They're here. Like you said. Like . . .'

'Mrs Farrow?' Ruth guessed. 'I'm sorry to trouble you like this, but . . .'

Jude Farrow shook her head. 'You must forgive William. He's had rather a shock lately. But we've talked all about it, haven't we, William?' She turned to him. 'Well, come on, dear. Let the people in. We're letting all the heat out. Go and put the kettle on. Let's all have a nice cup of tea. No reason why this has to be uncivilized, is there? That's a dear.' She motioned to Ruth and Felix. 'Please, do come in.'

Ruth followed her into the sparse hallway, then through to the lounge, her mind a blur. 'You seem to be expecting us, Mrs Farrow?' She sat in one of the armchairs as indicated. 'Did Miss Webster call to say we were coming?' Ruth asked, but she couldn't see it. From the impression given by Enid Webster, she wouldn't have called the Farrows to tell them their house was on fire if she could've helped it. Yet someone had clearly warned the Farrows of their visit.

'Miss Webster?'

'Enid,' Felix supplied, taking his place on a floral sofa. 'From Maldon. We've just come from there.'

Jude Farrow smiled. 'Ah,' she said, sitting next to Felix. 'You have been thorough. But then, she's an elusive girl, our Chloe, isn't she?'

The frown wouldn't leave Ruth's face. 'So you know about Chloe? Our search for her?'

'Why else would you be here, my dear?' Jude smiled assuringly. 'But it's all right. I've had a long chat with William, and we've decided to handle it as it comes.' She looked at Felix with a coy grin which made him even more uncomfortable. 'The truth will out, you know. But then, you always knew that, didn't you? Clever people, aren't you, with your X-ray machines and invisible microphones.'

'Mrs Farrow, I'm not sure we . . .'

Jude silenced him with a swiftly raised hand. 'No more games, please. They nearly sent me quite mad, you know. I can't do it any more.' She turned to Ruth with the sweetest of smiles. 'You win. All I ask is that you leave William out of it. The poor man has had quite enough to cope with over the last few days, finally finding out. And I can't stress this enough. He knew nothing about any of it. And I'll say that at the trial.'

Ruth met Felix's desperate glance, then looked quickly away. What the hell was happening? They were both as mad as each other. She thought of her own mother, equally rambling and ridiculous in her insane imaginings. What use would it be to ask Mrs Farrow anything? It was pathetic, a lost cause from the off, a ludicrous notion which had resulted in disturbing these poor people's lives. A selfish imposition – and Ruth felt flush with the shame of it. She wanted to leave, there and then, race back to find her mother, be at her bedside, where she should have been all this time, instead of buggering off on some useless half-arsed wild-goose chase.

But she sat, motionless, knowing and hating, yet resentfully accepting the reason why her legs wouldn't take her to the door. She'd rather be here, in the midst of someone else's insanity, a madness she would eventually leave, rather than suffer the dutiful permanency of her mother's dementia. From that, there was no escape, merely the merciful release of Death's forgiving embrace. Here, she could run at any time. So she stayed, knowing she could run. That no ties or bonds held her fast. It was a visiting madness, she was an embarrassed voyeur, uninvolved, uncomplicated by love and guilt.

Felix broke the stilted silence. 'Trial, Mrs Farrow?'

'Of course. After you've arrested me.'

'Arrested?'

'That's what you're here for, isn't it?'

'No, no, no . . .'

She took his hand in hers. 'But you're so clever, you police these days. Like I said, though,' she waved an admonishing finger, 'no more games, now. Nearly thirty years it's been, and I'm done with the guilt of it. I've told William everything I know – and, believe me, that was the hardest part, so telling you will be easy. Honestly, I feel as if a huge weight has come tumbling off my shoulders. Now, where would you like to begin?'

Jude Farrow sat straight-backed, wearing the expectant face of a nursery school teacher. Felix shifted uncomfortably. The situation was unbearable. Caught up in some paranoid fantasy, she clearly believed he and Ruth to be police officers. Yet he was intuitive enough to realize that to deny it would only add more fuel to the fantasy. He scratched the side of his temple thoughtfully, withdrawing his hand gently from Jude's. Maybe she did know something of use to Ruth. They'd come this far together, what harm would it really do to ask a few questions? Just words, after all. And if the poor woman really did believe they were police officers, what right did he have to demolish that fantasy? What if she had some crucial, telling detail that Ruth was searching for, and he didn't have the nerve to try to winkle it out?

And if she didn't, as seemed most likely . . . they'd leave, he resolved. Leave these good people to their own lives, head back to Chelmsford for a couple of pints, make the day last a little bit longer, laugh over their adventure, maybe take Ruth's hand in his . . .

His mind made up, Felix cleared his throat, ignoring Ruth's flashed warning. 'Mrs Farrow,' he began, 'what exactly can you tell us about Chloe Webster?'

34

'Guv?'

'Boot Sale?'

'Sorry to ring you at home an' all that.'

'Well?'

'Got something for you. Thought perhaps you'd like to know now, rather than first thing tomorrow, like.'

'Shoot.'

'It's, er . . .' a quick embarrassed cough, 'about one of your old mates, actually, Guv.'

'Not Jenkins again?'

'No, not him. His missus.'

'Ruth Jenkins?

''Fraid so, Guv.' The cough again.

'Boot Sale, for Christ's sake – spit it out, man. What's up with Ruth?'

'Bit difficult to say, really, Guv. What with her being a mate, and all that.'

'Then what the fuck are you ringing me for? I've had about four hours' sleep in the last five days, then the first fucking chance I get to put my head down, you ring me up and start acting the bloody fool –'

'She got herself arrested last night.'

A three-second pause. 'Ruth? Arrested?'

'Throwing bricks through shop windows.'

'You been on the piss, Sergeant? Or is this some sort of fucking wind-up?'

'Straight up, Guv. Video surveillance system picked it all up. Uniform nicked her last night playing the one-woman animal

217

liberation army in one of the local pet shops.'

'Ruth Jenkins?' Another three-second pause. 'On Christmas night, for Christ's sake?'

'Drunk as Ollie Reed on a day trip to the brewery. Took two of our boys to drag her in and nick her. Spent the night in the cells.'

'You're absolutely certain about this?'

'Hundred per cent, Guv. Had her in here . . . your office . . . first thing. Green at the gills, she was. Very contrite. Thing was, when she decided to play the Pied bleedin' Piper, she'd only gone and left her mother on her own back at the house. Turns out the old dear's certifiably crackers. She was hell-bent on digging her own grave – starkers in the front garden.'

'This is a dream, isn't it? Right now, I'm really asleep, aren't I? It's ten past four on Boxing Day afternoon and, in a minute, I'm going to wake up safe in my own lovely bed and forget all about this entire episode.'

'More like a fuckin' nightmare, Guv. It gets worse.'

'Don't tell me – the old woman has confessed to the Christmas Killings?'

'Behave, Guv. This is serious.'

A sigh. 'Enlighten me, Sergeant.'

'Well, while Mrs J's been guest of honour downstairs, I've run a little check on her. Turns out her maiden name was Golden.'

'Is that it? For God's sake, Boot Sale, I could've told you that any time. Ruth Golden. WPC Golden. I served with her back at Maldon in the sixties.'

'Appreciate that, Guv. But there's more.'

'Oh, God.'

'Load of stuff came back from the forensic lab at HQ early this morning, ready for us poor saps to file for the CPS if needed. Anyway, the 'anky's there, innit?'

A second sigh, slightly more tired than the first. 'The 'anky?'

'Handkerchief, Guv. Blue one taken from the Vietnamese girl's bedroom, covered in blood.'

'Well?'

'Lab couldn't find a single print on it.'

'So?'

'Chances are, it's the killer's, right? Dropped it at the scene or something. Maybe tried to tie the poor kid up first. See where I'm heading?'

'The nut-house?'

'Way I figure it, the thing must've been used in the struggle, to get covered in blood like that. And it's a snot-rag, Guv – of all the things you're going to hold tightly in your hands, it's got to be a bleedin' handkerchief, hasn't it? So if it belonged to the VC girl, it'd be covered in her dabs, wouldn't it?'

'Could've just washed it, Boot Sale. I'm sorry, Sergeant, it doesn't prove anything. The handkerchief went to the labs for a blood match as far as I can remember. It would have been extraordinary to get anything else from it.'

'How about this for extraordinary, then? Initials, bottom left-hand corner! R.G. 1969.'

'I remember, Sergeant, although it may be my only working faculty these days. Could stand for anything.'

'Ruth Golden.'

'Ruth?'

'Mrs Jenkins. Formerly WPC Golden, 1969.'

'Hang on, hang on. You're saying it's hers?'

'Forensics ran a fibre test on it. Now, as you know, those bastards are reluctant to put a sell-by date on yesterday's paper, but they reckon the rag is at least twenty years old.'

Davies thought for a second. 'And you confronted her with this, am I right?'

'This morning. In this office.'

'Jesus Christ.'

'Stay with me, Guv. It wasn't a fuck-up. She nearly had a cardiac when she clapped eyes on it. Went through the motions of denying everything, of course, but –'

'Denying everything?'

Now Mason waited a moment, collecting his thoughts. 'What I'm saying, Guv, is maybe she's the one who did for the student. I mean, who else knew the MO – the make-up? The boffins down at HQ reckon it was most likely a woman, so that fits. Way I figure it, Mrs J tops the girl to get her old man off the hook. Maybe they set the whole bleedin' thing up from the word go, knowing you'd nick her old man for the Sharansky number, then he could go bleating to whoever, demanding his cash for the exclusive.'

Davies struggled to keep a lid on it. 'Boot sale, as far as I can recall, Ruth Jenkins had an alibi for the afternoon Miss Xang died. She brought in a tape from the cab company exonerating her husband. Brought it in with Jenkins's mistress, if I remember correctly.'

Mason fought on. 'True enough. If we believe what they said. I mean, that all sounds a bit dodgy to me, doesn't it to you? Two women shagging the same bloke join forces to spring him from the nick? The more I think about this, the more the finger seems to point at Mrs J. Motive, opportunity, physical evidence strongly link her to one of the principal crime scenes.'

'Possibly link her, Sergeant.'

'Whatever.' Mason sounded a little deflated. 'Just thought you ought to know, that's all.'

Davies sighed. 'OK. Thanks.'

'I mean, it makes more sense than that load of old cobblers coming out of HQ. And it does tie in with the evidence that the second murder was done by a woman.'

Davies knew Mason had more. 'Anyone else know about your private theory? Butler, Knowles at HQ?'

'Not a dicky-bird to any of them. Only ones who are with me on it are Hassloff and Morgan. I've got 'em doing a low-level surveillance in a motor outside Mrs J's. And get this, Guv. She's been out most of the day. Got bailed by a fellow called Felix Pengelly, left with him, dropped back at her place for an hour round about lunch, then buggered off, God knows where . . .'

'Felix Pengelly?'

'Ran a check on him as well. Turns out . . .'

'I know who he is, Sergeant.'

'Another one from the Maldon days. Left the force in the mid-seventies.'

'Jesus wept. Felix Pengelly. You certain of this?'

'Ran his motor through the computer. It all checks. Odd though, isn't it? I mean, they have to have something going, don't they? He bowls all the way over here first thing this morning, then takes her off to her mother's twilight home for the terminally bewildered, before spending the next hour holding her hand in Hylands Park, then going back to her place for lunch. Hassloff and Morgan have been eyeballing all morning. What's up? Is the fat man giving her one, or something?'

Davies exhaled heavily. 'Where are they now?'

'Like I said, they buggered off after lunch. I told the lads to stay put outside the house, in case I needed them back here pronto. Something odd going on, though, isn't there?'

'I don't know, Boot Sale. I leave this investigation for one day, and you seem to head screaming into Never Never Land. What's the next move?'

Mason had already planned it. 'Way I see it, Guv, if there's anything going on between Jenkins and his missus, then we ought to get a wire-tap on the phone. I'm working on sorting permission for one when the court reopens for business first thing tomorrow. I don't see what else we can do. I mean, we can't pull her in again, can we? Not after the business with her old man. Butler would do his fucking nut if he thought we were off on any sort of tangent from the shrinks up at HQ.'

Another deep breath. 'All right, Boot Sale. Keep Hassloff and Morgan where they are. Low-level stuff, though. No fucking heroics. We see how it pans out in the morning. Maybe we need a warrant to search the house, look for any bloodstained clothing. I don't know. I just can't see it, for the life of me.'

'Got to admit, it's well dodgy though, eh?'

'Maybe, Sergeant.'

'Catch you first thing, then, Guv. I'm off myself in a mo. Night shift are going to clock up the fucking overtime sifting through all this shit for Knowles.'

'Still ploughing through the records, are we?'

'Bunch of arse, innit? Suicides, mostly. They're still banging on that their mystery woman is some sort of fucking serial number. I mean, this is Chelmsford, for Christ's sake! You and I both know there's a much more plausible explanation in Jenkins and Mrs J . . .'

'OK, Sergeant. You've made your point. Just make sure none of this leaks out, and keep the rest of the squad playing good little children for HQ, till we know any more. I'll see you first thing.'

'Sorted.' The final pause. 'Guv?'

'What?'

'Uniform have just told me that Jenkins has missed his bail appointment. Was meant to check in here between three and four today.'

'Probably pissed out of his brains somewhere. Send a couple of lads over to run him in. If he kicks off, stick him downstairs.'

'Very good, Guv.'

'Be nice to know we're pulling him for a concrete reason this time, eh?'

'Sure. Even better, to give him a good kicking ourselves, too. There'd be a bunch of us forming a fucking queue at his cell door . . .'

'Appreciate the squad loyalty, Sergeant. Better play this one by the rule book, though, eh?'

'Just wanted to let you know we're all with you on this, Guv.'

'You've just done it, Sergeant. Good night.'

'Night, Guv.'

35

Ruth watched with a dry throat as William Farrow made a dreadful hash of pouring tea. His wife tutted throughout, gently chastising her husband for his inability to complete the task, while all the time Felix rubbed his hands nervously, refusing to meet Ruth's gaze.

'Do you have any children?' Jude Farrow suddenly asked, dismissing William from the room as if he were little more use than a senile butler. Which, it occurred to Ruth, was probably the case.

'Just the one,' she replied, wishing to God she was with Marie at that very moment. What on earth was she doing here? It was all Felix's fault. If he hadn't asked about Chloe, they could have been on their way back to Chelmsford.

Jude sighed. 'William and I, we never could have any of our own. God knows, we tried, but this was years before the methods the youngsters seem to have nowadays.' She offered Ruth a digestive, and for the first time it occurred to Ruth that neither she nor Felix had properly introduced themselves. Yet here they were, drinking tea, four virtual strangers, seemingly bound together for any number of private hidden agendas. 'Science failed us, I'm afraid.'

'I'm sorry, Mrs Farrow,' Ruth replied, feeling guilty at her own daughter's effortless conception. She searched the sad green eyes of the little old lady opposite for any sign of what lay behind. Nothing. Just two lifeless eyes set in a chalk-white face made instantly forgettable by its near perfection. Not one mole, not one freckle, not one hair poked above her top lip. It seemed to Ruth that the woman's composed serenity had somehow rendered her characterless. She yearned to find just one tiny blemish that would breathe life into the marbled face.

Jude turned to Felix, spreading the conversation between her two troubled guests. 'The old people at the Maltings, they were our children, in a way, Inspector.'

'It's Felix, please,' he answered, feeling a sharp stab of guilt for being so economical with the truth. 'And this is Ruth. Ruth Jenkins. A very dear friend of mine.'

Jude nodded. 'As you wish, Inspector. Felix and Ruth it shall be.' She took a delicate sip from her tea. 'The problem with old people, I found, is that they die. Oh, we used to change them, spoon-feed them like our children, but eventually . . . they die.'

Ruth wondered if Jude was about to cry, lining the pale perfect face with two salty tracks of liquid humanity – allowing Ruth to console her, perhaps place a comforting arm round her shoulders. But it wasn't to be. Ruth remained uncomfortably struck with the woman's composure, pushing back whatever pained her, yet revealing the truth with seemingly good grace. A bravura performance? Or had Jude Farrow's sterility left her soul as barren as her life? Ruth listened on, almost hypnotized by the level tone gently filling the ordered room.

'Then things changed for us a little,' Jude continued. 'As you know, Chloe came to us after . . .'

'Her father died?' Felix prompted quietly.

'He was murdered. Don't play games with me. I'm not a stupid woman, Inspector, and I don't . . .'

'Mrs Farrow, please . . .'

Jude turned to Ruth, her voice as cold as ice. 'You've come for the truth, and I'm telling you.'

There was a dreadful silence for several seconds while Jude composed herself once more, running her hands along the creases of her tartan skirt, picking off pieces of fluff like fleas from an infested cat.

Felix made a show of finishing his tea noisily, before rising to his feet. 'Well, thank you very much, Mrs Farrow, you've been very helpful. We'll just –'

'You'll just sit down and listen, Inspector Felix!'

Felix glanced nervously at Ruth, looking for back-up. The

thing had gone too far. The woman was obviously upset, incredibly deluded, and most probably of no use in tracking Chloe Webster or the damned handkerchief. But how the hell were they going to get out of there? She seemed determined to make them stay, and nothing short of complete rudeness would allow them to go. He sat back down, victim of his own politeness and Jude Farrow's threatening insistence.

Jude smiled. 'Richard Webster was murdered, Inspector, as we all very well know. My sister Melanie killed him. Injected him with a syringe.' She pointed a bony finger towards her neck. 'Air bubble just here. Went straight to his brain. She'd read a lot of textbooks, you see. Found the neck was the best place to do it.'

Now it was Ruth's turn to object. Whatever was happening, she wouldn't let the poor woman suffer a moment longer under the present cruel misapprehension. Something the staff at her mother's nursing home had said came flooding back. Reality orientation, the American idea, always correct whatever bizarre or weird beliefs senile patients had. 'Chloe killed her father, Mrs Farrow. Not Melanie. We were there, that night. In Maldon police station. It was Chloe. A dreadful accident. But it was definitely Chloe.'

Jude turned to her and regarded Ruth as if she were the most stupid woman alive. 'Chloe thought that she did. And that's all we wanted. To make certain she thought that she'd killed him.'

'We?' Ruth asked, feeling a little uneasy.

'Melanie and I.'

'What for?'

'For Chloe, of course.'

'I'm sorry? I don't understand.'

'So I could have her, and Melanie could be rid of her. And Dickie. Melanie soon tired of him. And the life, stuck in the surgery, missing out.'

It was going too fast for Ruth, and her mind was becoming cluttered with Jude's ramblings. 'Mrs Farrow –'

'Jude, please.'

'Jude. What we're really interested in is an old keepsake of mine. A blue handkerchief. I gave it to Chloe on the night . . .

225

on that night. Now it's turned up again, and all we really want to know is how it got there. I had an idea Chloe might be able to help us, and that you might know where she is, so Felix and I . . .'

Jude lowered her voice. 'Don't you think I would have told you?'

The tone – biting, acidic – took Ruth by surprise. 'Sorry?'

'If I knew where she was. That's your damn job, not mine. And you know very well where the poor child is most likely hiding. How many more murders is it going to take before you stop her? Before you stop Melanie's obscene machine?'

'Murders?' Felix asked, braving the verbal conflict.

'The latest two,' Jude spat back. 'The old woman and the foreign girl in Chelmsford.' She shot a scathing look at them both. 'We all know Chloe's back at work again, so let's stop the foolishness. I'm done with your games. All of them. Done!'

Felix cleared his throat, subconsciously clasping his hands in prayer. 'You're saying that Chloe Webster murdered those two people. She's the Christmas Killer?'

Jude struggled to suppress her rage, settling herself back into the sofa, draining the tension out of her face once more, neutralizing the anger with a well-practised mask of benign calm. 'The saddest thing is,' she recalled, delving back into the past, 'Melanie and I both wanted what the other already had. I had money, time on my hands, a successful business, and a husband completely devoted to giving me all three.'

'Yet she had the child you always wanted,' said Ruth, relieved that the tone had reverted to clipped politeness. But how reliable was anything Jude Farrow said? The woman was obviously scarred, but by what? The past, the mind-numbing isolation of the present, or fear of what lay ahead – a life struggling with a disintegrating husband, punctuated occasionally by unexpected visits from passers-by, audience to the increasing madness of her fantasies? Ruth wondered if the meter man got the same treatment when he came to read the dials.

'Silly, wasn't it?' Jude whispered. 'So we decided on a swap, I suppose. No, let me rephrase that: Melanie decided. I was always the weaker one, despite her being the younger sister. Stupid. Followed little Mel around like a lost sheep, because she always got what she wanted. One look from those big green eyes of hers, and my parents' hearts would melt; they'd give in to her every whim.' She turned to Felix suddenly. 'I so wanted to be loved like her.'

He mustered his most understanding smile. 'Of course.'

Jude offered him another biscuit. 'I was already godmother to Chloe, and Melanie . . . well, you must remember, Inspector, this was the sixties. Times and opportunities were changing for women. Word got round, even as far as Great Totham. And Melanie's head was full of it. It burned in her soul. Women now had the chance of proper careers, to unshackle themselves from the kitchen sink. She used to tell me endlessly of the life she could lead, if only . . . if only she didn't have Richard and Chloe.'

Felix refused another chocolate bourbon. 'Why not simply divorce?'

'Too lengthy. Too unreliable. And she needed the money. Life insurance. Besides, she'd still have been burdened with dear Chloe. Melanie was an all-or-nothing girl, Inspector. She had to cut all the strings, or none at all.'

'The good mother,' he muttered.

'It's not for us to judge, Inspector. She had her reasons, and I'm afraid I had mine. With Richard dead, Melanie promised me I would take custody of Chloe, leaving her free to pursue her dreams. All we needed was a plan which would make it credible that Melanie no longer wanted her own daughter.' There was a long silence. 'One day, Melanie hit on it. She told me that if the police and the courts were convinced Chloe had killed her father, then she'd have a valid reason for rejecting her. Emotional upset, you know. It seemed obvious to us that I'd be awarded custody.'

'And you went along with all this?' Felix asked, gradually being drawn into the story.

'I didn't believe she was serious at first. But as the weeks went on, I realized Melanie was becoming obsessed with the idea, making plans, feeding me with her ambition. Dangling Chloe like a big carrot before my eyes.' Jude shook her head sadly. 'Then I discovered she'd begun the affair. But I don't have to tell you about that, do I?'

'No, Mrs Farrow,' he glanced quickly at Ruth. 'We know she had a lover.'

'I couldn't understand it at first. It seemed so stupid. So dangerous. I mean, a policeman, of all people.'

Ruth's heart missed a beat. 'A policeman?'

Jude nodded. 'One of yours, from Maldon. And I couldn't for the life of me work out why. Until it happened. Until the night she killed Dickie. Then I understood, well enough. She'd been so very clever, you see.'

Ruth tried to catch Felix's eye, feeling suddenly uncertain of him as he glanced away. 'Because', she said, putting the pieces together, 'he couldn't have mentioned the affair, for fear of ruining his own career.'

'Like I said,' Jude said, 'Melanie had worked the whole thing out, down to the finest detail. She knew she would be one of the major suspects – she had so much to gain. She also worked out that the local police would be asked about her good character. And that this young man would lie his mouth off in order not to be discovered seeing a married woman.'

Ruth looked a second time at Felix, noticing he was trying to mouth something silently towards her. She turned away, unable to face him. Was that what he had been trying to say in the car, the reason for the uncustomary anger? That he had been Melanie Webster's lover at the time she plotted to murder her husband?

She was glad when Felix finally spoke aloud. 'Why didn't you tell Richard Webster any of this? Or your husband? Somebody – anybody?'

Jude turned to him. 'Because, by then, I had a dream. A chance of my own child. My own little girl. Who wouldn't die like all the old ones at the Maltings. Who would bring me life, colour, joy, and happiness. Fulfilment, Inspector. Truth was, I wanted Chloe more than I wanted to save Richard. Far more.'

'So what happened, Jude?'

'All I had to do was drive a car.' A tear had finally broken loose from its fleshy moorings, running quickly to the corner of Jude's mouth. She spoke in a barely audible whisper, eyes fixed to the far wall. 'Melanie had noticed that Chloe had become totally engrossed in one aspect of Dickie's work. What he called his "sleeping machine". It was her first real encounter with death, I suppose, and it fascinated her young mind. While Dickie was understandably reluctant to go into great detail, Chloe found an eager teacher in her own mother.

'Only it wasn't all talk. There was plenty of play. Every Wednesday afternoon, I'd drive over from Danbury to collect Melanie for her weekly shopping trip. Dickie liked to keep their car at the surgery in case of any emergencies he might need to attend, so Melanie was more or less housebound. And she had such a wicked temper that, frankly, I think Dickie was rather glad to be rid of her for the afternoon. We'd shop, then pick Chloe up from school, before popping back to the Maltings at Danbury for another hour or two.'

'Your old people's home?' Ruth asked, with an ominous feeling growing deep inside. What if the old woman was right? What if Chloe Webster really was the Christmas Killer? What if she'd kept the handkerchief all this time and dropped it while murdering the student girl? What if . . . ?

Jude nodded. 'And that's where the games began.'

'Games?'

'Teddy Hospital, she called it. I was horrified, absolutely horrified. Melanie would stand at the top of the stairs, sending little Chloe's favourite teddies tumbling down. Then the pair of them would decide which bears couldn't be saved, which ones were going to have to go to heaven. Chloe loved the game, playing with her mother, being the big grown-up nurse.

'Melanie had covered an old icing syringe in silver foil, to make a sort of replica of the real thing back in Dickie's surgery. She'd let Chloe put the wounded teddies to sleep. One pretend injection straight into the neck. Then they moved on to dollies. Always the same thing. Melanie would throw them down the stairs, Chloe would put them to sleep.'

Ruth felt rather faint. 'You mean, she trained Chloe to kill her own father?'

'Simply to think that she had. That was the point of it all. As long as Chloe was convinced she had sent her daddy to heaven, then Melanie knew she'd have created the perfect tragic accident, and its innocent confessor.'

'That's dreadful.'

But Jude hadn't heard. 'And she made heaven sound so wonderful. So different to life on earth. So magical. And Chloe, of course, lapped up every word. Maybe that's the saddest part of all of this. Chloe herself.'

'Chloe?'

'All she ever wanted to do was please people. Make them smile, care for them. Melanie understood this full well. And used it to her own filthy advantage. That poor child had such a loving, giving nature, and all she wanted was the best for everyone. Even at that age. Even at seven years old.'

Ruth nodded solemnly, remembering the wriggling child on her lap, the innocent face shining with the purest conviction that she'd done nothing wrong. That Daddy was in heaven. That Daddy was happy now. 'And on the night of the . . . murder?'

'Dickie had a cold. A really bad one: 'flu, most probably. He'd had to close the surgery and he lay moaning in bed for two days, making the most of it.' She turned to Felix with just the smallest hint of a smile. 'You know how men do, Inspector.'

Felix nodded back encouragingly.

'I came over as usual on the Wednesday. Melanie was over the moon about it, and once we'd collected Chloe from school, I understood why. All Chloe wanted to know was if it was the right time to send poor Daddy to heaven. Wouldn't he feel much happier with Jesus and all the angels? That was part of it, you see? To get Chloe to make the connection. To have her think it was her idea. To please us all by doing it, playing Teddy Hospital for real with Daddy.'

Ruth found herself equally absorbed in the narrative, hanging on Jude's every word, unable to reconcile the growing feeling that although much of what she said had the inescapable ring of truth, one or two central points threw up worrying inconsistencies. Most importantly, why was Jude Farrow telling them anything at all, regardless of the fact that she harboured the delusion they were both police officers? It was the strangest thing, to be sitting in the well-ordered lounge, listening to the macabre tale unfold, tear by wretched tear.

'We went back to the surgery at about seven that night,' Jude whispered. 'Dickie was still groaning in bed. Melanie made sure that the door to the surgery was unlocked, making some hushed

230

excuse to show Chloe the real syringe Daddy used, ensuring it was accessible to young hands. Then we put Chloe to bed herself, and . . . simply waited.'

'Waited?' Ruth asked, half-dreading the answer, following the tragic scene in her mind, feeling the awful tension of the little girl, lying awake, listening to her father's moans, remembering the games with Mummy, the talk of heaven and all the angels . . .

'It had to be up to Chloe, you see,' Jude replied. 'Had to be her idea. There was really nothing else we could do. The scene was set. We just sat in the kitchen and waited. About half an hour later, we heard her move, following the footsteps above our heads as she crept downstairs, into the surgery, then back up again. I felt sick, knowing it was my last chance to stop her. But I didn't.'

Felix said gently, 'And Chloe took the syringe up to her father. And stuck it in his neck. Just like Teddy Hospital?'

Jude turned to him, both eyes pleading for understanding. 'It all happened so quickly. I heard Dickie cry out. Then Melanie raced upstairs and brought Chloe down to me. She was so happy, so pleased to have helped her daddy be rid of his suffering.'

'But he wasn't dead yet, was he, Jude?' Felix prompted. 'Melanie was up with him, doing it properly. Re-injecting him, like the textbooks had shown.'

The sobbing woman nodded, a tiny, barely perceptible movement. 'As she'd anticipated, Chloe's strike had barely broken the skin before Dickie woke up in pain. She quickly soothed him back to bed. Then – like you said – murdered him as she'd planned. A second, lethal injection.'

'Then came downstairs and told Chloe that Daddy had died, right? And the poor kid was totally convinced she'd done the deed?'

Jude nodded again, looking away, unable to face anyone in her pain. 'I called the ambulance, while Melanie set about working herself up into a state. She had to be convincing, you see, when the ambulance arrived. Had to be mad at Chloe in the police station.'

'That was all an act?' Ruth asked. 'Melanie's screaming?'

'And it worked, didn't it?' Jude gave a little laugh, amused at some part of the tale Ruth and Felix weren't privy to. 'Only thing Mel and I were terrified of was the autopsy. If they'd discovered two puncture marks, we'd have been sunk. But they didn't.' She turned to both of them, still smiling. 'That's what clinched it for us. Everyone took the word of a little child as the truth. No one even thought to doubt dear little Chloe. Melanie had programmed her dreadfully well. Frighteningly well.'

'And you never breathed a word of this to your husband, Mrs Farrow?' Felix asked.

'Not until just the other day. How could I? I was trapped, in too deep. Part of something monstrous, yet handsomely rewarded. For a while, at least.'

'It went wrong?'

'Not at first. After the fuss died down, Melanie set off with some new man, and, as planned, Chloe came to live with us. Melanie had put on another prize performance before the adoption committee, tearfully explaining how she couldn't stand to be in the same room as the little girl who had killed her beloved husband.'

'And you were granted custody?'

Jude nodded, drying her eyes. 'But the longer she stayed with us, the worse things became. Every day, I saw something to remind me she wasn't really mine. A look, a phrase, a tone of voice; bit by bit, everything she did reminded me of my sister. I would only ever be Aunty Jude. I couldn't cope. I started drinking. Too much. Far too much. Then the killing started.'

'Killing?'

'The old ones. Clients at our home. Chloe hadn't moved on. She seemed stuck in the killing mode, put there by her mother. She began sending the old ones to heaven.'

'And you knew about this?' Ruth asked, aghast.

'It was very convenient, I'm afraid. I'm sorry if that sounds terribly callous, but that's how it was. I just wanted everything to end. It had all gone so horribly wrong. I grew to hate the old ones, grew to despise their constant neediness. Chloe . . . she became like one of those little elves in the fairy story, mending the cobbler's shoes at night as he slept. She . . . fixed them for me, when they became difficult. And I was too drunk to really care most of the time. Life had no meaning. I'd gambled on a child and lost. One man had already died, the others didn't seem to matter after that.'

A look of anguish crossed Felix's face. 'How many, Jude? How many do you think she killed?'

'Nine. Ten, possibly. Like I say, it's difficult to remember. I wasn't myself then. It was all slipping away, and I didn't care. Melanie had created a very efficient and loving euthanasia machine. She was filling heaven with as many poor souls as she could.' She turned to him. 'Still is, Inspector, as we both very well know.'

Something popped unexpectedly into Ruth's mind. A long lost comforting memory, eradicating all doubts about Felix and a possible affair with Melanie. She felt impelled to look over to him and smile reassuringly, but when she tried she saw only his worried face, clouded with confusion.

'The Christmas Killings,' he said slowly. 'Chloe?'

Jude Farrow merely nodded.

'You have no idea where we can find her?'

Jude shook her head. 'There was a fire. Late one night. At the Maltings. Many died in the flames. It sort of brought me to my senses. William and I almost lost everything, including our lives. We were finished as a business. Had to start over, do what we could. I sent Chloe on her way. She must have been sixteen. Gave her what little money we had left and begged her never to return. It was the last I saw of her.'

'She set the fire?' Felix asked.

There was a long pause. 'I did, Inspector.'

'You?'

'I wanted her dead. It had to end. All of it. Chloe, the Maltings, everything. I was drunk, wasn't thinking straight. Just did it.'

Ruth nodded, identifying all too recently and reluctantly with the sudden rush of glorious insanity drink obligingly provides. But at least her brush with drunken stupidity had only caused minor abrasions to three mice and an African Grey parrot. Here was a woman who had burnt people to death in their beds as they slept. And had lived with the dread guilt of it ever since. Little wonder she was so completely paranoid. Guilt seemed to have eaten away at her soul like a cancer, urging the truth from her tortured remains.

She wondered whether Felix was thinking the same, that it was time to call in the real experts, DCI Davies and friends. She checked herself. Not Davies. Not yet. Not until . . .

Jude wrapped both arms round herself. 'But it didn't work. Chloe survived the fire. So . . . I suppose I threw her out. Gave her the money and told her to leave. Until very recently, William simply thought she'd run away. And that hurt him very badly. He loved little Chloe, loved her as the daughter he knew he could never give me, that I could never provide for us both.' She faced Ruth, eyes blazing in defiance. 'And I've had to live with that. His pain, his sorrow, his loss. For all these damn years. How easy do you think it was, to send her away, the little girl I'd killed for?'

Ruth stared silently back, unable to make any response.

'And you haven't heard from her since?' Felix asked.

'I'd get the occasional letter. I made the mistake of writing back to her when we were staying in lodgings before we found this place. I gave her this address. God knows why. Maybe part of me needed to know my little Chloe was still safe. Anyway, there I was, always running down to beat William to the post, desperate he wouldn't know she was still writing to us. Postcards, mostly. Chloe in Great Yarmouth, Southend, Clacton – coastal resorts. Then, sooner or later, I'd read about another one, a lonely old man found dead in such-and-such a place. Police have no clues. Open verdicts, mostly. Accidental deaths, sad statistics of an uncaring age. But deep down, I'd know, simply know, Chloe was still sending them to heaven.'

'And you ignored it?'

'Up till now. The last two. Christmas Killings, they're calling them, aren't they?'

Felix nodded.

'She sent me a Christmas card at the beginning of December. Chelmsford postmark, Inspector.'

Felix paused for a minute, composing himself. 'Mrs Farrow . . . Jude, you have to understand. Ruth and I, well, we aren't police officers any more. What you've told us . . . perhaps it's better you tell the police about it. The real police. Uniformed officers, Mrs Farrow. I mean, they'll treat you with respect and . . .' He looked to Ruth for support, drowning as he was in a tidal wave of embarrassing truth and toe-curling guilt. 'And who knows?' he heard himself saying. 'Maybe you're wrong about all of this. Perhaps Chloe's alive and well and living with a husband and two kids in a semi-detached in Romford.'

Ruth was on her feet in an instant, hoping to God Jude was still too absorbed in her own distress to have heard. 'We have to be going now, Jude,' she said quickly. 'One final thing. Please think back. Do you remember Chloe ever having a blue cotton handkerchief?'

But Jude Farrow was too far away to hear, locked in a time when dreams shattered into a thousand deadly fragments, each mocking her barren, blinded ambition. Laughing at her cruelly from within the darkest corridors of her mind.

36

Blue-grey exhaled smoke from two Marlboro Lights quickly filled the groaning Austin Morris as it began its nocturnal journey back down Danbury hill towards the twinkling orange streetlights trying their hardest to illuminate Chelmsford.

The rapidly frosting road was empty, the majority of the population seemingly content to sit out what remained of the Christmas break in the sleepy luxury of sofas and armchairs set lazily before a hundred thousand televisions showing repeated Hollywood blockbusters and dismal Christmas sitcom specials.

Ruth broke the silence between them, a silence which had lasted from the moment they excused themselves from the Farrows' bungalow to seek claustrophobic refuge in the freezing car.

'I really thought it was you, at first.'

'I know you did, Ruthie.'

She laughed quietly to herself. 'Stupid. I was almost jealous in a way.'

'Jealous?'

'Then I let logic get the better of my emotions. Come on, girl, I said, think realistically about this. What woman in her right mind would've had an affair with PC Pengelly, as he was?'

'Charming.'

'What I mean is, you weren't exactly the catch of the day, were you?'

Felix gripped the steering wheel a little tighter. 'You obviously didn't think so.'

'Not then, Felix. No.' She let it hang in the thick smoky air for a second. 'What did you make of all that, anyway?'

Felix sighed. 'To be honest, I don't know what to think. There she was, telling us all this stuff, this . . . nightmare about the kid, and all I could think about was the sister.'

'Melanie Webster?'

'Right. I mean, how much would you have to hate your husband, your life, your child, to cold-bloodedly murder him, then brainwash your seven-year-old daughter into taking the rap for it? It's just . . . evil.'

Ruth took another deep drag. 'Maybe. Maybe not.'

'Maybe not?'

'Maybe Melanie Webster wasn't the wicked little sister Jude Farrow would have us believe.'

'You're saying that poor weeping woman was lying to us? Come on, Ruthie, I know she was rather paranoid, but the whole thing had a hideous ring of truth to me. Just like she said, we took the little kid's word, didn't we? Never really occurred to us to look any further. And I knew, Ruthie, I knew Melanie Webster was playing around, and yet . . .'

'For God's sake, Felix, stop beating yourself up on that one. All you had was pub gossip. Conjecture, that's all. Besides, we weren't even handling the investigation proper. All we did was babysit Chloe until CID arrived from Colchester. It was up to them to investigate all the angles, and you well know it.'

He wound down his window and flicked a glowing butt outside into the blackness. A welcome rush of cold night air filled the car, clearing the fog of smoke between them. 'And I suppose, clever clogs, you've also worked out why I couldn't really say anything to CID about young Melanie?'

'The mystery man in her life?'

'Frank Davies.'

It was the final piece in the puzzle for Ruth, who sat in quiet contentment for a few moments, assessing the fit in her mind, recalling the day's conversations and her own bank of freshly awakened memories. Frank Davies – Melanie's secret lover. Now that did make sense.

'Let me guess,' she said. 'You found out a copper was involved and had a word with Frank?'

'And he told me to mind my own goddamned business.'

'Which, like the slightly awkward yet hugely likeable guy you were, you did.'

'Don't take the piss, Ruthie. Please. Davies was a star, a by-the-book hotshot, destined for the big time. There was no way I was going to grass him up. I rather stupidly felt, that, yeah, it wasn't any of my business. And perhaps he'd remember me for my loyalty later on. You know, a favour for a favour.' He shook his head sadly. 'Hell, I was only young. And what would have been the point in telling anyone? Frank would've denied the thing, and it would have been wonder boy's word against mine. So I let it pass.'

'Felix! Will you stop wittering on about it? No one's blaming you but yourself.' Now it was Ruth's turn to abandon her cigarette to the ravages of the freezing night. Once done, she sat with both hands on her lap, getting all the pieces in order for airing. 'Aren't you intrigued?'

'Intrigued?'

'As to how I knew it was Frank, and not you?'

'I don't know, Ruthie,' Felix wearily replied. 'I'm beginning to get this horrible feeling I've got Miss Marple in the car by mistake. The sooner I get you home . . .'

'We're not going home.'

He brightened a little at this. 'Pint, then?'

'Not yet.'

'Bollocks.'

Ruth ignored him. 'All this stuff Jude Farrow told us about little sister Melanie being the dominant one, the mastermind. Did you buy that?'

'Go on.'

'I mean, it didn't exactly fit with what Enid Webster told us this morning, did it?'

'More or less,' Felix replied. 'Stuff about her being pissed off with the country life seemed fairly accurate from both accounts.'

'But the rest of it, Felix,' Ruth insisted. 'All that crap about Melanie's plans for the big time, the ruthless business woman prepared to murder for her freedom. Think back. She ran off with a bookmaker and ended up dying a lonely old woman in a tower block in East London. Hardly fits with the frustrated Anita Roddick image, does it?'

'Maybe it all went sour for her. Guilt took away her edge. I don't know.'

'Then there was the "performance" Jude would have us believe Melanie gave at the police station. I don't know about you, but from what I remember, it seemed pretty bloody genuine to me. Oscar-winning stuff. I just don't see how it's possible to fake that. Not unless . . . not unless she really thought Chloe had actually killed him.'

'Oh, come on, Ruthie . . .'

'And if she was that clever, why run the risk of letting Chloe do it at all? Why not simply doctor her husband's breakfast or something far more reliable? All this brainwashing, the Teddy Hospital, it just doesn't seem possible from a silly tart who ran off with a bookmaker.'

'But you've got more, right?'

Ruth nodded, registering that they were fast approaching Chelmsford's Army and Navy roundabout on the outskirts of the quietened town. 'Something Jude said. About the timing.'

'And?'

'Think back, Felix. To the old days. You, Frank and I in Maldon.'

'I'd rather not.'

She pressed on. 'The night-shift system. Remember?'

An easy one for the exhausted driver. 'We all had three a week. Me and you. Me and Frank. You and Frank.'

'And the following day?'

'Free until five that night, the next shift.'

She savoured the moment. 'And Frank and I did Tuesday nights together. Leaving him free on Wednesday afternoons.'

'So?' None of it was crystallizing for Felix.

'Wednesday afternoons, Felix. The time Jude said she'd spent with Chloe and Melanie.'

'Ruth, I'm very tired . . .'

'Just listen, please. It's important. We know Frank was seeing Melanie Webster. An illicit affair. We know they were both "free" Wednesday afternoons. Just suppose Jude Farrow has been rather economical with the truth. Suppose the real arrangement between the two sisters was for Jude to take Melanie to her young lover for an afternoon's secret fun, while she babysat little Chloe. Suppose it wasn't Melanie who Frankensteined Chloe into the perfect killing machine, but Jude herself. Remember what she said, Felix? That she'd have done anything for a child of her own?'

Felix negotiated the roundabout, before proceeding down Parkway and stopping at a set of red lights. On the other side of the dual carriageway, a group of police officers in yellow striped jackets were pulling over vehicles from the fluctuating stream of traffic. But this wasn't a stop on suss drink-driving operation. There were too many of them for that. The ever-present police helicopter hovered overhead, catching the scene in the white circular glare of its halogen searchlight. If little was obvious to Felix inside the car, outside it was readily apparent the search for the elusive Christmas Killer was extremely high profile.

He reluctantly mulled Ruth's theory over. 'So Chloe goes back to the Maltings to play games with broody Aunt Jude, while Melanie plays a few of her own with Frank?'

'Exactly.'

A car hooted from behind, causing them both to jump. The lights were green. Cursing, Felix pulled away, his mind swimming with unresolved detail. 'But why bother telling us any of it? Why not simply keep shtoom? I mean, if you're right, this stuff's nearly thirty years old. Jude Farrow's managed pretty well so far. Why the false confession now?'

Ruth paused for an instant, watching another foot patrol stop a group of excited revellers. 'I think she really believes that Chloe's the Christmas Killer.'

'Jesus wept, Ruthie. The woman was bonkers. Delusional. You know that.'

'Even so, I think Jude's convinced that Chloe murdered those two people, and that she's close to getting caught. Maybe she thinks Chloe will spill her guts about the whole deal, and simply wants to put her side first. A warped version of events, implicating the dead sister who couldn't deny a word of it. Christ sakes, Felix, I don't know. But maybe the whole thing does make some sort of sense. I gave Chloe the handkerchief. It was found at one of the murder scenes. You remember, it's where we started, and now we've heard some more . . . and maybe . . . maybe we're all to blame. I don't know.'

'So we go to the police, right? Tell them what we know?'

'Get real, Felix, we'd be laughed out of there in seconds. Mason'd have a field day with me. He already thinks I might have killed the student.'

'Right,' Felix acknowledged. It had been a long day, and he wasn't thinking straight, becoming edgy and irritated with the whole package. 'So it all ends here? Half-truths, uncheckable facts, untraceable people, dead witnesses? And what about you?' He felt the first warning signs of his earlier anger rising up to re-visit him. 'I notice you're not saying whether you believe all this stuff about the latest murders. Because we both know Jude Farrow could be making the whole fucking deal up from some twisted corner of her mind. Maybe it's your turn to "get real", Ruthie. Here was a woman openly admitting to burning little old people in their beds, for Christ's sake!'

'There's plenty we can do, don't you worry.'

It took a supreme effort of will to stop himself from saying something he might later regret. Instead, as his panic-attack counsellor had so expensively instructed him, he ground his teeth and counted silently to ten. Then twenty. Gradually the rage retreated for another day, disappearing like the aftermath of a foaming wave back into the black ocean of his anger. He vowed to play more sport in the New Year. Give his aggression the chance to find a healthier release. Snooker, maybe, or darts. Dominoes, he decided.

'Who's worrying?' he replied, pessimistically anticipating that Ruth had yet another card to play.

'The key to it is to check Melanie's movements on a Wednesday afternoon. Find out if she went with Jude and Chloe or not.'

'She's dead, Ruth,' he quietly replied, hoping to God she wasn't about to send him on a hunt for a spirit medium working the twilight hours of what must have been the longest Boxing Day in history.

'Agreed. But the last I heard, Frank was very much alive.'

241

37

Thirteen minutes and forty-seven seconds later, they drew up in front of Frank Davies's imposing detached home, Felix making an unintentional show of braking loudly on the gravel as the security light caught their arrival.

It hadn't been difficult to find, Ruth remembering the route out of town into the darkened Essex flatlands towards the picturesque village of Writtle. Frank's large, Georgian home stood with a group of similar ivy-clad properties bordering the village green. Stepping from the car, she recalled the previous July, the annual Davies' barbecue. Doug and her arriving in his taxi, with Ruth insisting that they park away from the cluster of Mercs, Jags and BMWs on the forecourt. The sudden dread feeling that everyone would know her shoes were from a charity shop, and praying Doug wouldn't get pissed and out of order with the potent mixture of sunshine, police and drink surrounding them on all sides. And Frank's polite but grimacing smile when she'd offered him the litre-bottle of Rioja and twenty economy burgers – supermarket own-brand, naturally.

Not that the wealth and ostentatiousness was any of Frank's doing. A DCI's wages wouldn't stretch to one-tenth the monthly mortgage for this chateau. No, Frank had married the money, and seemed to have lived fairy amicably with it for the last twenty years or so.

For Felix, it was his first visit to the place, and he greeted it reverently with a low whistle. But it explained a lot. Explained why Frank had never chased those early dreams of the Chief Constable's position he had looked so ruthlessly designed for. The money had changed all that. Blunted the ambition, the drive to accumulate more wealth. Why bother, Felix thought, when he was obviously fucking loaded?

'Kept this bloody quiet, didn't he? Jesus Christ, who the hell did he marry, Ruthie? One of the Gettys?'

Felix found himself slightly overawed by the opulence bearing down on him out of the night sky, and was suddenly homesick for the trivial comforts offered by his tiny flat. He watched Ruth march straight up to the holly-wreathed front door, trying his best to persuade himself that it mattered how you lived your life, not the number of bricks you wrapped it in.

Davies opened the door.

'Happy Christmas, Frank,' said Ruth, quickly stepping inside.

'Ruth . . . I . . .'

'I know. You weren't expecting us. Believe me, it's important.'

'Us?' Davies replied, totally bemused.

Felix followed Ruth into the elegant hallway. 'Long time no see, Frank.'

Davies refused the outstretched hand. He appeared flustered, like he'd just risen from a nap, confused at the unexpected interruption. Ruth watched his fevered mind working overtime to explain their presence.

'If this is about Hassloff and Morgan,' he blustered, 'then I have to put my hands up and say I did authorize the tail, but only to appease my sergeant. He's got it into his head that you're tied into these murders, Ruth. Seems he reckons a handkerchief found . . . but you know about all that, don't you?'

'I spoke to that idiot this morning, Frank,' Ruth confirmed. 'It's what started me thinking.'

A bored, gum-chewing boy wandered into the tinsel-strewn hallway. 'Wha's 'appening, Dad?'

'Oh, God. Go to your room, Gareth. Now. And tell your mother I'll be in my study for a while.'

Felix and Ruth exchanged mock-impressed glances before following Davies upstairs, a silent procession heading for the far room at the end of a long corridor.

'And how is the good Mrs Davies?' Felix asked.

'Pissed. It's Christmas, what do you think?'

Felix was thinking all sorts, but kept it to himself. Mostly, as they stepped into the small study, Felix pondered how sad it was that Davies had apparently felt the need to construct in miniature what he assumed was a carbon copy of his office at New Street police station. A small desk, fold-up chair, phone, fax machine, and the obligatory display of framed photographs chronicling the rise of the owner-occupant from PC to DCI, completed the small-scale mock-up in a rather ineffective fashion. Fine for an egotistical dwarf, Felix concluded, but spatially challenged to take all three of them.

Davies made a show of offering Ruth the foldaway chair, then settled himself rather uncomfortably on the corner of the desk. Felix beamed back and contented himself to lean against the wall, dislodging a smiling photo of a younger Sergeant Davies as he did so.

'Careful,' Davies growled, proving time was no great healer as far as his relationship with the awkward portly man opposite went.

Ruth looked at them both, before settling her gaze on Davies. 'Puts me in mind', she said brightly, 'of a similar occasion, nearly thirty years ago. The three of us, crammed into a tiny cell. You, Frank, looking worried to buggery.'

Davies scanned both expectant faces, before swiftly retreating to his earlier position. 'Like I say, Ruth. First I heard of it was a phone call from Boot Sa– Sergeant Mason earlier this afternoon. I just needed the day off, following all the . . . business with Doug. Anyway, Mason told me about your antics with the pet-shop window, then how he'd stumbled upon the initials R G on a handkerchief found –'

'At the second murder scene,' Ruth quickly cut in. 'You don't have to tell me all this, Frank.'

'Right.' Davies ran a hand through his short grey hair. 'I was just trying to explain why I agreed to the tail. I mean, it's just precautionary. To prove . . . to prove you're not involved, in my mind.'

'You've been following us?' Felix asked, beginning to re-discover his sense of humour. Davies had authorized some kind of surveillance operation? On him and Ruth, for God's sake? Shit, the poor bloke must really be feeling the strain. Felix had seen indications during the televised press conference:

Davies on his feet, pathetically trying to shout down a horde of baying journalists as the despairing press liaison officer looked on, open-mouthed. 'Why, Frank?'

Davies tried hard to find something interesting to look at through the small dormer window. A pointless task, the night rendering the smooth pane ebony black. 'To prove Mason was wrong about Ruth,' he offered weakly. 'That it was all just a coincidence.' He turned to her earnestly. 'Ruth, I never for one minute . . .'

'It's no coincidence, Frank. The handkerchief's mine. I recognized it immediately.'

'Rubbish, Ruth. You're in the clear. Mason checked with the woman from Whizzcabs. Says she was with you and Felix when the student was killed. You're not involved. And I'm sorry, really sorry, that I sanctioned –'

'Frank,' she said sharply. 'We're all involved. Me, Felix, you.'

'Especially you, Frank,' Felix echoed.

'What's all this about?'

Ruth looked him straight in the eye. 'Melanie Webster, Frank. And a young PC Davies.' She watched as he shot Felix a filthy look, Felix merely nodding by way of reply. A thin film of perspiration was beginning to form on the flustered DCI's top lip. 'This goes no further than this room, Frank. But there are things we need to know.'

'Things?' he replied, a little too quickly. 'Things about Melanie Webster? You honestly think I have the time, the brain-space to trawl up distant bloody memories to satisfy you?' He pointed at Felix accusingly. 'It's him, isn't it? Been bad-mouthing me, hasn't he?'

'Frank. It wasn't like –'

The finger still shook in Felix's direction. 'He knows all you need to know about Melanie bloody Webster. What the fuck do you have to ask me for? Some kind of thrill, is it? Joining in the goddamned world party to bash Frank Davies? Well, I just don't need this. Any of it! I've taken enough shit this week from your old man, top brass, the fucking press, the whole bloody shebang!'

Ruth maintained her calm, feeling a grain of genuine sympathy for her ex-colleague's plight. 'Frank,' she said reassuringly.

'I gave that handkerchief to a little girl called Chloe Webster on the night her father died. Remember her? The girl whose mother you were seeing at the time?'

'Of course, I remember,' Davies lied, frantically racing through his own idling memory banks. The woman? Melanie Webster, by God he remembered her. Still thought of her occasionally when the urge wasn't strong enough to fully satisfy Mrs Davies's voracious sexual appetite. But a girl . . . Yes . . . maybe. And then a wave of long-forgotten, suppressed guilt broke from a distant chamber of his mind, drenching him with its awful intensity. Oh, shit! For Christ's sake! The daughter . . . Melanie's kid . . . that night . . . oh, fuck!

'The kid injected him, or something,' he tried as nonchalantly as possible. 'So?'

Felix took up the thread. 'We all thought so. At the time. Mainly because someone talked to CID and assured them that Melanie couldn't be a suspect. That the young vet and his wife appeared to have the happiest marriage in Maldon.'

'And that was you, Frank,' Ruth assisted. 'You talked to CID, didn't you? Had to tell them what a wonderful mother and loyal wife she was, because you were terrified of what might happen to your career if you told the truth about your lover. Right?'

Davies said nothing.

Felix added, 'It goes no further than this room, Frank.'

Ruth asked, 'Was it back at your place?'

Davies frowned. 'What?'

'The affair. With Melanie?'

'I fail to see what –'

'Please, Frank. It's very important. Did Melanie Webster come to you on Wednesday afternoons?'

What little colour remained drained from Davies's face. He looked shamefully about the tiny room, caught on the back foot, victim to a body blow from the past, a politician at the centre of yet another sleaze allegation. 'This was years ago,' he said defensively.

'This is now, Frank. The Christmas Killer? I'm certain it all started back then.' Ruth turned to Felix, then back to Frank. 'We think that little Chloe grew up with all the wrong messages, Frank.'

'The daughter,' he mumbled to himself, head gently drooping as he recalled his own scepticism inside the dark, gently humming Offender Profiling Unit. A kid, fucked up by some childhood tragedy. Unable to move on. Was this it? Was this what he'd missed? Had the killer been there, all along, locked silently away in the tangled mess of his earliest, and only, career mistake? The anger began to wane, replaced by something more sinister, irrational. An exhausting cocktail of fear, shame and regret. He looked up from his midriff, feeling whatever fight remained drain from his aching body. And nodded. 'She was dropped off by her sister.'

It was music to Ruth's ears. 'Wednesday afternoons?'

A second nod. Guilty, Your Honour.

'How did you meet her, Frank?'

'The sister, again. Whether by accident or design, I don't know.'

'Design,' Ruth replied.

Frank slowly rolled his head to relieve the tension in his shoulders. 'Older, she was. Ran an old folk's home up in Danbury. Used to make shopping trips to Maldon. Came up to me one day asking for directions. We got chatting. It was near the end of my beat. Had coffee together. Suppose I told her too much, but I was . . .'

'Young,' Felix helped. 'We all were.'

'Anyway, next thing I know I'm sort of seeing the pair of them out together. More coffee. More chats. I was . . . flattered, in a way. Melanie was . . . well, let's just say she was what I wanted at the time.'

'No strings, you mean?' Ruth asked, seeing how easily it could all have happened. How the young uniformed policeman bursting with repressed hormones could have been so deviously used by a woman desperate for her sister's child.

'Pretty soon, we didn't need the coffee. Jude . . . Farrow, I think her name was, started to drop Melanie straight off at my place. Then pick her up after.' He paused for a moment, massaging his frowning brow. 'So . . . that night . . . when the kid came in, when the accident happened . . . I mean, what could I say to CID? I was the bloody golden boy . . . They wanted the local opinion of Melanie . . .' He tailed off into an awkward silence.

'So you lied, Frank. To save your skin.'

He turned to Ruth once more. 'I don't know what I did. And that's the truth. They were asking me all these questions, and all the while I was thinking, there's no way, no way she would've killed the guy like that. Just didn't make sense. I knew her, for God's sake, better than any man – other than the deceased.' His eyes bored into Ruth's. 'She just didn't have it in her to kill him. It wasn't what she wanted. So I went with what everyone else was accepting. That the kid killed him by mistake.' His gaze returned to the darkened window, a porthole into the bleak night beyond. 'Though how all this gets us any fucking closer to your handkerchief . . .'

Ruth interjected, 'You're right. Melanie Webster didn't kill her husband. But neither did little Chloe. You were used, Frank. Didn't you ever stop to wonder why this Jude Farrow woman was delivering her sister gift-wrapped to your door every week?' She paused. 'No, you've already answered that. Too young and innocent. She was what you wanted. Why bother analysing it at all?'

'Something like that, yeah. Look, I'm not the only copper who's made a mistake, you know. Jesus, I could give you –'

'Frank,' she interrupted. 'We don't have time for any more postmortems. Jude Farrow set you up. Knew you wouldn't risk blemishing her sister's character – so bolstering Chloe's bizarre claim to have killed her father.'

'But that's what the kid was saying, for God's sake,' Davies insisted. 'Over and over. Sent him to heaven, or something. I remember all that crap well enough.'

'And that's all it was,' said Felix grimly. 'Crap. The kid was brainwashed, coached for the show while you were seeing its mother.'

'Jude Farrow killed Richard Webster,' Ruth calmly announced. 'In order to gain access to the child she could never naturally have. And to her dying day, I suspect Melanie Webster thought exactly as we did. That her own beloved daughter had killed her husband.'

'Dying day?' Davies croaked.

'I'm sorry, Frank.'

He waved the sympathy aside, and attempted the beginnings of a smile. 'Don't worry. Past, isn't it?'

'I know it's come as something of a shock.'

'You can fucking say that again.'

'Felix and I only found out today. Like I say, your sergeant's little chat put the absolute fear of God into me. I had to do something. So once I remembered giving the handkerchief to Chloe, we set off to try and find her.' She stood, and to Felix's complete amazement, planted a kiss on the humbled DCI's cheek. 'If it's any consolation, Frank, my closet's got a few old bones rattling around inside there, too.'

'And mine's got to be a close runner for Highgate Cemetery,' Felix added, embarrassed by the sudden show of affection. A thought stirred lazily at the back of his tired mind. Surely he couldn't be jealous of one little peck? He put it down to the rigours of the long day, but noticed how quickly it vanished the moment Ruth sat back down.

'And now,' she announced, smiling at both men, 'Felix and I have a little story for you. It's called "What became of a girl named Chloe Webster?" Are you sitting comfortably? Then I'll begin.'

38

December the twenty-seventh.
Seven thirty-four in the morning.

Chloe Webster turned the pistol in her hands, marvelling at its lethal weight. She tried lifting it with one hand, wrist cramping from the unfamiliar effort. The other was necessary to steady the wobbling barrel trained on its terrified target. The first shafts of dawn broke through the attic skylight, illuminating both captor and prey.

'Morning, Mr Jenkins,' she said, revelling in his fear. The temptation to pull the rusting trigger and end it there and then was almost too great. But she had other plans for the bastard pretender, plans she'd been working on through the night, as he'd slept, concussed from the pistol's handle, brought down with such sudden ferocity the previous afternoon.

Ha! How she'd laughed at that. Boxing Day, and she'd scored the biggest knockout in the land!

Mr Fabian's pistol. Dear Mr Fabian from Southend. Leaving his service revolver for her as unspoken payment for his sweet release from a world which had moved on, unable to stop and listen to his pitiful worries for the time it would have taken to unravel them.

She walked over to Doug, ripping the masking tape from his whitened lips. A thin trail of caked blood ran from a tiny cut in a large bruise on the crown of his head.

And that blow. That wincing collision of ancient gun metal on unsuspecting scalp. How the dollies had laughed at the falling clown before them!

Watching the imposter crash with such force to the floor, as

250

if every bone in his treacherous body had suddenly powdered, his structure vanishing, flesh collapsing under flesh, muscles folding, sinews stretching and tearing as he . . .

Crash, crump, slap! The gloriously edifying sounds of skull on fireplace.

She'd revelled in every moment, gagging the unconscious lump on the floor, kicking it, hating it with such intensity that, at times, it was difficult to remind herself Jenkins had a purpose. That in a very real, if not accidental sense, he was a vital part of it all. His own greed had secured him the role.

The Vietnamese girl had suffered terribly because of him, but even that horrifically gory maul had been necessary, playing its ghastly part in the overall drama and leading up to this: the capture of the Judas man and, if all went well, much-deserved public understanding and sympathy for her plight, her sacrifices and her vision of the future.

People would remember Sulee Xang, Chloe had decided. Remember the supreme sacrifice she had unwittingly made for the cause. Chloe envisioned her as a latter-day John the Baptist, a forerunner, precursor of the new truth. And as her brand new Sulee dolly had been quick to point out, the good man in question had also left this poisoned life suffering a fatal neck injury. Saint Sulee – it had rather an appealing ring to it.

The time, the signs, everything was right. She had to act now. A chance, that's all she was asking. A chance to be heard. Let the people judge, let them decide if her way was a better way.

Doug lay where he'd spent the night, tied to the chair, his broken head lying on the dusty grate. It was her original plan to have him upright in the chair, but he was simply too heavy. On reflection, she rather liked having the bastard at her feet.

His neck craned to see her, an enormous effort, veins standing out on scarlet temples, the head wound re-opening slightly. A tiny tear of blood ran into his blinking eye. He'd seen the gun.

'Jesus,' he gasped. 'What the . . . ?'

She stooped over the heaving, trussed body to check the knotted electrical flex. 'Wake up, Judas man. I've got a gun and it's loaded. Took me a while to figure out how to get the bullets in, though. Hey! Look at this. Watch!' She held the pistol tantalizingly close to his head, flicking the chamber-release mechanism and spinning the loaded cylinder just inches from his face. 'Thirty-eights, these bullets are, or so it says on the box. Very old, though, all of it. Pretty dangerous, I'd have thought. Still, I put a bit of bicycle oil in all the moving bits, and everyone else seems to think it'll work.'

Doug turned his head once more, feeling the weighted agony of his previous encounter with the pistol. Jesus wept! What the fuck had he blundered into? This journo, this Styles woman, was some sort of headcase! He struggled to remember how and why he might possibly have ended up bleeding on a cold floor in a room full of dolls and an insane woman pointing a pistol at his head.

But, it wasn't her, was it? The Styles woman, she'd been a blonde, a bit of stuff, sophisticated elegance. Then he saw the largest doll of them all, propped on the single bed, one eye open, the other obscured by a yellow lock of synthetic hair. Hair he recognized from the previous afternoon. Her hair. Hair she'd worn as she led him, teased him, lured him expertly to her lair.

A wig. The bitch had worn a wig. And now it adorned a cheap plastic doll. Jesus Christ!

'Who the hell are you?'

She said nothing.

'Please,' he moaned. 'My head's killing me!'

'Oh, stop bleating!'

Doug fought to control the pain, his breathing and his temper. Something about the woman told him she was deadly serious. The gun was real, he had no doubt of that. Not that he had any firearms experience himself, but it looked the part. Convincing. And the truth was, so did she. After all, she'd got him back to wherever the hell he was, knocked him out, tied him up, then kept him overnight whilst working out the firing mechanism of an old army service pistol.

He tried to relax his muscles to slacken the flex, relieve the freezing cramps. She was sitting on the bed, flicking back her short brown hair, levelling the barrel, closing one eye to take better aim . . .'

'Jesus, don't!' He cried in pure, unadulterated terror. He wet himself.

'I expect you wonder why I'm doing all this, don't you?'

'Please, put the gun down. Please.'

'You caused an acquaintance of mine to go through a lot of pain. You defiled the memory of another.'

'Please,' Doug implored. 'Miss Styles, I'm begging you. Just let me go, eh? I won't say a word to anyone.'

'Oh, do shut up, Judas man!'

A new avenue suddenly opened in Doug's terrified brain. A way out of here, a solution! The Old Bill – they'd come to his rescue at last, extricate him from whatever hell he'd wound up in. 'My bail!' he said quickly. 'The police expect me to sign at the station twice daily. Eight in the morning and three in the afternoon. They're already going to be scratching their heads, love, wondering where I got to yesterday. And when I miss this morning's they're bound to send someone round to me mate's. They'll be after me. All the Old Bill.'

Chloe stared blankly back, completely unfazed. 'Your "arrangements", Judas man, are insignificant. The police probably sent someone over to your friend's place last night. And what would he have told them, eh? What information could he offer to assist their enquiries?' Her voice took on a terrible, mocking tone. '"I'm sorry, officer, I fell asleep. When I woke up, he was gone." But don't fret, Judas man. We'll be seeing a lot more of the police, later on.'

'What are you saying?' he moaned, hopes dashed, numb with pain.

'My dear Mr Jenkins,' she replied, giggling a little, 'I really didn't lie. You're still going to make the front pages. "Britain's Saddest Man" – isn't that what they've been calling you? But I'm going to put an end to that, too, just like I promised. Course, the bit about the money was really a big fib.' The gun moved slowly in her hands, tracing an invisible path over his contorted body. 'But I'm going to give you something far more valuable in return, Judas man. I'm going to give you immortality.'

'Please,' he begged. 'I need the toilet.'

'You've just been.'

'You know . . . the other . . . sort.'

'I'm not untying you, so you may as well go in your trousers. I don't mind, I can always open a window.' It amazed her how easily humiliation came to her. She'd spent a good deal of the night worrying how this first half-hour might pan out, working through endless permutations of the present power struggle. But none had resolved themselves as easily as the real situation. The gun, of course, empowered her, but she had to have the anger there first, and her rage was very real. Now she wanted answers.

'Why didn't you tell them?' Chloe barked.

'Tell who what?' Doug responded, unable to figure any of this out. Not the woman, the place, the situation, the gun, the whole 'Judas man' bit, and those wretched goofy-looking dolls. And now this, crazy questions from nowhere.

'The police. And don't piss with me like you don't know, fart-face! Why didn't you tell them she was already dead. Answer me!'

Doug's sweating brow creased in painful bloodied confusion. He'd seen something like this once before. Late-night television. An alternative female comic, mincing, squinting and squeaking as she pretended to be a naughty muddy-kneed schoolgirl. It was happening now. But there was no comedy in it, just a manic edge, threatening to ride out of control. His eyes were rooted to her two forefingers, wrapped round the trigger.

'Who?' he moaned.

'Ida. Ida Sharansky.'

The old woman! Back from the bloody grave to haunt him again! A thought occurred, another chance. 'OK, OK,' he conceded, struggling to steady his breathing. 'You win, Jayne. Tell you what, love. You untie me, and I'll tell you the bloody lot. Whatever you want to know. Promise. It's just that I can't concentrate down here, and . . .'

'Too late!' Chloe shouted. 'You lose! I already know the answer, Judas man. You wanted the credit for yourself. Wanted to steal my idea, my glory. Didn't you?' She approached him slowly, jabbing the pistol muzzle into his shaking belly. 'You saw her sitting there, all beautiful as I'd left her, and you thought, "I'll have a bit of that." But you're too greedy, Judas man. Too stupid. Had to go after your thirty pieces of silver, didn't you? Had to steal Ida's purse as well.'

'Jayne,' Doug insisted, 'I really don't know . . .'

More tape brought a swift end to his pathetic pleading. She checked her watch. Fast approaching eight o'clock. Time to start making her move. Speeches needed to be memorized, sermons polished to please the still-sleeping congregation.

Chloe coshed him once again, for good measure. The intention wasn't to knock him out, just to release a little of her own tension. He moaned through the thick black tape.

Yes, she decided quickly, violence was OK. Permitted, maybe. Especially on the Judas man.

39

Frank Davies knew that if ever his faithful sergeant had nursed
any aspirations of a thespian career, it would've been strictly
walk-on parts. Third spear-carrier at the local amateur dramatics'
Shakespeare; man-seen-walking-dog-in-back-of-shot; strictly no
acting required. Mason just didn't have the ability to disguise
his emotions. His thin, pointed face gave instant access to his
current thoughts and feelings. And at that moment, as they
both sat drinking their third coffee of the morning in Davies's
New Street office, Mason's expression said, 'What the fucking
hell's my guv'nor on about?'

In truth, Davies couldn't blame the man. The half-hour he'd
just spent painstakingly reiterating the previous night's conversation with Ruth and Felix had seemed plain ridiculous even to
him. Yes, he'd been sparing of his own part in the Chloe Webster
drama – he'd rather not let Mason know about that indiscretion
– but overall, he reflected, he'd more or less recounted the tale
word for word. So why did the whole damned thing still sound
so completely implausible? He'd never gambled, even on the
Grand National, so why had he taken such long odds on a little
girl called Chloe Webster? Career-ending odds?

Because, maybe, deep down, it was time to face up to the
one mistake which had subconsciously haunted him every time
he had been made up to a higher rank. A lust-fuelled error
which had sat on his pipped shoulder throughout, whispering,
'What if, Frank? What if they knew about me? About you and
Melanie? How far, Frank, how far would you have climbed, if
they'd known about me?'

And in the early hours, as he'd sat in his darkened living room with a glass of ten-year-old malt in front of the dying embers of last night's fire, it had come to him. Staring down, three-quarters of the way up the ladder to success, it really wasn't so far to fall into the safety-net of his own professional integrity. So he'd gone to bed, and prepared to jump.

'If it sounds unbelievable, Alan,' he said eventually, hoping first-name terms might help, 'then that's how it is. And if I'm coming over like someone who's just done a bunk from the nut-house, then I apologize. But what else have we got? Thin air, from what I gather. Two dead bodies and just thin bloody air.' He looked at the clock on the wall. Eight forty. 'I've got a briefing with Knowles and the crew from HQ at ten this morning. I'd like to take them something they can use. I'd like to give them Chloe Webster.'

Mason shuffled uncomfortably. 'No disrespect, Guv,' he mumbled. 'Just that this has come out of the blue for me, you know? I mean, it's a lot to take on board.'

Davies nodded, sensing the weight of disappointment from the slumped figure opposite. It was one of the cruel ironies of rank that Mason was forced to indulge his superior officer's whims, regardless of his own wishes. They both knew this, which made the atmosphere even more uneasy. 'Penny for them, Alan?' he offered. 'Off the record?'

Mason thought for a moment. 'It's just . . . well, it's just that . . . it's like you've given in on the Jenkins link, you know? Like you're suddenly all fired up and running with what those fucking computer-shrinks up the road are waffling on about. Fucked-up kids and stunted whatnots. Serial killers, all that old cobblers. And I know, I'm just certain, that if we put some heat under Jenkins's old lady, we'd fucking come up trumps with the whole deal.' He looked at the black-and-whites pinned to the wall. 'You sit there going on about something which may or may not have happened thirty years ago, and all I can see is two freshly dead stiffs that never got their turkey this Christmas. I just . . . feel it could be another . . . you know, cock-up on our part, if we go all the way with this. And I don't know that either of us needs any more shit hitting the fan. Sorry, Guv, but you asked.'

Davies pulled at his bottom lip. He'd have said the same,

word for word. 'Please, Alan,' he asked softly, 'let's run with it for just this morning. I need your help.' He looked out into the open-plan squadroom, seeing the rest of the demoralized CID team arriving for yet another day's slogging through the records. 'I've got to tell them all this in a second. Just be with me on it. Prepare the ground a little for me. Please?'

Mason nodded, trapped by rank. 'So what's the plan, then?' he asked, making a show of appearing convinced. The bad actor, stuck in a role he hadn't the faintest how to play.

'We find her,' Davies replied. 'Plough the records, trace her movements. If anything, just to rule Chloe Webster out of it.' He smiled at Mason. 'Look, if it turns out to be a crock of shit, I'll be the first to put my hands up and say I'm a dickhead, right?'

'This is all still a hunch, though, isn't it?' Mason softly insisted. 'There's no evidence, is there?'

'Apart from the handkerchief? No.'

Mason frowned as he turned over the tale in his mind. 'So, you reckon that Chloe Webster got given this handkerchief by your mate Mrs J, over thirty years ago, then dropped it when topping the foreign girl?'

'Look, I know it sounds . . . just indulge me, OK? We've got a killer using lipstick on the victims. A killer who got severely pissed off when we were about to cite Jenkins for the Sharansky fiasco. A killer who killed again, who wants us to know they're still out there. And I know this pisses you off more than anything, Alan, but yes – like it or not, Chloe Webster does fit the profile from HQ.' Davies didn't know what else to say. Nothing probably. Nothing would convince the doubting sergeant. 'Just try Chloe Webster, please. Electoral rolls, council tax lists, driving licences, anything. Just find her.'

Mason rose from his seat and turned for the door. 'I'll tell the others you want a word in five minutes, then, shall I, Guv?'

Davies held his gaze for a moment, trying not to blush. It was back to business. 'Very good, Boot Sale. And I . . . erm . . . appreciate . . . you know . . .'

But Mason had already gone to spread the word. Five minutes' grace. It was all he needed. Time to settle an old score. Davies quickly picked up the phone, called directory enquiries, then punched in the number they gave him.

A woman's voice, older but still vaguely as he remembered. 'Two-five-nine-two?' Unmistakeably Jude Farrow.

'Remember me? It's PC Davies, giving you your wake-up call.'

A silence. Then, predictably, 'I'm sorry, I think you must have . . .'

'I've got your number, Mrs Farrow, don't you worry about that. And let's not hang up, eh? I'm a Detective Chief Inspector now. I'll have half the Essex Constabulary on your doorstep in seconds.'

Another silence. 'What do you want?'

'You've been speaking out of turn, Jude, to some old friends of mine.'

'I've said nothing.'

'Blaming Melanie for Dickie Webster's death.'

'I've done no such thing.' Panic in the voice. Fear.

He bluffed, recalling Ruth's description of the woman's rambling paranoia, a mind trapped by ridiculous fantasies of police surveillance techniques. 'It's all on tape, Jude. The woman was wired.'

A longer silence, Davies almost hearing the mind race, madly searching for a way out.

'Every word of it was true. Melanie killed him. I was downstairs with Chloe. I only told the truth.'

'Crap. We both know Melanie couldn't have come up with a scheme half as devious as that. You used us all, Jude. Me, your sister, and most of all the little girl you wanted for yourself. Chloe, isn't it? Chloe Webster?'

Short, shallow breaths.

'Didn't you?'

'You can't prove a thing.'

'Oh, I don't have to.'

'I'll stick by what I said. And next time I'll name you, Detective Chief Inspector. I will.'

Davies laughed. 'That's what you're relying on, isn't it? That I'll keep my trap shut?'

'You slept with a murderer.'

'But I know different, now. A murderer set me up to sleep with her sister.'

'You can't prove any of it. Melanie's dead.'

'That's why I've got nine officers looking for Chloe. That's why I'm about to brief the Serious Crimes Squad about your nasty little life. We get Chloe, and we get the truth about who played Teddy Hospital with her. Remember that, don't you, Jude? Ran your lying mouth off about Teddy Hospital to people you shouldn't have.'

'You wouldn't dare!'

'Wouldn't have the bottle, you mean? Try me, Jude, try me. I've had a good thirty years in the force; haven't done too badly. The truth is, I can afford to come as clean as I want.'

A hissed warning. 'It would be the end of your career!'

Davies laughed again. 'Don't you worry about me. The pension fund's swelling quite nicely.'

'Just you try it, and we'll see –'

'See you on the front pages of the tabloids, Jude!' Receiver down, business finished. Frank sat and waited for the feeling of euphoria which never came. Outside, the squad went lethargically through routine tracing procedures, shaking their heads and whispering to each other. Mason had obviously stuck loyally to the task, telling them the guv'nor had a new suspect, and that all would be revealed during the briefing.

He looked from face to bemused face, and found he couldn't blame them one iota. They wanted it over and done. No more false arrests, no more stick from HQ. Just the quiet life again. A few nicked motors, harmless break-ins, traditional punch-ups. But no more murders. They'd done with murders.

An hour later, Mason wandered lazily back into Davies's office and stood awkwardly before his guv'nor. Without waiting to be asked, he started to read from a computer printout. 'Chloe Charlotte Webster. Born 1962 to Richard and Melanie Webster of Great Totham, Essex. Several known addresses, principally the veterinary practice of the same village. Legally adopted by Mr and Mrs William Farrow of the Maltings Residential Home for the Elderly, Corely Way, Danbury. Registered with two local schools, primary and secondary.'

Davies waved him on.

'As you said, Guv, the reason for the adoption is given as: "Mother unable to cope with personal stresses of daughter following accidental death of Richard Webster, husband and father, respectively." She stayed there until seventy-six when the place was destroyed by fire.'

'And?'

Mason shrugged. 'That's it.'

'That's it?'

'All there is. Chloe Webster disappears off the map.'

'Killed in the fire, you mean?'

'She wasn't listed among the victims.'

'Arson?'

'Fire Inspector's report couldn't make a definite conclusion either way. It was an old building, stuffed full of bedding, timber, furniture, the lot. Bloody thing went up like a tinderbox. Tragic, really. The old ones were cooked, mostly. The Farrows moved on to several addresses, ending up back in Danbury themselves. Whether they took the girl with them is anyone's guess.'

'School records?'

Mason consulted the printout. 'After the blaze, she attends three schools in the Danbury area over the next two years. First and second dump her after a few months citing "strange behaviour". Then she's sixteen, up and out of the system. Records dry up. She vanishes.'

'Strange behaviour?'

He shrugged. 'S'all it says. No details.'

'And since then – bugger all?'

Mason sighed. 'No bank account, credit rating, driving licence, criminal record – nothing. Either she's dead, or done a bunk overseas, or lived the last twenty years totally cash-in-hand, travelling everywhere on the bus.' He paused, sensing his superior's disappointment. 'I'm sorry, Guv. There's nothing more we can do. God knows if this woman's alive or dead. Could be living on the fucking moon for all the good it does us.'

Davies massaged his tired face in his hands. He looked up. 'We've got to find her, Boot Sale. If she's . . . involved, then she was most probably living in Chelmsford when the two killings happened. Rented accommodation, maybe. Check with the local landlords. I really want to give Knowles something tangible. Else I'm going to look like . . .'

Mason shuffled unnecessarily from foot to foot. 'Very good,

Guv,' he lamely tried, accepting the impossibility of the task. Needle in a fucking haystack time. A cocked-up crusade to verify yet another crock of shit from the guv'nor. 'There is just one other thing . . .'

'Well?' Davies asked.

'Our old pal Jenkins.'

Davies moaned. It was the last name he wanted to hear.

'He's now missed two bail appointments. Yesterday afternoon's, and this morning's. Uniform spoke to the geezer who's putting him up yesterday evening. Said he hadn't had a sniff of Jenkins since lunch time. Apparently they'd both had a skinful, he'd crashed out, then, when he woke, Jenkins had done a runner.'

Davies sighed, wondering how much a luxury cruise down the Nile would cost at that time of the year. For one. One severely pissed-off Detective Chief Inspector. He'd check it out after briefing DCI Knowles and company. He'd need a walk, and the travel agent's was as good a place as any.

'Send Uniform back round to the bail address, Boot Sale. The stupid bastard's probably sleeping off a cheap hangover. And this time, be sure they bring him in and nick him.'

40

Human beings never failed to amaze her.

Even though she hadn't had time to make a foolproof plan, the ease with which she had managed to prod Doug down busy streets full of eager shoppers scouting for the best sales bargains, with hands tied and a pistol held to his back, totally mystified her.

Those who noticed the weapon either hurriedly turned away and pretended they hadn't, or assumed it to be part of some harmless stunt. Admittedly, her hastily concocted disguise may have been the deciding factor to discourage unwanted interest: Chloe in her balaclava, Doug shuffling in front, hands behind his back, wearing a cardboard sign telling everyone he was part of a fancy-dress sponsored walk. He also had a small red bucket hanging from his reluctant neck, jangling with a few pieces of change from Chloe's purse and Doug's trouser pockets to heighten the effect.

A gorilla mask completed the bizarre scenario, ensuring Doug's anonymity from any who might recognize the loathsome murderer Chloe perceived him to be.

Indeed, by the time she prodded Doug round the corner at the upper end of the herringbone-paved High Street and headed down Market Road towards the imposing stone and glass County Hall offices, they'd been walking for nearly twenty minutes completely unmolested. Even more surprising, there was an extra £2.49 in the bucket since they'd started

Reaching their destination, she tore the sign from his neck, forcing him up the wide steps in front of the vast expanse of sheet glass marking the huge atrium entrance to County Hall. For a second, Doug thought the automatic revolving doors offered a chance of escape, all too quickly dashed as Chloe stepped smartly in behind, the pistol never leaving the small of his back as they entered the bright, unsuspecting greenhouse together.

'Please,' Doug begged, a pathetic muted whine from behind the grinning mask, 'I must sit down. My head really hurts, love. Think I'm going to be sick.'

'Keep walking,' she replied happily, marching him to a small brown room at the far end of the tiled floor marked 'Hallkeeper's Office'. To her left stood the atrium's centrepiece: two glass-fronted lifts sliding silently to the four floors which framed the steel edges of the lofty space. Each rose gracefully from behind a bubbling moat of Koi carp, up through a latticework of silver pillars and suspended gantries which accessed rows of hi-tech council planning offices on each floor.

As Doug had often complained to other drivers on the taxi-rank, the Chelmsford architectural and town-planning division of Essex County Council seemed to have spent a great deal more time and effort designing their own premises than those of the rest of the town. The magnificent atrium was hung with trailing plants, and dotted with tall trees lost in the vastness of the echoing surrounds. This was council opulence at its most extreme; designed to impress, guaranteed to intimidate.

'Please be careful,' Doug warned vaguely amused passers-by. 'She's got a gun. Stay away.' They smiled back, disbelievingly, the children waving at the talking gorilla.

The atrium itself was unusually crowded, providing a warm sanctuary from the bitter cold outside, access to the main library, and a series of stone benches around its edges for the use of smokers on the council's staff, banished to pursue their solitary habit outside the office.

Chloe adjusted her balaclava one last time and approached the Hallkeeper's Office. Two bored security officers sat watching a bank of television monitors for any sign of trouble. She walked to the open window, peering inside, the pistol at Doug's neck. 'Excuse me,' she said politely. 'I have a gun and I'd like you to listen.'

The younger of the two officers tutted and approached the window, chewing gum, looking her up and down as though he'd just spotted her on the dance floor. Even she had to admit that the seriousness of her request was somewhat undermined by the small crowd of excited children who had gathered around the comical duo.

'Piss off, love,' he unwisely replied. 'And take those scabby kids with you. They're scaring the fish.'

Deciding she had no other option, Chloe pointed the pistol into the air and squeezed the heavy trigger.

Boom!

The noise was unbelievable. For a second, everything seemed to freeze as the explosion ricocheted around the glass walls. Then there was a high-pitched whistling, followed by a shower of myriad tiny shards of razor-sharp glass falling to the polished floor, sent tinkling to the ground by the bullet's lightning exit through the roof.

She smiled, thanked the Lord, Mr Fabian and the spirit of her father. It worked. The bloody thing still worked!

Then the screaming started. Gradually at first, as the nearest children backed away, eardrums stinging from the blast. Next cries of 'A gun!', 'She's got a gun!' from the startled group of adults frantically searching for family before scurrying towards the exits. As the panic set in, Chloe was surprised to discover that the only people who appeared unmoved were the two men nearest the offending weapon, completely frozen in open-mouthed fear.

'Excuse me,' she asked again, basking in the aftermath of the handgun's power. The smell of burnt cordite was as sweet as victory itself. 'Do you have a mobile phone? I'd be ever so grateful.' She took the proffered piece of black plastic from its shaking owner. 'It's just a borrow, thanks,' she teased, quite enjoying the game, nerves disappearing by the second. 'Oh, and by the way, I'll be taking my friend into one of those lifts over there. I really don't want to be disturbed for a while, so I suggest you evacuate these premises immediately, or . . .' She winked at the petrified man and whispered, 'I'll blow your fucking head off.'

He nodded, then began racing round the tiny office, bumping into his equally terrified colleague, in his haste to alert all those remaining in the building to the danger that lurked below.

Satisfied that they would soon be left alone, Chloe prodded Doug back towards the curved Plexiglas lifts, whispering in his ear, 'Nearly time for your big moment, Judas man. Hope you're ready for your fifteen minutes of fame.'

'Feel dizzy. Sick.'

'Oh, do shut up moaning. It's quite ruining the atmosphere.'

'Can't breathe properly.'

She sighed and began pulling at the back of the rubber mask, freeing his pink sweating head. He gasped, taking huge lungfuls of the air-conditioned environment. 'What about my hands? My wrists are killing me.'

'I'll kill you, if you carry on. Just move, murderer!'

'I never killed anyone,' he insisted. He'd had time enough to fathom that this insane woman was probably connected to the trouble he found himself in over the old woman's purse. Relative, or something? Lunatic grand-daughter come to . . . to what? What on earth were they doing in the bloody council buildings? 'The coppers pulled me for that, Jayne. Like I was going to tell you, there's this DCI down there, has a thing about me. Tried to slot me up . . .'

'Boring! Boring! Pants are on fire, Mr Judas liar!'

They waited by the carp pool, watching as the last few frightened council employees quickly fled the atrium. Behind, similar sounds told of the library's evacuation. Chloe thought about firing another shot or two to speed the process, but decided against it. They'd have the place to themselves in a moment, and besides, guns were dangerous, and bullets precious.

She reached into the red bucket dangling farcically at Doug's shaking midriff and pulled out a piece of the previous night's homework. She dialled the first number on the page, humming happily and watching the gold-and-white Koi swimming lazily as she waited for an answer.

'News Desk, please,' she requested. 'Your leading crime reporter, if possible. Thank you.' She lifted the phone to Doug's mouth, holding out the paper before his eyes. 'You can read, can't you?' she hissed suddenly.

A voice cut in before he could answer, asking if he could be of any assistance.

At a nod from Chloe, Doug started to read aloud, ignoring the

266

sweat which ran into his eyes. 'Hello,' he faltered, 'and good
. . . morning. My name's Doug Jenkins, the Judas man . . . and
I have something very important . . . to say.'

'Jenkins?' the voice replied. 'That toerag who robbed the old
dear in Essex while she lay dead? What d'you want, then?'

Chloe nodded again; Doug swallowed hard and pressed on.
'I am the sick . . . selfless man who by his own pathetic actions
decided to . . . con-confess to the killing of Ida Sharansky in order
to take another's . . . glory for myself, thereby necess . . . necess
. . . necessit . . .'

'You on drugs or something, pal?'

'Necessitating . . .' Doug cried, unable to decipher any more
of the handwritten text.

Chloe took the phone back, cursing his incompetence. 'Listen,
you fat parasitical slug,' she spat at the unseen tabloid reporter.
'Get all of your so-called journalist friends down to Chelmsford,
now. County Hall. You can't miss it, it'll be the place surrounded
by police as I tell the world the truth behind the so-called
Christmas Killings. I've got the sicko who made me bungle the
second one, a gun, and very little patience.' She terminated the
call and turned to Doug. 'See how easy it is? Just needed a little
feeling, that's all. Now then, shall we take a ride in one of these
rather wonderful lifts? I think we will. In a moment. Let's have
some more fun first.'

She walked him back across the empty atrium towards the
curious crowd gathering near the glass entrance. She levelled
the weapon and fired for a second time.

Boom!

Another deafening report as a large pane of glass shattered
twenty feet above the heads of the screaming crowd. In seconds
the steps were empty.

'That's better,' said Chloe, walking Doug like a zombie back
towards the Koi pond. There they boarded the lift and she took
them high up to the third floor. Doug slumped against the cool
Plexiglas, staring disbelievingly at the silent space below.

'I reckon', said Chloe, checking her watch, 'we've got about
five minutes before the police arrive. Filth, you call them,
don't you?'

'Sometimes,' he mumbled.

'Enjoy it, then, Doug. The calm before the storm.'

'I don't understand. Any of this.'

She sighed, dropping on to her heels, training the pistol on his fearful face. 'In case you haven't noticed, Doug, this is a gun. I've been firing it in a public place. That makes me a naughty girl, the sort of naughty girl the police send their own men with guns to kill.'

'They'll kill us both,' he protested weakly. 'Stuck in here, we're sitting targets.'

'You are,' she agreed casually. 'Definitely the bigger of the two of us. Couldn't really miss a lump like you.'

'Let's go now, before they arrive. I'm a cabbie. I know this town, the routes. We could slip out the back . . .'

'Strange if you die, Doug,' she pondered. 'I mean, what is it that you'll be remembered for, eh? How has Douglas Jenkins made his mark on this sorry world in which we live? What's your contribution, eh?'

'Please,' he begged. 'There's still time.'

'I think you'll go down as rather a sad statistic, myself. A five-minute nobody. I was there, Doug, the day you did your little stand-up routine in the magistrates' court. You thought the whole world would laugh along, didn't you?'

'Like I said,' he said softly, 'they didn't know the half of it. I never murdered anyone. I nicked her money, that's all.'

'I was a good friend of hers.'

'What can I say?'

'It's what you shouldn't have said.'

'Like what?'

'Like confessing to Ida's murder.' She was becoming angry now, incensed by his stupidity. Hadn't he even stopped to think it through?

'Jayne, I swear . . .'

'Then why did they hold you for so long, Doug? You claimed it for your own, didn't you?'

'I've got form,' he squealed. 'They reckoned I done it, that's God's honest. I never confessed to nothing. You have to believe me. Please!'

Her face clouded with total contempt. 'You'll be remembered as a dog-poo,' she concluded. 'Me? A saviour.' She pushed the gun hard into his unshaven cheek, pressing his puffy head into the curved glass. In the distance, several sirens told of an approaching army of police.

'And if I'm not mistaken,' Chloe whispered, effortlessly removing her balaclava, 'that's the cavalry on its way.' She re-checked her watch. 'Less than three minutes. I'm impressed. A fine response time from the boys in blue.'

41

It took Jude Farrow over an hour to write just fifteen lines.

As she'd written, the phone had rung once more, most probably William, the letter's unknowing recipient, calling from the supermarket to ask if she wanted anything special for supper. It pained her to think of him pushing the steel trolley down rows of tins, fresh vegetables and herbs, searching for this week's exotic ingredients at the keenest prices.

But she never answered the phone, unable to listen, let alone reply. Instead, she'd tried committing everything she wanted to say on to one page of Basildon Bond.

He deserved more, so much more, but even now, even at the close, she wanted to spare him as much as she could, unable to bear him knowing the full truth. Not dear, kind William. It had shattered him to hear the half of it – God knows, the truth, the whole truth would kill him. To know that his own wife had . . .

At times she thought she might cry, feeling the bubble rise at the back of her throat. But no tears came. She remained quite numb, sitting at the kitchen table, trying her best to make some sanitized sense of it all, watering it down, seeking and failing to justify the unjustifiable.

Nor was there the feeling of relief she'd anticipated. She'd imagined the scene many times, telling herself that when the time finally came, a huge burden would be lifted. That in some small way, she might find a moment's peace from the madness, her reward for a lifetime's effort of living a nightmare, shielding her loved one from the awful truth.

And what sort of a life had it been, cursed by nature never to experience the joy of holding her own newborn? A fundamental human right, denied by ineffective fallopian tubes. Cursed by time to miss the advances of science giving fresh hope to today's generation of infertile women. Many had been the occasion when, in the dead of night, she'd woken sweat-soaked from another nightmare, and had to grip the mattress with all her might to prevent herself from running straight for William's sharpest carving knife and plunging it into her barren womb.

And all the time he'd slept on, inches away, a lifetime apart.

She sealed the letter in a plain blue envelope, placing it in the exact centre of the formica table. Now was the moment, this was the time. William might be back at any second, and Detective Chief Inspector Davies, that young buck so easily baited by the chance of free love with Melanie, had seemed ominously serious. Perhaps, she mused, he'd reached the same decision as her – time to end it all.

The burning . . . the flames . . . their screams . . . the intense heat burning her cheeks. Standing on the street, praying she wouldn't see the girl, her dreadful creation . . . wishing her dead like the rest . . . And then seeing Chloe, smiling . . . knowing it was all in vain . . . that others would die and follow the rest . . .

Jude walked into the lilac bedroom for the last time and fetched a pillow, returning to the kitchen and removing the grill shelves from the spotlessly clean oven. Next, she placed the pillow on the bottom and lay down on the floor, her head resting on the soft cotton inside the cold iron box.

She wondered how long it would take, whether Melanie and Dickie would be there to meet her. She'd heard tales of a great white light, growing in intensity, racing to embrace you in absolute universal love as you left all your worldly worries and cares behind. That would be nice, she thought, and so welcome.

Shifting position, her left arm reached out for the control panel, turning the large knob slowly clockwise to start the comforting hiss of escaping gas by the side of her head. She settled back down, taking great breaths of the North Sea's gaseous bounty.

William would live. Understand why she couldn't. And if not, he'd join her. She'd be waiting, watching, arms outstretched, head bowed in eternal shame. Maybe they'd be allowed to start over, spirit children given to them in the netherworld, a heavenly family finally allowed to live and love as they'd never known before.

Heaven was going to be as wonderful as she'd painted it to an eager young mind so many years ago . . .

Within seconds her eyelids felt heavy, and Jude started to vomit. But there was no panic. She saw Chloe's teddy tumble down the stairs for the final time, and at last a sense of blessed relief began to slowly filter through her already unconscious mind.

42

'All right! All right!' Ruth cursed as she raced downstairs in her nightshirt to open the pounding front door.

Mason practically fell into the hallway. 'Guv'nor needs you, Mrs J. Fucking balloon's gone up!'

It was too much, too frantic, too early for Ruth. She stared at the breathless figure uncomprehending. 'You'll have to do better than that, I'm afraid. You're here to arrest me for the murders, I take it? Another stab in the dark, Sergeant?'

'Please,' he begged. 'The car's waiting outside. Seems your Chloe Webster may have finally decided to show herself.'

Ruth blinked in shock. 'Chloe?'

'Someone's gone berserk in County Hall, got herself a gun and a hostage. Been putting calls through to the papers saying she's the Christmas Killer.'

'Give me a minute.' She raced upstairs to change.

Mason heard a muffled conversation, then was surprised to see Felix wander downstairs in Doug's towelling dressing gown. 'Blimey,' he said. 'You don't waste much time, do you? Jenkins has only been gone a few days, hasn't he?'

'On the contrary, Sergeant,' Felix replied, quickly dressing from a heap of crumpled clothes left lying by the sofa. 'I've wasted the best part of thirty years.'

Ruth joined them in less than two minutes, dressed in jeans, baggy jumper and trainers. 'Well, let's go, then.'

All three hurried out into the bitter cold and the waiting police car. Sitting on the back seat, Felix felt the beginnings of a panic attack looming up to strangle his sanity, destroying his reason with each blast of the siren blaring over their heads. He fought the urge to throw up as the speeding car raced towards town, parting curious traffic in its wake, lurching from one side of the frosty road to the other. Instinctively, he reached out for Ruth's hand, keen for the reassurance of warm flesh in his own clammy palm.

Minutes later, they had arrived at County Hall, pulling up behind several iron-meshed transit vans spilling blue-capped marksmen on to the street. The front of the building was a hive of activity. A lone chopper hovered overhead, and several uniformed officers with megaphones struggled to contain and push back the growing crowd.

'Follow me,' Mason instructed, leaping from the car and running towards a black van surrounded by armed police. Ruth was never more than a metre behind, watching from the corner of her eye as more armed men swarmed into the glass-fronted building. Then she was level with the van itself, Mason helping her inside, Felix breathlessly following as the metal door slid shut.

A familiar voice cut through the gloom – Davies, excited, urgent, eyes fixed on a television monitor set within a bank of equipment at the far end of the van's cramped interior. 'Can't be sure till we get a line in there, but we think it might be her.'

'Chloe?' Ruth asked nervously.

Another voice, this time from a stooped figure she hadn't seen at first, crouched by the monitor, wearing a headset, microphone pressed to his lips. 'Pictures coming through, sir.'

They all craned for a view of events inside the atrium. The image was unfocused, wobbly.

'Can't you sort the fucker out?' Davies urged.

'Give it time,' the Tactical Armed Response officer replied, whispering frantic instructions into the microphone.

The van door slid open once more, and a figure pushed past Felix. Ruth turned to see a tall bearded man in plainclothes.

'Ashe,' he announced. 'Negotiator, Serious Crimes. You DCI Davies?'

Davies nodded.

'Rest of the squad's on the way down. DCI Knowles, orders are to stay put, contain the situation until he shows. OK?'

Davies shook his head. 'Listen. Until your pals arrive, I'm in charge. I say what the goddamned orders are, Ashe. I fucking give them!'

'Serious Crimes are . . .'

'Aren't fucking here!' Davies replied, trying to ignore Felix's muffled cry of 'You show the bastards, Frankie!' He turned back to the monitor. 'We've got one woman, one hostage, one gun that we know of – Shit!'

It was plain for all but Ashe and the TAR officer to see. Ruth, Felix and Davies all stared in frozen shock at the flickering screen. There could be no doubt. It was Doug, sitting in the lift, hands on head, gun held to the back of his sweating neck by a crouching figure behind.

'You know her?' Ashe asked the stunned vanload.

'Both of them,' Ruth replied quietly, eyes rooted to the pathetic figure on the small screen. 'My husband.' She sighed. 'And the woman's name is Chloe Webster.'

'We don't know that yet,' Davies insisted. 'We can't assume . . .'

'Demands?' Ashe interrupted.

'Your damned job isn't it, Mr Negotiator?'

Ashe nodded at the silent weapons man. 'Your mob in position?'

'Two minutes ago. Eight on each floor. Seventy per cent sight-line on the woman.'

Ashe took a deep breath. 'Well, let's see what the crazy bitch is after, shall we? Give me five minutes.' He turned to Ruth, and she could smell the garlic he'd eaten the night before. 'Your old man . . . ?'

'Doug. Doug Jenkins,' she whispered, staring at her husband's broken face, and thinking how he looked for all the world like one of the startled animals she'd seen late on Christmas night, blinking sadly as the brick left her freezing hand. Yet, curiously, she felt no desperate urge to free him as she had with the occupants of the pet shop. There was something sadly inevitable about his situation, something pitiless, somehow deserved.

'Fine,' Ashe replied, placing a comforting arm on her shoulder. 'Don't worry, love. Ninety per cent of these do's go off peacefully.'

'And the other ten?'

But he was already gone, pushing past Felix once more, leaping from the van to find the nearest flak jacket.

43

Doug stared in horror as dozens of high-powered assault rifles pointed towards his glass prison. His breath began to steam the curved insides. Throat too dry to beg for mercy, he sat silently, fingers interlocked on top of his head, sweat pouring from him.

And thinking. Trying to come up with a way out of the living hell he found himself in. If he could just stay calm, he told himself over and over, let the professionals do their job, he'd be out of there. She'd be dead, and he'd be walking out a hero. With a hero's story to tell; a hero's story to sell . . . Why the fuck didn't they gun the stupid woman down? They had enough firepower. Shoot the cow, for God's sake, get it over with!

The atrium was eerily silent, save for the bubbling of the carp pool thirty feet below. Armed police stood, knelt and lay stock-still, spaced around the steel gantries and behind open-plan office windows, weapons raised, safety-catches off.

'They'll kill us if we don't go down,' he finally managed to croak, weak with fear.

She whispered into his ear, keeping her head tightly behind his. 'Not yet, they won't. I've seen this sort of thing on the telly. They need to find out who we are, then what we want.'

'I just want to live.'

'We all have to die some time, Judas man. Fact.'

'Please, Jayne, not like this.'

'It's Chloe,' she sighed. 'And can you imagine a better way to go? The world's media at your feet? You wanted your shot at the big time, here it is. Relax and enjoy.'

'I don't want to be shot.'

'You won't feel a thing, I promise. The bullets will be here before we even hear the bang.'

A lone figure walked slowly through the large revolving doors, making for the centre of the shining floor, stopping deliberately to look up at the lift before raising a loud-hailer to his lips.

'Here we go,' said Chloe, excitedly. 'Show time.'

The amplified voice filled the atrium. 'My name's Paul Ashe, and I'm a trained negotiator with the Essex Police.'

'Seems like a nice man,' she giggled. 'A very nice man.'

'Can you hear me up there?'

Chloe shouted back through the glass, 'Say pretty please! Didn't they teach manners at negotiating school?'

'It's a little too serious to waste time playing games.'

She waved the gun. 'Who's playing?'

'We're ready to deal,' Ashe replied. 'What is it you want out of this? Tell me, and I'll do my best to sort it out before anyone gets hurt.'

'The newspapers!' Chloe yelled back. 'I know they're out there. Let the journalists in. I have something to tell them.'

Ashe shook his head. 'No can do, Chloe. It is Chloe, isn't it? Chloe Webster?'

She bristled at the name. 'Then the scumbag dies, Mr Megaphone!'

'And maybe you too, Chloe. I have to warn you – make too many threatening moves with the gun, and the armed police have orders to open fire.'

'Couldn't give a monkey's!' Chloe shouted back. 'Your choice. Let the journalists in, or you get two dead bodies on your conscience!'

'And then what? You'll let Mr Jenkins go?'

A frown crossed her face. How on earth did the little weasel know so much? 'We'll talk after.'

'Not the way we do things, Chloe. Doesn't sound like much of a deal from our end. How about you come down from there, then we sort something out with the papers? Saves anyone getting hurt, doesn't it?'

'Best I can do,' Chloe replied, quickly learning to despise Ashe. Smug, she told herself, too goddamned smug. Obviously thinks I haven't got the nerve to . . . She jammed the gun barrel into the back of Doug's head with renewed vigour. 'The papers! Now! Unless you want your nice new Christmas jumper covered in bits of his brains.'

Two marksmen nearest the lift instantly readied themselves. Doug yelped and screwed his eyes tightly shut, waiting for the explosion which would blow him into oblivion.

'Give me five minutes,' Ashe replied, slowly backing towards the revolving doors.

'Fine!' Chloe shouted after him. 'Make it ten. We're not going anywhere!'

44

Frank Davies had a big problem, all eighteen stone of it sitting petrified in a clear glass lift. Doug Jenkins, alive, for the moment, fairly well, and crouching painfully on the brink of media stardom.

How the hell could he be cursed like this? Davies's mind struggled to comprehend the injustice of it all. If he did his job correctly, and Doug walked away unharmed, an army of newsmen would want his story. And Davies knew full well what that would lead to: Jenkins pissed in some hotel, running his mouth off to a bunch of sleazy hacks, entertaining them with his own potted theory of his wrongful arrest for the Ida Sharansky murder, and the DCI who had not given up on hounding him after thirty years.

And no matter what Doug's previous relationship with the tabloid press had been after his pathetic little show in court, they'd be queueing for the exclusive now, chequebooks waving at the first mention of a senior investigating officer.

If he'd had it in his power, he'd have ordered the TAR officer to open fire there and then, obliterating Doug, the girl and the whole sorry story. Then there was Knowles to consider, racing down from HQ to take over. Take the bloody credit for everything. Probably arriving any minute now . . .

Ruth and Felix both jumped as the van door slid open. For an instant, the noisy commotion outside flooded the small van, fading quickly as Ashe slammed the door behind him.

'Well?' Davies asked. 'Is she serious?'

Ashe ran his fingers through his hair. 'Who can say? She wants the reporters in. Maybe that gives us a lever. Your hunch about the name ... She definitely reacted when I called her Chloe Webster.'

Ruth's eyes never left the flickering screen, watching Chloe, so cool, calm and confident, a woman utterly convinced of her own actions.

Mason appeared at the van door. 'Guv? Got a posse of Wapping's finest here, champing at the bit. Apparently she rang the news desk half-hour back, plugging some sort of exclusive on the murders.'

Davies turned. 'For fuck's sake, Boot Sale! Keep them away,' he growled. 'As far back as you can. We already have our journalist.'

Mason's bewildered face searched the darkened van, finally realizing that all eyes stared back at him. 'Me?' he whined. 'Go in there? With all those shooters?'

Davies smiled. 'Reagan and Carter would've been straight in there, Boot Sale, bluffing it out.'

'You pulling my pisser? This is real life, not the telly.'

'Think of it as a spot of undercover work. Temporary transfer, if you like.'

'You're kidding!'

'She wants to speak to a journalist, Boot Sale. Get a flak jacket and a notebook and pen. Now.'

The colour drained from Mason's face. 'Pretend, you mean? Me, with all those guns?'

Davies turned to Ashe for back-up.

'If you act the part,' Ashe conceded, 'she won't know the difference. I'll be there to hold your hand. All we're doing is buying some time until my guv'nor arrives. She can't shoot you, she's trapped in the lift.'

'No fucking way!'

Ruth cleared her throat. 'I'll go.'

'Great idea,' Mason shot back. 'Magic solution.'

Davies shook his head. 'Not on, Ruth. No way.'

'You said yourselves the risks were minimal.'

'Police business,' Ashe replied.

She crouched down and talked directly to Davies. 'It's got to be me, Frank. I'm the one she's most likely to trust. One of the only people who knows the full story. Right from the beginning. Yes?'

'Ruthie,' Felix pleaded.

'It started with me. It finishes with me.'

Chloe Webster's voice suddenly cut through the gloom. Muffled, edgy – a nervous child singing to keep her spirits up.

The weapons officer turned to Frank. 'Why are we waiting?' he said, as they all listened to the familiar tune. 'She's getting anxious.'

Ashe came to a decision. 'We wait for the Regional Squad to arrive. Those are our orders. Not to piss about seeing if we can pass off a member of the public as a damn journalist!'

'Please,' Ruth urged. 'You're in charge, Frank. Let me talk to her. She can't shoot me. There's no danger.'

'Fucking circus!' Ashe cursed, turning to Ruth. 'Jesus Christ, what happens the moment your husband recognizes you? Your cover's blown. Maybe he dies. Finito. Maybe she turns the gun on you. Who knows? It's ridiculous! Insane! You're untrained, and personally involved. Forget it!' He turned to Mason. 'If anyone goes in with me, it's him.'

'When hell freezes over,' Mason muttered.

Davies suddenly found five pairs of eyes staring at him, waiting for his decision. And that was when the thought struck him. They'd all turned to him. Ruth was right, until the big boys arrived, he was still in overall command. But not for long; the precious moments ticked away. 'She goes in,' he announced. 'Get a jacket on, Ruth.'

Ashe was incensed. 'I cannot sanction a member of the –'

'I said, she goes in!'

'Give me the radio,' Ashe demanded. 'I need to speak to my people about this.'

The TAR officer added his own mumbled reservations. 'Puts the civilian in considerable jeopardy, sir. Have to question the wisdom of your decision.'

Davies ground his teeth in pure frustration. 'We've got a suspect with a gun at a hostage's head, demanding to talk to a journalist. She's getting impatient. We've also got someone who's prepared to play the role for us, who has knowledge of the suspect. It's my decision, and mine alone. She goes in. Now – not after you've farted around talking to your mate Knowles, OK? Now!' He turned to Ruth. 'You ready for it?'

'DCI Davies!' Ashe raged. 'This is sheer bloody madness!'

'Hear, hear,' Felix added softly.

'Just take her in, Ashe,' Davies calmly insisted. 'If the shit hits the fan, you can tell them I plugged it in.' He stared at the negotiator, daring him to defy the order.

'I'm far from happy about this.'

'Stick it in your report, then. Do it, Ashe. Stop whining!'

'Don't think I won't. Gross misconduct from a senior officer . . .'

'Your objections have been noted.'

Ashe turned away, furious; too outranked to object any further. Ruth prepared to follow him out of the van.

Felix suddenly said, 'I'm going, too.'

'What?' she said softly. 'And leave me with nothing to come back to?' She leaned over and whispered into his ear. 'Remember Steve McQueen on the motorbike, trying to make it over the wire? Well, this is my chance to make my own great escape. From the past.' She kissed him on the cheek.

He swallowed hard. 'See you in Switzerland, Ruthie,' he weakly replied, before turning away as she stepped outside.

Two minutes later, Ruth stood surrounded by armed police outside the atrium entrance. The flak jacket was heavier than she had expected, far heavier, cutting into her armpits uncomfortably. Ashe remained grim-faced as he gave her a notebook and pen, then adjusted her microphone and earpiece, giving her a direct audio link back to Davies in the van. She turned briefly, looking at the large crowd watching from the other side of the street.

'Never mind about them,' said Ashe. 'Let's just get this pathetic party piece over with.'

'It is my husband up there,' Ruth objected. 'I do have an interest, you know.'

'But no bloody training, love. That's the problem.'

'Didn't do you much good, though, did it, from what I saw? Chloe was laughing at you.'

Ashe pretended to ignore her. 'Does she know she's got your old man up there with her?'

'God knows,' Ruth replied croakily. 'I haven't seen him for the best part of a week, and her for over thirty years.'

'This isn't funny.'

'It's the truth.'

He sighed and wired himself up for sound. 'Assume for the moment she has no idea he's your husband. Keep it as simple as possible. We go in, you play the reporter. Chances are, she's got some sad little statement to make. Just take it down, assure her it'll make the front page of tomorrow's editions. Then let me do the rest. OK?'

She nodded, wondering if it was too late to ask to go to the toilet.

Ashe shook his head. 'Sheer bloody madness.'

A voice crackled in Ruth's earpiece. 'Ruth, it's Frank. Right with you, every step.'

'Bollocks,' she whispered nervously. 'You're sat drinking coffee in that bloody van.'

Frank went on: 'If you can get her to leave the lift, the gun boys reckon they can drop her with a leg shot. Go carefully. And Ruth, follow your instincts. They haven't let you down so far. Ashe is playing a waiting game. We can end it, maybe.'

It was time to go. The armed police parted to allow Ruth and Ashe to enter through the revolving doors, Ashe first, Ruth three shaking steps behind.

Suddenly she found herself half a dozen paces back, frozen by the surreal quiet of the huge empty atrium she knew so well. She had passed through many times on her way to the library, sometimes stopping to rest a while, smoke a Marlboro and admire the fish. Now, as she looked cautiously round, all she heard was distant water bubbling over the slate stones beside the bottom of the lift shafts. As she looked up, an involuntary shiver coursed through her. Kneeling marksmen peered down, weapons trained on the stricken couple high above her head. She forced herself to follow their aim, catching her first real glimpse of Chloe and Doug. She was too far away to make out if he had spotted her.

Ashe raised the loud-hailer. 'We've done what you asked, Chloe. This is Josephine Bell from the *News of the World*.'

Ruth watched transfixed as Chloe bobbed up from behind Doug. Then came the muffled command, brash, confident.

'Prove it!'

Ashe passed Ruth the megaphone, nodding encouragingly.

Trembling, she raised it to her lips and pressed the trigger, sending her croaking voice high into the glass roof. If ever there was a time for the heart to rule the head, this was it, staring her in the face, peering suspiciously down from high above. 'I can't, Chloe. Because I'm not a reporter. But you might remember me as WPC Golden.'

Ashe cursed and made a grab for the megaphone, but Ruth held firm. 'I knew you as a child, Chloe. I was there the night your father died.'

Davies hissed into her earpiece, 'Careful, Ruth. Don't give the whole game away. Not yet.'

But Ruth wasn't listening. She was desperately concentrating on the tiny head thirty feet above, searching for any reaction. 'I sat you on my knee, at the police station.'

'Send me the journalists!'

'I gave you my handkerchief, Chloe. To stop you crying. Remember? WPC Golden. Ruth Golden. R.G.'

There was an interminable pause and a single bead of sweat trickled down Ruth's back. Ashe grabbed at her arm, determined to march her back outside.

Then Chloe's voice cut through the heavy silence. 'Come on up!' she cried. 'Third floor, handguns, saints and murderers. Slowly, though. Any screw-ups and the idiot gets it!'

Davies's voice again, excited, trying to appear calm, but failing. 'Do it, Ruth. Exactly as she says. Slowly. We'll cover you every step of the way.'

Ashe reluctantly loosened his grip and nodded, pointing silently towards a set of steel steps rising beside the lift shafts. Swallowing hard, her dry tongue resting on her lower teeth, Ruth walked falteringly towards the stairway and began to climb, heart pounding with each agonizing step.

To her left, marksmen in blue caps nodded silent encouragement as she passed, offering the quiet reassurance that if she stopped a bullet, her assassin died also.

She continued climbing, wishing she was anywhere else in the world. It was as if her legs moved themselves, completely disconnected with any common sense her brain still possessed, propelling her towards the inevitable. Fearfully, she realized how vulnerable her head was, the perfect target for Chloe's gun. A jumble of images and memories fought for space inside her mind.

At last she stood on the third floor, placing herself between three TAR men and the steel lift doors, breathing deeply, trying to muster whatever reserves of courage remained.

'Chloe,' she managed to say, 'I'm here. Open the doors.'

Another dreadful pause during which Ruth felt her knees begin to shake uncontrollably. Then the lift doors glided open.

Ruth recoiled in surprise with the intensity of it all. After thirty years, Chloe Webster stood smiling before her.

'It's been a long time, WPC Golden,' she said simply.

Ruth stood motionless, hypnotized by the innocent smiling face. Short, mousey brown hair framed the hazel eyes and small mouth perfectly. It was, without doubt, one of the kindliest faces Ruth had ever seen, glowing with compassion and silent understanding of its own purpose. 'Hello, Chloe,' she stammered. 'I didn't know if you'd remember me.'

'How could I forget? It meant so much to me, the handkerchief. So kind. It's a wonderful thing to bring kindness to others, don't you think?'

Ruth dared to try to see further inside, just catching Doug's back and his arms crossed above his head, unable to reconcile the shaking body with the man who had shared her life for so many years. But all she saw was a body, disconnected from her by its own stupidity. The past, her time with Doug, had ended with his affair. How could that trust ever be rebuilt? When this was all done, and she sat down with Doug to talk it all through, Ruth knew she would never take him back. It was time to move on. For all of them.

So there was little concern in her voice when she asked, 'Is he all right?'

'Judas man?' Chloe replied brightly. 'He's fine. Doesn't smell too good, but otherwise better than he deserves. He wanted it all for himself, you know. The glory.'

'Chloe,' Ruth pleaded, fighting for a level, reasoning tone of voice. 'They really want you to come out now. They want you to give them the gun. Give me the gun, if you like. Will you do that for me?'

She shook her head. 'Not yet. Sorry. Maybe afterwards. I need

286

to tell everyone what really happened. About my plans to help the suffering. But it's so good that you're here. I wonder if Daddy sent you? I need you to tell them all for me. You understand, don't you, WPC Golden? You were there when it all started. You knew the truth right from that night. You agreed with me. Understood. Daddy was in heaven, with all the angels. Remember?'

Ruth closed her eyes, searching for the answer. 'I can't do what you want, Chloe.'

'Why not?'

'How many? How many people have you killed?'

A frown appeared. 'Released. No one understands! I release them. Send them to a better place. Where the others wait. You've read the Bible, haven't you?'

'How many, Chloe?'

'Don't push her, for fuck's sake!' Frank's urgent voice hissed.

Chloe's face softened. She realized that she'd need to explain further. Maybe WPC Golden was rather stupid. Like everyone else. Maybe she needed to have it all spelled out. 'It doesn't matter. Numbers are unimportant. The point is they're all happy now, just like Daddy. Every one of them, up there with the angels, at peace for eternity. Thanks to me. Thanks to what everyone told me. Numbers are unimportant.'

An argument had erupted in Ruth's earpiece as the TAR officer tried to persuade Ruth to move away from the open lift door, allowing his men an opportunity to drop their prey, whilst Davies urged her to stay put, keep talking.

'Besides,' Chloe concluded, 'does a doctor count the number of patients he saves?'

'You kill them, Chloe,' Ruth replied evenly, eyes fixed to the gun pointing at Doug's head.

'Release them!' Chloe insisted. 'Why won't you listen to me?'

Ruth took two shallow breaths. 'Because you're wrong. People aren't animals. You can't put them down. We call that murder, Chloe.'

The gun made its way silently from inside the lift to point directly at Ruth. Chloe held it in both hands, shaking from the strain, voice cracking. 'You'll be telling me there's no such thing as heaven, next.'

'What do you want, Chloe?' Ruth felt no fear facing the gaping barrel. Her adrenaline system was already in overdrive, pushing her on, determined to see her through.

'Just some recognition. And money. Lots and lots of money.'

'Rather cheap, isn't it?'

Chloe smiled. 'Not for me, silly. For the others. Money's going to make it so much easier for them. It's going to build a special place where they can go if they want to go to heaven. You know, like a hotel, or something. Nice rooms, with carpets and pictures. Proper equipment to help them with their journey. Dignity, that's what the money would buy. Your chance to end it just as you like, when you want, where you want, surrounded by others with the same feelings. That can't be wrong, can it?'

Ruth thought of her own mother, desperate to die, knee-deep in freezing mud, a sagging, wasted human being bent on leaving a world which offered nothing but the atrophy of mind and body. 'Ida Sharansky?' she found herself saying.

'Exactly. She wanted to go, WPC Golden. I could tell. Her friends, husband, they'd all moved on. She wanted to go.'

Ruth took a step closer to the lift, deciding it was time to reveal all. 'Chloe, listen to me. Listen carefully. I've found out some things. About your father. You were tricked, Chloe. You never kill– released him.'

She grinned. 'He was the first.'

'We've spoken to your Aunty Jude, Chloe. We know what really happened that night.'

Chloe looked bemused. 'My Aunty Jude?'

'She killed him.'

Chloe began to laugh, lowering the gun, one hand to her mouth.

'She killed him because she wanted you for herself.'

'Stop it. This is ridiculous!'

'Please, Chloe. Just think back to that night,' Ruth pleaded. 'What happened after you'd injected your father?'

'He went to heaven. He wanted to go, too.'

Ruth fought to calm herself. From the back of the lift she heard Doug whimpering like a wounded beast. She thanked her lucky stars he hadn't confused Chloe even further by telling her he was married to the woman currently standing outside. It was probably the most sensible thing Doug Jenkins had ever done in his life. Perhaps such close proximity to death had improved his brain.

'You were only young, Chloe. A child. You were tricked. He had 'flu. Bad 'flu. But he wasn't going to die.'

Chloe began chewing on her bottom lip. 'I sent him to heaven.'

'What happened after you injected him?'

She blinked, reaching into the past. 'Mummy came and took me downstairs. I told her what I'd done. I think Aunty Jude went upstairs to see Daddy. I remember noise. He took a long time to pass over.' She looked slightly shameful. 'But like you say, I was only a little kid. I used his syringe, only it didn't have anything in it. Fortunately for him, I must have got lucky, sent an air bubble to his head.'

'And you were downstairs with your mum, all the time?' Ruth pressed.

Chloe nodded. 'I think I remember Aunty Jude calling us up. He'd gone by then, of course. It must have taken nearly ten minutes.' Her voice dropped to a whisper. 'Sorry, Daddy.'

Ruth swallowed hard. 'Listen to me. That was when she – your Aunty Jude – killed him, Chloe. When you were downstairs with your mum. She had the nursing experience, the medical knowledge it would take. She even told your mum you'd done it. But all the time, it was her. Your Aunty Jude.'

'Rubbish,' Chloe replied. 'Even you, WPC Golden, even you told me he was in heaven, that I'd done no wrong. The handkerchief, remember?'

'I didn't know then!' Ruth shouted back.

'Know what?'

She felt totally exhausted, head spinning with it all. 'The games, for one thing. Remember those? Teddy Hospital, with Aunty Jude after she'd dropped Mummy off at that house?'

Chloe looked totally stunned. 'That was our secret!' she snapped. 'She never told you any of that! That was our secret, and she'd never, ever, ever tell anyone that!'

'You were tricked, Chloe. A very wicked trick, so Jude Farrow could have you to herself.'

The shocked face was changing, darkening, the eyes narrowing. 'I've only ever helped anyone. Tricks? This is a trick! Your wicked lies!'

Davies cut back in once more. 'The gun! See if you can get the gun!'

'Please, would you give me the gun, Chloe?' Ruth held out a trembling hand.

'You liar! You lied to me!'

Ruth's earpiece crackled with a mêlée of frantic voices. Only Davies encouraged her to stay put, telling her to try and lure Chloe from the lift.

'Then come with me now,' said Ruth calmly, finding inner strength as she looked into the confused face. 'Come to the cathedral. Show me where heaven is. Prove to me it exists. Show me I'm wrong, Chloe. Dear God, I'd love to be wrong. I'd love the chance to believe in something else besides all this.' She laughed, an echoing cry ringing round the atrium. 'You know, Chloe, after the week I've had, if I knew for certain I could just check out and wake up feeling fabulous on my own fluffy cloud, I'd commission you myself!'

'Never mock my faith,' Chloe warned ominously.

'Careful, Ruth,' Davies hissed. 'Don't fuck with her!'

'Clear the sight-line!' The TAR officer yelled in her ear. 'Get out of there! Now!'

Ruth looked briefly around, aware that armed officers had crept dangerously close, unseen by Chloe. 'Go on, Chloe. I dare you. Prove it,' she said belligerently. 'I'm open for conversion. Show me your choirs of archangels. Let's go to the house of God and see who shows up, eh?' She held out a hand, eyes blazing, challenging the woman who had never matured a day beyond the wriggling child on her lap. 'Come, Chloe. Walk with me.'

Chloe held Ruth's penetrating gaze, searching that well-remembered face. But it had changed. The kind police lady had gone, replaced by a hardened cynic. She watched Ruth turn away and take two small steps back towards the stairs.

There was really only one way to prove she was right. Only one way to show WPC Golden the truth, the power of her selfless humanity.

She took a step from the lift and raised the gun.

'Away! Now!' implored the TAR officer in Ruth's ear. 'Out of there!'

Ruth turned once more, standing between Chloe and police rifles.

'Get out of there! Get out! Get out!' The TAR officer screamed. 'She's out of the fucking lift! Let the snipers take her!'

But Ruth stood rooted to the spot, watching in sheer terror as Chloe pointed the shaking pistol back into the lift.

'It's this easy, WPC Golden,' she boasted, 'to send someone to the other side.'

'Chloe! Wait –'

'Move woman! We can take her! Fucking move it!'

'Here's your proof.' Chloe smiled. 'One minute the murderer's here with us, the next . . .'

Ruth saw Doug beginning to scramble clumsily to his feet, totally panic-stricken. 'No!' he pleaded. 'No! No!'

'What's he got to live for, eh?' said Chloe coldly. 'All-around idiot, this one. Thief, lecher, totally motivated by greed. A disaster. Waste of a life.'

Davies again. 'The gun, Ruth! Get the gun!'

'Please,' Ruth begged. 'Let him go. Put the gun down! They'll kill you!' She glanced quickly into Doug's terrified eyes. He just managed to mouth 'Help' before Chloe offered him her ultimate salvation.

'Bye-bye, Judas man!'

The revolver exploded in the heavy silence.

Chloe screamed in sheer elation as she watched Doug's disbelieving head disintegrate when the bullet struck home. The force of the shot hit him like a giant hammer, sending his dying bulk flying backwards, crashing through shattered Plexiglas to fall obscenely through the air.

Ruth passed out before the final sickening splash as he landed in the carp pool below, allowing the marksmen their first clear view of the pistol-wielding target.

A volley of shots rang out and Chloe fell, clutching her leg and screaming in agony.

Inside the darkened transit van, Frank Davies took off his headset and held his face in his hands. It was finished, finally over. As Felix charged outside to find Ruth, he began to cry, overwhelmed with guilt and relief.

His career had almost certainly ended with one fatal shot, but Jenkins was dead, and so too the exclusive. He would be blamed, of course, but not damned and reviled. They had the Christmas Killer.

Maybe there was a God in heaven, after all.

45

February, the following year

For the second time in as many months, Ruth's terraced home played reluctant host to a crowd of sombre relatives and friends in mourning clothes. Ruth herself had opted for the long red dress again, certain her mother would have approved.

Felix stood at her side, watching Frank Davies make his way over with a half-empty plate of egg-and-cress sandwiches.

'It's official,' he said quietly. 'Got the news last week. Top brass have seen fit to post me to some leafy little station in Suffolk. Retirement country. Had to, really, didn't they? Couldn't have some bloody maverick running New Street.'

'You weren't to blame, Frank,' Ruth replied. 'The awful thing is, I'm damn sure it was exactly the way Doug would have wanted to go. Gunned down in a blaze of tabloid glory. And if Chloe was right about that afterlife stuff, he's probably up there now, cursing the fact he didn't make any money out of the deal. Or trying to broker an exclusive with the *Heaven Times*.'

Davies hung his head slightly. 'Right. But you know as well as I do, Ruth: I broke every bloody rule in the book. Ashe saw to it that I was made sacrificial lamb for the whole bloody mess.'

She smiled. 'Part of the reason I left the force, Frank. No room for anyone prepared to take risks. Besides, how could you have known that Chloe was going to shoot him? I was more at risk, listening to you in my ear, telling me to keep her talking.'

Felix glimpsed a slight look of embarrassment cross Davies's face. Why he'd chosen to leave Ruth for so long directly between Chloe and the marksmen was hard to fathom, but ultimately nobody's business but Frank's. Besides, Felix had had his share of idle speculation over the last few weeks, and was firmly set on looking to the future rather than dwelling in the boggy mires of the past.

'Guess I'm just lucky they didn't dish the old P45,' Davies acknowledged. He looked at Ruth. 'But I'm sorry. Really sorry about Doug. And your mother.'

'It's been a hard time. Not easy. Not easy at all. I do miss him – Doug. And my mum. What is it about death? Our one inevitability, yet we're all hopelessly unprepared for its arrival. Yeah, a strange time.' She took Felix's arm. 'But not all bad.'

Davies managed a small smile. 'We must meet up some time. Chinwag over the old days, eh?'

'What about the new days?' Felix suggested. 'Make a change, wouldn't it?'

Davies nodded, kissed Ruth on the cheek, shook Felix by the hand, then made his excuses and left. In the far corner of the crowded lounge, a young nurse waited patiently until most of the stragglers had left before plucking up the courage to fulfil Rene Golden's last wish. She walked over, clutching a shoebox under her arm.

'Mrs Jenkins?' she asked nervously. 'I'm so sorry. Your mother was a real character. I liked her a lot.'

Ruth smiled. 'You're from the home, aren't you? It's nice of you to come. Funerals are always so damn glum, aren't they?'

The nurse returned the smile. 'I wanted to come, really. Though I guess you've had more than your fair share of funerals, what with your husband . . .' She blushed, ashamed to have given herself away as a tabloid reader quite so easily. With little else happening, Doug's spectacular death had made headline news for several days, and she'd spent many tea breaks amazed at the sensational revelations of the case featuring Mrs Golden's daughter.

She proffered the box, keen to change the subject. 'Before Rene . . . passed away, she asked me to give you this.'

Ruth took it, confusion clouding her face. 'Are you sure?'

'She was most insistent.' The nurse lowered her voice. 'Though I'd be grateful if you wouldn't mention it to anyone. I'm not supposed to place bets for any of the residents, and some say it's gambling, don't they?'

Ruth opened the box and gasped. Felix very nearly swore in surprise.

'Four numbers, she got,' the nurse explained excitedly. 'On two hundred tickets! Came to twenty-eight thousand, four hundred and sixty pounds. Took the post office nearly an hour to process all the winning slips. And when I brought it back, Rene simply kept it in the box. Your little nest egg, she called it. It's all there; you can count it if you like.'

Ruth was too stunned to say anything, staring at the crisp, clean notes, neatly packed in the innocent-looking box.

'There's a note at the bottom,' added the nurse with some relief, glad to have handed the cash to its rightful recipient. 'It's addressed to you. I haven't opened it.'

Ruth delved through the money to find a scented blue envelope marked simply 'Ruth'. She felt a lump rising in her throat as she opened it and pulled out a short letter in her mother's familiar hand. She read it twice, through gradually misting eyes.

Dear Ruth,

Didn't get as much as I hoped for you, but this should tide you over. I'll sort it away for you until the right time, after which it's yours.

Don't think ill of me, but when your time's up there's little point in hanging around. Christmas made me realize that. And that it had to be me, not you, who did the hard work. They'll tell you I fell down the stairs, but I want you to know I didn't go in some stupid accident.

I decided where and when. I hope the next life comes as easily to you as it will do for me.

Your loving mother,

Rene Golden

P.S. Don't forget to buy some new blouses for next term.

The smile didn't leave Ruth's face for the next twenty minutes.

46

July

She stood painfully in the white-walled reception, leaning heavily on two crutches. The metal pins in both legs were still agony, but the doctors assured her she'd be able to walk again eventually. And she was a fighter. By God, she could fight. And she'd do it because she had to – others depended on her.

She savoured the smell of disinfectant, waiting for the strip-search, an intimate examination by rough female hands. She knew the drill by now; six months on remand had taught her well.

She couldn't wait to be in amongst them, sharing their pain and sorrows – offering the final earthly solution. Then they'd understand. Finally come to realize who was right. Even the judges, ridiculous men insisting she swear on a bible before giving evidence. How she'd wanted to cry out, right there in the crowded court, that all the answers they sought were right under their noses, concealed within His Holy Book.

She heard them, calling out from lonely cells just a wall's width away. Poor tortured souls crying for release.

'For a minimum of twenty-five years,' the judge had said. Stupid man! When would he understand, she wondered, when would he finally stumble into the bright, loving light of the truth? At the end – when they all did. As they passed to the other side.

And now to this place, this dustbin of fucked-up humanity. Human shit-bin. Oh, yes, she'd learned a lot on remand, the other women teaching her much better swear words.

But maybe, she suddenly thought, maybe everything had led

her to this present incarceration. Every step of it, from her first nervous fumblings with the needle, to the media circus in the lift. Perhaps this cesspit was her natural ministry. Jesus himself hadn't shrunk from the vilest open-sored lepers, had he? Now, she could really set about her business with those who needed her services the most. And she wasn't one to shrink from the task, no matter how it might disgust her.

She knew she'd find the first one within minutes. There would be so many to choose from. So much good to do.

She'd start immediately – the soother of screams, the enemy of sorrows, the guide to the light.

Chloe Webster was the happiest woman ever to be admitted to a high-security mental institution.

And she started immediately . . .

The Judgement of Strangers

Andrew Taylor

It is 1970. In the London suburb of Roth, David Byfield, a widowed parish priest with a dark past and a darker future, is about to remarry. And throughout that summer the consequences of this marriage reverberate around the sleepy little village.

Blinded by lust, Byfield is oblivious to the dangers that lie all about him: the menopausal churchwarden with a hopeless passion for her priest; his beautiful, neglected teenage daughter Rosemary; and the sinister presence of Francis Youlgreave – poet, opium addict and suicide – whose power stretches beyond the grave.

Soon the murders and the blasphemies begin. But does the responsibility lie in the present or the past? And can Byfield, a prisoner of his own passion, break through to the truth before the final tragedy destroys what he most cherishes?

Tense, brooding and atmospheric, *The Judgement of Strangers* is the second novel in Andrew Taylor's acclaimed Roth Trilogy.

'Taylor is marvellous and devilishly clever'
FRANCES HEGARTY, *Mail on Sunday*

ISBN 0 00 649654 7

The Wire in the Blood

Val McDermid

Young girls are disappearing around the country, and there is nothing to connect them to one another, let alone the killer whose charming manner hides a warped and sick mind.

Nobody gets inside the messy heads of serial killers like Dr Tony Hill. Now heading up a National Profiling Task Force, he sets his team an exercise: they are given the details of missing teenagers and asked to discover whether there is a sinister link between any of the cases. Only one officer, Shaz Bowman, comes up with a concrete theory – a theory that is ridiculed by the group . . . until one of their number is murdered and mutilated.

Could Bowman's outrageous suspicion possibly be true? For Tony Hill, the murder of one of his team becomes a matter of personal revenge, and, joined again by colleague Carol Jordan, he embarks on a campaign of psychological terrorism – a game where hunter and hunted can all too easily be reversed.

'Stunningly exciting, horrifyingly good'

RUTH RENDELL

ISBN 0 00 649983 X

On Beulah Height

Reginald Hill

They moved everyone out of Dendale that long hot summer fifteen years ago. They needed a new reservoir and an old community seemed a cheap price to pay. They even dug up the dead and moved them too.

But four inhabitants of the valley they couldn't move, for no one knew where they were. Three little girls had gone missing, and the prime suspect in their disappearance, Benny Lightfoot.

This was Andy Dalziel's worst case and now fifteen years on he looks set to relive it. It's another long hot summer. A child goes missing in the next valley, and old fears resurface as someone sprays the deadly message on the walls of Danby: BENNY'S BACK!

Music and myth mingle as the Mid-Yorkshire team delve into their pasts and into their own reserves of experience and endurance in search of answers which threaten to bring more pain than they resolve.

'All Reginald Hill's novels are brilliantly written, but he has excelled himself here: and has, too, put together an intricate narrative with the complex ingenuity of a watch-maker'   T. J. BINYON, *Evening Standard*

ISBN: 0 00 649000 X